GROWING UP
YANOMAMÖ TODAY
BY FAITH, NOT BY SIGHT

Growing Up Yanomamö Today By Faith, Not By Sight

Michael Dawson

GRACE ACRES PRESS

CULTIVATING JOY

LARKSPUR, COLORADO

Grace Acres Press
PO Box 22
Larkspur, CO 80118
www.GraceAcresPress.com

Printed in United States of America
25 24 23 22 21 20 19   01 02 03 04 05 06 07 08

Print ISBN - 978-1-60265-062-6
Ebook ISBN - 978-1-60265-063-3

Grace Acres Press also publishes books in a variety of electronic formats. Some content that appears in print may not be available in electronic books.

Library of Congress Cataloging-in-Publication Data:
Names: Dawson, Mike, 1955 August 2- author.
Title: Growing up Yanomamo today : by faith, not by sight / Mike Dawson.
Description: Larkspur, CO : Grace Acres Press, [2019]
Identifiers: LCCN 2019006973 (print) | LCCN 2019010694 (ebook) | ISBN 9781602650633 (ebook) | ISBN 9781602650626 (pbk.) | ISBN 9781602650633 (ebk.)
Subjects: LCSH: Yanomamo Indians--Venezuela--Religion. | Christianity--Venezuela. | Christianity and culture--Venezuela.
Classification: LCC F2520.1.Y3 (ebook) | LCC F2520.1.Y3 D39 2019 (print) |
   DDC 278--dc23
LC record available at https://lccn.loc.gov/2019006973

DEDICATION

Dedicated to my beautiful wife Keila, who puts up with all that is required to live in the jungle as a missionary's wife with grace and dignity, and at the same time provides me with a calming sanctuary and refuge from all the stress that goes along with living and ministering to primitive peoples.

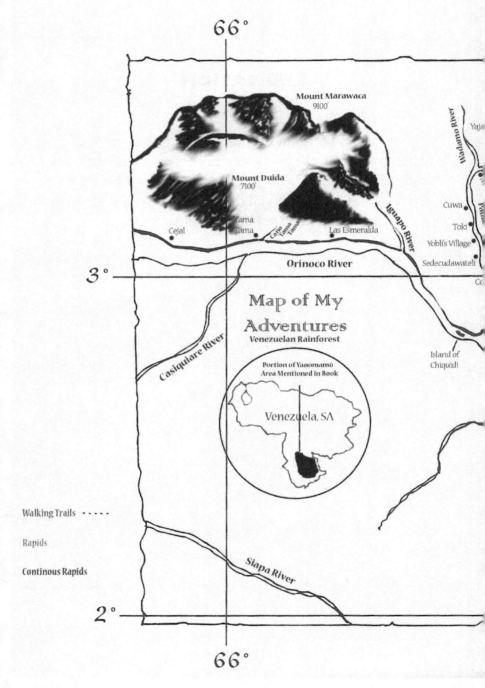

Map of My
Adventures
Venezuelan Rainforest

Portion of Yanomamö
Area Mentioned in Book

Venezuela, SA

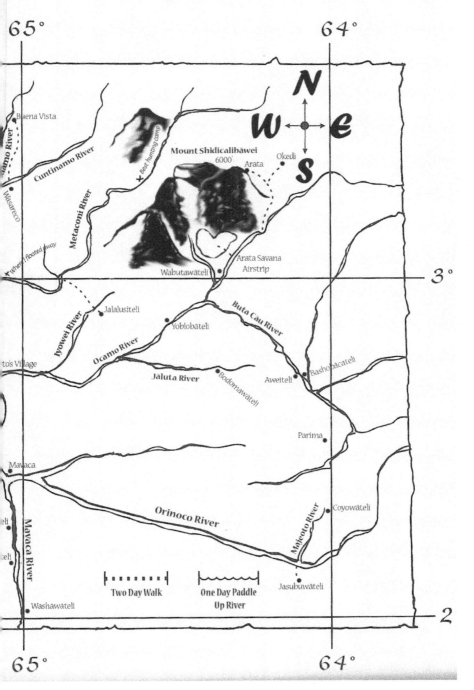

TABLE OF CONTENTS

PREFACE

Joe and Millie Dawson left the USA for Venezuela in October 1953, with three small children in tow, to work with the New Tribes Mission. Their fourth child was born two weeks after they arrived in the little town of Puerto Ayacucho. Millie's time in the primitive local hospital was not a good one. Because she spoke no Spanish, she had no idea what was going on, and Joe was not allowed in the room. One month later, the family of six loaded what meager supplies they could fit in a dugout canoe and set off up the mighty Orinoco River, excited to finally meet the exotic Yanomamö and eager to start building a relationship with this seminomadic, monolingual people — despite the fact that no outsiders spoke the Yanomamö language, so they knew communication would be extremely difficult.

The primitive culture of the Yanomamö is controlled by their witchdoctors. Despite having a knowledge of the Supreme Being, whom they called *Yai Wanonabälwä* or *Yai Bada*, they were held prisoner by demonic influence, and were frequently in conflict with other villages and peoples. After the first six months, the mission leadership felt that Millie and her four small children were possibly being exposed to more danger than New Tribes cared to be responsible for, so Millie was told she had to go downriver and wait for Joe to come down when he could. Realizing that his wife and family were a critical part of his calling and mission, a haggard Joe traveled back down the river six months later, determined never again to be separated for that long from his family.

In early 1955, the mission leaders insisted that Millie give birth to child number five in town, against her and Joe's wishes to remain with the Yanomamö and not be separated. They asked the mission leadership to reconsider, but their request fell on deaf ears. It was just too dangerous up there, and besides, who would deliver the baby?

A couple of weeks before the team was to head back up into the jungle, one of the local ladies, who had recently become a Christian, became ill. When her family urged her to go to the hospital, she told them she was prepared to meet her Maker. If God wanted her to live, He could heal her in her bed, and if it were her time, there would be nothing the meager hospital could do but prolong her agony. She stayed in her own bed at home, witnessing to her friends and relatives who came to visit her, and did in fact recover. The head of the missionaries commented on this lady's faith. "I wish I had missionaries with this faith," he said. "Now we missionaries, with all our talk of living by faith, would have run out to town with our tails tucked between our legs. How I wish I had a few missionaries with the faith of this lady!" he exclaimed.

Joe and Millie immediately looked at each other. This was just what they had been discussing with this man! As soon as the leader finished, Joe slowly stood up. "You are so right, we need to trust God more. Millie and I are willing to trust the Lord for the birth of our child in the jungle." The leader looked at Joe for a long moment and slowly nodded. Joe's and Millie's excitement and peace confirmed the Lord's leading in their lives. If they were nervous, they did not show it. Thankfully, Millie had an easy birth: both mother and baby—yours truly—were fine.

Joe and Millie continued to work with New Tribes Mission until 1990, when they retired after many years of service. Through their trust and faithfulness to their calling, God had established a strong, functioning, indigenous church in the village of Coshilowäteli and had translated the New Testament into the Yanomamö language. This would be the time that most retirees would be looking for a rocking chair, but God had different plans for these brave pioneers, who at this point took yet another step of faith. Along with Bautista Cajicuwä, formerly one of the most powerful witchdoctors and now an elder in the church at Coshilowäteli, they formed Mission Padamo and continued working. Clearly God was granting Mission Padamo a continued open door with the indigenous communities of Venezuela.

So, God guides in the lives and affairs of men. More than sixty years ago, when my dad and mom were arguing for the right to have mom join the team and have her baby in the jungle, no one knew that a resolution would be signed in late 2005 giving New Tribes Mission three months to vacate all tribal areas. But God knew! He had a way planned far in advance to get around this resolution.

They have endured some incredibly challenging times during their work, especially the deaths of their daughter-in-law, Reneé Dawson, in 1992, and their granddaughter, Mikeila Dawson, in 2006. Nevertheless, it is obvious that the hand of the Lord has guided, strengthened, and comforted them every step of the way.

In spite of much opposition from the Enemy, many souls have been won. As a matter of fact, there have been more conversions to the Gospel of Jesus Christ in the past ten years than in the previous fifty years combined. In past seminars, there have been anywhere from twelve to fifteen converted witchdoctors studying God's Word with an intensity that has to be seen to be believed. Due to uncertainties with the Venezuelan government, half of our missionaries have had to depart; we are at best a skeleton crew. However, we believe God's purposes will not be thwarted, because

He is raising up missionaries from within the Yanomamö people to help with the work and stand in the gap, making our work now truly an indigenous mission.

INTRODUCTION

When I started thinking about doing another book, I went back through letters sent to supporters and to my Facebook posts to refresh my memory on all that has happened here since I wrote *I Can See the Shore*. But you can't make a book out of disjointed stories stacked hither and yon on top of each other, so in trying to tie the stories together, I went back to the end of *I Can See the Shore* and tried to pick up my train of thought from that book and carry it forward into this one.

That was a mistake. It has been more than twelve years since our little Mikeila was taken to glory and, to be honest, there has not been a day that she has not been missed. But life does go on. Here were my thoughts from twelve years ago, from *I Can See the Shore*. I remember writing the words:

> [T]here have been so many times that all I could see was the fog…. [How] I desperately wanted and needed to see the shore. Well, it took a little three-year-old to make me look up and over the fog … and see the shore. And when I finally did, it was as if I were seeing the shores of heaven! The Bible speaks highly of the faith of a child, and I long to have my own faith be as the faith of a child. As I said before, I long for the day when my faith shall be sight and I shall see the Lord!
>
> [But then] the funeral was over and I sat in my office more in shock than trying to do anything. I sat there wrapped in my thoughts, barely aware that Mia had walked in and was sitting in Mikeila's little blue rocking chair that I had placed right

beside my desk. I was suddenly snapped out of my morose thoughts by something Mia was saying, more to herself than to me.

"This is Mikeila's little chair," she said to herself. "Mikeila sat here and Uncle Gary came and prayed for her. Then Jesus sent His people to talk to her and take her home to be with Jesus."

Like I said, she was talking to herself, rocking in Mikeila's little chair. I got down on my knees beside her and asked her,

"What did you say, Mia? Who came and took Mikeila to Jesus?" My voice shook as I asked her the questions.

She was not bothered by my questions. "Daddy, Jesus sent people to get Mikeila to take her up to be with Him. She told me goodbye and not to cry, that she was OK now. Why are you crying, Daddy?"

Now, I don't know what Mia saw. But I do know that ever since Mia was old enough to be aware of anything, she and Mikeila had been inseparable. Mia normally took longer naps than Mikeila, but as soon as she woke up, if Mikeila were not in the room, Mia would not rest until she could be reunited with her sister. Her first question was always, "Where is Mikeila?"… Since that day, though, Mia has never once asked where Mikeila is. She has remained steadfast that Mikeila is in heaven with Jesus.

"I miss my sister very much," she said just the other day. "But she is in Heaven with Jesus now. Daddy, why did Jesus have to take my sister to Heaven?" she asked me.

"I don't know honey, maybe He needed her for a job." I told her, not sure myself why Jesus would have taken my beautiful little girl.

"Like do you think His room was messy and He needed a little girl to clean it up for Him?" Her little face was so earnest all I could do was smile and hope she did not see my tears.

There continue to be tears, but as we journey through this life, we continue on as the song writer says: "I walk into the unknown trusting all the while." How do we do it? Well, it is because "**we walk by faith and not by sight.**"

1
JUNGLE PLAGUES AND OTHER SCARY MOMENTS IN THE HOME

A first-term missionary, after finding a bug in his cup of coffee, throws the coffee out, carefully washes out his cup, replaces it, gets another cup, and pours himself a new cup of coffee. A second-term missionary, after finding a bug, scoops out the bug and continues drinking his coffee, albeit with a small grimace of self-pity. A veteran, in contrast, scoops out the bug, eats the bug, and frantically searches for another one. Well, sorry, even after thirty-eight years as a full time missionary, I don't fit the stereotype. I had a bunch of ants in my powdered milk and sugar one day and didn't catch them until too late. But with all the food shortages here in this country, I could not just throw it away because three of the items most difficult to find here are — you guessed it — coffee, sugar, and powdered milk (huge sigh).

◈ ▣ ◈ ▣ ◈

I had to smile at a message I received from my son Stephen. He was complaining because a bag of chocolate toddy (a drink mix) that I had taken to him was expired. Well, folks, under socialism one does not have the luxury to even look at expiration dates, brand names, or anything else. If an item is available, one grabs it and is grateful. I remember when my parents would regale us with tales of buggy pasta, buggy rice, buggy oatmeal, and … well, you get the picture. My younger siblings would smile a tight little smile of tolerance for their parents' stories of bygone times. By the time they came on the scene, we had moved past the effects of the then-dictator, and my parents' support level had increased to a point at which we could be a bit choosier—but not me. I remembered crunching through more bugs than I cared to enumerate.

◈▣◈▣◈

An old Yanomamö guy asked me for rice the other day, and I gave him a bag of our carefully hoarded stash, only to have him look at it carefully and hand it back to me, showing me the bugs. "It's better this way," I told him with a straight face. "This rice already comes with its own meat supply." He was not amused. The only point in all this is to say *vote carefully*, because elections have consequences. A politician might sound fine, but the results are inevitable: empty stores and empty stomachs. It took less than twenty years for this country [Venezuela] to go from one of the richest South American countries to one of much hunger and anguish, and I don't think we have hit bottom yet.

◈▣◈▣◈

At different times, I have mentioned the bothersome little *nigua*. It is a small flea that burrows into your body, which would be offensive enough, but then it has the audacity to lay its eggs in you, which grow and grow by feeding on you. Now, how many of you all have ever had a flea in your toe—or anywhere else on your body, for that matter? If you haven't had one, count yourself lucky! I have one just a-chompin' and a-chewin' and it is driving me batty! To make it worse, it is under the bottom side of my big toe where I can't get at him to get revenge. I keep asking Keila to help, but so far she swears there is nothing there.

This had been going on for about two weeks. The itch in my toe was driving me crazy. With my ever-expanding girth, I can no longer get that close to said toe, so I begged my wife to check my toe and please remove said offender before it ate too much of me. She assured me I did not have a *nigua* in my toe. During the ensuing days, I continued begging her to verify that I did not have a *nigua*, as my toe was not only itching, but was also swelling and discolored.

As I said, this went on for two weeks. Finally, I had to make a trip to La Esmeralda and Keila went with me. On the way back upriver, our boat was so slow that I asked her to please take a closer look, as she had nothing better to do. Imagine my surprise when she said, "Well, I guess it is big enough to take out now!"

◈ 回 ◈ 回 ◈

Somewhere I read that "to lie down in the jungle is to yield, wholesale, to insect life. This will either take advantage — by biting, sucking, probing — or casually accept a chance to inspect, up nostrils, within ears, by eyeballs, wherever it chooses." I got to thinking of all the times — right in my own house, in my own bed — that this has proven to be all too true. I could bore you with many examples, but here is one story from the past to prove my point.

I was sleeping fine when all of a sudden, I had such a splitting pain in my head that I despaired of ever waking up. Contrary to my first thought, I did in fact jerk awake. Keila turned sleepily toward me and asked me what was wrong.

I grinned sheepishly in the dark and told her it was nothing, just a dream. The words were no sooner out of my mouth than the pain about drove me to my knees. I realized something alive had burrowed into my eardrum and was heading deep! Something crawling around in your eardrum in the middle of the night is a sensation you would have to experience to believe, yet I wouldn't wish it on my worst enemy! Whatever it was in my inner ear felt as large as a Dungeness crab, just a-biting and a-clawing, heading for my center lobe (as I am not medically knowledgeable, I'm not sure what the center of the brain is called)—but that dinosaur was heading deep! By this time, Keila had woken up sufficiently to join the battle.

Shining a bright light into my ear only drove whatever it was deeper. Between short respites from the pain, we discussed options and she finally decided to pour a bit of olive oil into my ear. Not sure what a medical professional would say about that remedy, but almost 300 miles from the nearest hospital and a doctor's advice, one tends to grasp at straws. I put my head down and she poured away. Whatever it was, it liked the oil even less than it had the light, and once again started digging. Its efforts would have put a ditch digger to shame, I'll tell you. But the second time she flushed my ear out, its efforts to dig clear through to the other side ceased. Now I am left with merely a bit of an oily ear, still wondering what in the world that was.

◈回◈回◈

The Bible tells about the plagues in ancient Egypt, so many people are familiar with them. As a kid listening to this story, I always felt a bit smug that the plagues posed no danger to the Israelites. I so associated with them! Their power was my power! I felt haughty and superior to the Egyptians, and felt they got only what they deserved. My smugness is now gone, as I too am in the middle of a plague!

We have been plagued with beetles. Don't sneer! I will hold up this beetle plague against most of the plagues that smote the Egyptians except the obvious few. I can almost hear you all muttering, *Why beetles? How can beetles be a plague? Dawson is just whining again!* Let me just say, don't try to sit in a dark room to use a computer with thousands of senseless beetles flying and buzzing around. I am, and they have no purpose other than to crash into me at full flight speed! I can hear the ones outside tapping to get in. The ones inside fly into my hair and into my face as the light reflects from the computer screen off my glasses. Anyway, I am about ready to scream! I sure don't understand Pharaoh, because if I were holding any people here, I would get up immediately, get dressed, and run and tell them the good news: YOU ARE FREE TO GO! But alas, I am just being plagued by these miserable beetles in the dark of the Amazon night for no purpose that I can see.

I read this beetle plague story to Keila and she commented, "Thousands? Come on, there are only hundreds!"

I said, "Who's counting?"

After a thoughtful pause, she said, "You know, you might be right. I find them in my laundry and in my dishes. I find them in my toilet, in my dirty clothes, and in my clean clothes! Thousands, there must be hundreds of thousands!" So, see, I am not just whining!

◈▣◈▣◈

As if the beetles were not enough, I am also up to my eyeballs in frogs! Along with dangers presented by insect life in the jungle and in my home (which is also in the jungle), is the innocent-looking, cute (according to my sisters), little tree frog. Although I live in the Amazon jungle, I have maintained many times that the most dangerous place in this jungle is right in my own home. Take this story for an example: I was attacked by a frog! Not the first time either!

"A frog?" I can hear you ask with skepticism dripping from your vocal cords. "What about the anacondas, the jaguars, the …?" (the list is endless).

Keep your anacondas and jaguars, I say. For me, the frog is about all the excitement I can handle! They have, at various times, almost put me into cardiac arrest. Although as something to write about, it lacks the shock value of an attack by a jaguar, a bear, or a snake, if I had my druthers, I'd avoid the frog attack before any of the other animals mentioned, regardless of how much it lacks in value as letter material. The truth is, I don't have to worry about anacondas, jaguars, or bears in my house—at least not yet. However, I have yet to find a way to keep out the slimy tree frogs that have nothing better to do than wait for a really gloomy night, then jump on you, and either splat right on your face or elsewhere on your bare skin. You want a cardiovascular workout? That will give it to you! Thus, I still maintain that one of the most dangerous animals in the Amazon rainforest is the lowly, slimy tree frog.

Here's an example of a frog attack. There are many other documented examples of tree frog attacks in my writings: so many that the casual reader might get the idea that I have developed a phobia of some kind against them—and the casual reader would be right!

Here's what happened. While heading to the restroom, I had the misfortune to step on one of those slimy tree frogs. To say he was not happy would be a gross understatement, but to be honest, I was even less happy than the frog was, and clumsily danced around trying to get off him as quickly as possible. I did finally get off him and we each went our separate ways, albeit a bit more shaky and jittery than we had each been before that fateful midnight meeting. At least *I* was jittery!

Did that frog appreciate how quickly I had tried to get off of him? Not for one moment. He made a flying leap that took him to the sink, then from there to my leg, and he used my leg as a springboard to further catapult himself out of my reach. But to add insult to injury, as a show of his great contempt for me before leaving my leg, he committed a small wet indiscretion on my leg. I could just imagine him chuckling as he headed on. One of these nights I am going to go into cardiac arrest trying to extricate myself from the clutches of some stupid tree frog!

However, shortly after this terrifying incident, I suffered a real animal attack that made the frog's indiscretions pale in comparison. I was walking over to visit a friend. His dog was standing by the door and gave no indication of being upset or unhappy in any way, but as I walked by him, he jumped up and tore into me with a vengeance!

The fight was loud, really loud. I was screaming like a banshee, and the dog was barking and growling furiously. Multiple bites were given, and even the dog got some bites in. One was on my lower leg and the other was high enough on my leg that I will be sitting precariously for a while.

◈ 回 ◈ 回 ◈

I complain about the frogs, but these are probably toads. I'm not sure what the difference is. You see, in Yanomamö you can't just say *frog* or *toad*. If you see something, you have to call it by its real name. There are *bloabloamö, mocas, jasubuli*, and *yoyos*, to name just a few. Forgive me if I don't know whether I am plagued by frogs or toads, but whatever they are, they are making a mess out there! In case you are wondering, the ones in my airplane hangar are *yoyos*.

The plague started slowly, as I am sure many plagues do. I didn't even realize we were about to be overrun, as I was busy with many other things. One day Keila found a frog in her laundry sink, which caused no end of loud squeals for help. Knowing that the cause of her squealing was a harmless little tree frog, I reminded her that after twenty-three-plus years as a front-line missionary, she should be able to deal with a little tree frog. Well, that advice did not go over well, but it did cause her to try and deal with it herself. (By the way, when frogs are bothering Keila, they are harmless. It's only when they are attacking me that they become the most dangerous animal in the rainforest.)

I watched as she got a dustpan and shooed the poor, hapless frog onto it with a rag, then quickly covered her prisoner with a pitcher. She yelled at me to open the door, which I was glad to do. She took the frog out about twenty feet from the house, released him, and he took off in huge bounds back toward his sanctuary: Keila's sink! My back was to the door, so I didn't realize I had failed to close it in all the excitement, and I was trying not to fall over from laughing at her frantic contortions to get away from the frog's spritely springs. We never did find him, so Keila was back to forking her clothes out of the laundry sink with the broom.

From there, unfortunately, they have multiplied and have moved over to my airplane hangar next door. I have got to do something with the frogs in that hanger. Mercy! Cleaning up after them seems like I am mucking out after a group of bears. (I can't remember the correct group name for bears. Oh, yeah, it is a sloth of bears.) Anyway, it feels like I am mucking out after a sloth of bears living in there. This morning, in the dim light of dawn, I saw one frog that was as big as a cardboard box, and no, I did not think of taking a picture. Anyway, figuring that this was one of the main ones I'd have to be cleaning up for all the time, I looked for something to do war with it and evict it from the premises. I carefully crept up on it … only to find that it had changed itself into a cardboard box! I never knew frogs could do magic! Now, not only do I have to put up with frogs pooping in my hangar, but they know magic as well! We all have our crosses to bear, I suppose. By the way, the group name for frogs is knot, colony, or army. I'm not sure which group I have my troubles with, but

I think it's probably a colony because they look like they have moved in to stay!

Then, one night at 9:00 p.m., I went out to shut the generator off. There was an extremely large frog sitting right in front of the door, just waiting for it to open so he could jump through it and begin depositing large indiscretions that I would then have to clean up. "No thank you!" I told him, and moved him, none too gently, out of the way with my foot. Then turning to the door, I unlocked it, taking at the most two seconds. Before opening the door, I turned back to where I had last seen the frog, to make sure he had not gotten back to the door. HE WAS GONE! I looked diligently for him, to no avail. I then went in and turned the generator off and came back outside and spent another five minutes looking for that frog. Not that I wanted him for anything, but I was perplexed as to where in the world he could have gotten to. I never did find him. He would have had to be a super frog to get out of sight that fast, and there was just nowhere for him to hide.

◈▣◈▣◈

I'm not sure where the frog went, but there must be a connection, because the next morning at 5:30 a.m. I had a bat in my bed! In reality, I can take or leave the ever-present bugs: they are just part of the ambience here, like the rain, the sun, and the jungle. But one thing I refuse to accept are bats in my bed! I am sorry, but that is totally beyond the pale. A bat in one's bed has absolutely no redeeming value at all. When it comes to bats, I admit I do a bit more than whining! It so destroys my sleep that the next day I am worthless. I can't even think of the right words to convey how much I utterly dislike—no, I *abhor*—bats in bed.

I had to take a patient down to the little government clinic about fifty miles below us on the river. We got back late and Keila and I unloaded the boat of tanks and whatnot by flashlight because it was already dark. Shining the flashlight around, I spotted a bat on the wall. It was low enough that I thought I could pop it with a hammer that was conveniently lying on a nearby barrel. I crept up to the unsuspecting bat and tapped it lightly on its head. Well, I tried to tap it. Crazy thing—very unsportsmanlike, I tell you—it not only moved its head out of harm's way, but then fluttered over and landed on my chest!

Thankfully, Keila was screaming loud enough that it drowned out my own slightly less shrill screeches. I do dislike bats! Especially one that is frantically trying to save its ears from all the screeches by trying to burrow further into my clothes. The trick with screeching is just to make sure you stop before your wife does, and you might possibly get away with it.

◈ ▣ ◈ ▣ ◈

I was sleeping like a baby when, all of a sudden, I was awakened by a brutal slap on the cheek. I jumped up with my eyeballs bouncing in their sockets. "What, what … ?" My beautiful wife calmly held out her hand with a smudge on it. "There was a mosquito on your cheek and I killed it!" she happily told me. Now my question is: was she my protector, or was she possibly taking out hidden hostilities against me?

◈ ▣ ◈ ▣ ◈

We desperately needed meat, so I decided to go night hunting. What a night! We left a bit before 5:00 p.m. under beautiful blue skies. At 7:00, a storm came up that you would have had to be huddled under to believe. It was still pouring at 3:00 a.m., so we turned around to just come home. It was still raining when we got back. Fortunately, I didn't drown. If I had not been so cold, I could have batted the fish out of the water above me, as they wouldn't have been able to tell where the river quit and the rain started.

We didn't get the meat we needed, but I learned something that night. No, it wasn't that I don't have the stamina for rain and miserable conditions like my brother Steve; I have always known that. What I did learn that night is that I have, sad to say, gotten spoiled.

"Shame!" I hear you mutter. "Shame!"

And you are right! Shame! I figured out that night in the pouring-down rain that I would much rather get my meat from a buffet line at Golden Corral or even a McDonald's drive-through than have to sit huddled down on the cold, hard board seat of a miserable dugout canoe in the torrential rain.

◈ ▣ ◈ ▣ ◈

I had thought I would work for a few more hours on some different things I've been trying to finish up, but I had to give up. I hate to admit it to all of you who think I am some kind of a jungle macho man, but the moths got so bad, swarming me at my computer, that I gave up.

It would be one thing if they would just stay on the screen of the computer. I think I could adjust and peer around them to continue working, but what gets me is their playing ping-pong between the screen of the computer and my glasses. What is *really* bad are the ones that get thirsty and land on me to drink the sweat off my body—a sweat that has built up, I might add, during my attempts to chase the crazy moths away. Enough is enough. Goodnight!

2

THE FINALITY OF DEATH AND THE COMFORT OF THE GOSPEL

The reality of Bautista's homegoing was brought home by Mia in a sad but bittersweet way. Through the many years I knew him, I would give Bautista any kind of food and whatnot, and Keila would remind me of how short our supplies were. I would always paraphrase the verse that talks about giving a righteous man a cup of cool water and reaping a righteous man's reward. I would say: "Look, if I can reap a righteous man's reward with just a cup of cold water, how much more of a reward can I get by giving a righteous man a bag of rice, or a bag of pasta, or a _____ [fill in the blank]." (Let me make it clear that I was not being facetious: I truly knew him to be a righteous man.) Keila, though possibly not convinced by my reasoning, would at least stop fighting it and we were all happy. Because of this, Mia took to calling Bautista "your righteous man." As in, "Dad, your righteous man is calling you," or "your righteous man is outside," etc. Today, she mournfully announced, "Dad, your righteous man is gone now." And it really sank in.

◈ ▣ ◈ ▣ ◈

Working with the Yanomamö tests our faith daily because death is something that we have to deal with way too often. My wife, Keila, teaches preschool, and I remember walking back from the funeral of one of the little preschool girls who passed away from malaria, my eyes full of tears for her parents, Jacinto and Leticia, and the rest of her family who took her death so hard. I remembered shaking my head in frustration. Hers had been the third death that week! The sad thing was that so many of these deaths from malaria might have been avoided.

I know for a fact that if we still had access to the needed treatments and/or air support for emergency flights like we used to have, we could do more for the people. We keep trying to do what little we can. Meanwhile, malaria and other tropical diseases continue to kill at an alarming rate. Some fifty years ago, Carson's *Silent Spring* was written with erroneous information regarding DDT, which led to that chemical — the *only* pesticide that works effectively against malaria-carrying mosquitoes — being banned. An estimated fifty million people in Africa alone have died since the use of DDT was outlawed. Neither time nor space allows me to go into detail about the lives that have been affected by all this, my own included. There are those who are happy with this (Wurster, "Green Fervor, Red Blood," Oct. 8, 2010), and then there are those who are do-gooders but ineffective (Limbaugh, "When Liberal Ideology Results in Mass Death," April 29, 2013 podcast). Rush finished up with this: "So, you could say the biggest killer of young African children is not AIDS, it's not war. It is DDT being banned. And you'd be right."

◈ ▣ ◈ ▣ ◈

Carlito, a skinny kid who moved to our village after the death of his father, was a special friend of our son, Ryan. Our house rang with the laughter of these boys growing up. Shortly after we lost our air support, Carlito got really sick. We did what we could for him, but at that time, we were stymied by a regulation from the government saying that anyone helping with medical matters had to be certified. My brother and sisters had years of experience and knew tropical medicine, but they were not certified and had no chance of ever being certified with this new government. So, we watched helplessly as Carlito got sicker and sicker. The government-promised airplane to medivac him never showed up. We waited for more than a week, but then gave his family enough gasoline to take Carlito down to Puerto Ayacucho by boat. It was obvious that all the government promises had already been forgotten.

But the trip by river was too long. A few days after they got him down to Puerto Ayacucho, we received the news that Carlito had died. The government then promised to have the body flown home, but for some reason, the plane just dropped his body off in La Esmeralda, saying a helicopter would bring it the rest of the way. All day the family waited, and the next day dragged on slower and slower. The village could not wait any longer, so we sent a boat down to pick up Carlito's body where it had been dropped off, because it was now obvious to all that no helicopter would be coming.

After waiting two days for Carlito's body to be brought home, his family from here and his home village were almost hysterical when the motor was heard pulling into port. The crowd moved as one person, so tightly were they all packed together, as they rushed to the boat landing. The crush of bodies almost swamped the boat as the men chosen to pick up the coffin fought their way through the wailing, keening mourners to do this last service for their friend. The noise of the crowd by this time was at such a crescendo that it was hard to hear anything specific or coherent, just the noise. All of a sudden, above this noise came a harsh beating sound. I was taken by surprise, as the Yanomamö do not use any form of drum, but it did sound like a badly beaten drum. I then realized that it was all the people beating on the coffin in their grief, imploring their loved one to get up and come out.

I sensed the urgency everyone felt as they started the funeral fire, as time was of the essence. Bodies don't last long in the extremely high heat of the Amazon jungle and it had taken a long two days just to get the body home. Because the Yanomamö cremate their dead, the coffin had to be opened and the body removed. When the coffin was opened, I cringed at the stench and wept at this added insult to my poor friends.

The men who were making the fire decided that it was now hot enough. I watched as the body was removed and laid in a hammock. This was difficult because rigor mortis had already set in and the body would not conform to the shape of the hammock; somehow, though, he was placed in it and the ones designated to do this job braced themselves for this last deed. At a signal, the hammock ropes were untied, and with the hammock swaying between them, the two ran out to the fire, fighting their way through the crowd, which tried to delay the last action as long as possible. Finally, they were close enough to heave their burden onto the flames, with the wails by this time a frightful sound. Additional lengths of firewood were quickly thrown on, covering the body for the last time.

I was standing possibly twenty feet from the fire and had to move back because of the heat from the now blazing inferno. The crowd of relatives was still there, many of them continuing to reach in for one last touch. I honestly had no idea how they could stay that close to the blazing fire. They danced and wailed their grief. I cried with them. I knew Carlito was in a better place, but I cried because their grief was contagious.

As I cried, I noticed once again the fluid movements of the mourners. The Yanomamö are such a graceful people. Even in mourning, their steps are a dance and their crying is a unique song from each individual person: a song telling about the person who has died and his or her relationship to the person singing the song. It might be about a fishing trip they had gone on together, or maybe about his skill as a hunter or fisherman ... even a basket the person had made might be sung about. Each person had a piece of the dead man's belongings. This is one of the last displays of his earthly possessions. They will be hidden away after the funeral pyre has burned down and when the bones are disposed of, they will be brought out one last time and then destroyed.

Have you ever smelled a body burning? Once experienced, that smell is something you will never forget. The fire burned down and the bones were gathered. Then came the hard part. Because Carlito was originally from another village, his family from there wanted to take his bones back with them. The bones would be used in a traditional *leaju*, where they grind the bones into a powder, mix them in a plantain drink, and drink them. When Carlito came to this village, he married a girl from here. Our village has given up the traditional *leaju* since the Gospel has taught them that their hope and confidence in being reunited with their loved one is based on the finished work of Jesus Christ. Carlito had a friend tape a message for his family when he knew his end was near. Through their tears, they heard him speak with obvious pain in his voice and his message came through clear. "I know I am God's and I am going to His land. Don't be sad for me."

Normally, these types of issues are never resolved peacefully, and often result in loud shouts, threats, and sometimes even blows and clubs. In the worst-case scenario, shots and arrows fly. But God gave Pablino, one of the leaders here in Cosh, real grace and wisdom as he dealt with Carlito's family members. "My friends," he said, "we are all grieving for the same person. You are suffering and we are suffering as well. Let's not add to our grief by shouting and yelling. I propose that we split the basket of bones, you take your basket and have your bone drinking *leaju* and I will take my basket and bury them here in my house. We grieve over our loss.

The person we are grieving is not here, it is not going to matter to him what we do with his bones. He is already at home with God. I know he has gone to be with our God. You do not believe this. That is OK. Now don't call me when you are going to drink your bones and I won't call you when I bury my bones. But let's don't argue over this." His suggestion was met with nods of approval; although each of the head men still had to have their say, and the meeting would last another hour or more, it was a done deal.

This death is just one more in a long list of deaths that brings into full focus how terribly important air support was and is for this entire area. I don't know if it would have saved Carlito's life: it very possibly would have, as he would have made it to the hospital days earlier instead of having to be taken out by river. It would also have made the return of his body so much easier, faster, and less traumatic for the villages.

❖ ▣ ❖ ▣ ❖

Without air support, and now without the most basic of medicines, death is becoming all too frequent. We had been called to come up and pray for Sergio's and Dada's little boy—just shy of three years old—but it was not to be. He died shortly after we finished praying for him. Malaria had claimed another victim here and we were, of course, crushed. Deaths are so hard, especially for a young couple, and this little boy was their first death. The funeral fire was made and we stood around with tears in our eyes watching the young, bereaved couple wail their grief. I further grieved with the couple, knowing that in spite of the fact that they were both born and raised here in a Christian village, neither one of them had ever made a personal confession of faith in Christ.

That's why I was shocked when, on the following Sunday morning, Sergio and Dada stood up in front of the church and asked to be allowed to say something to the congregation. Sergio's nervousness was obvious, but gripping the microphone he started. "My friends," he began, swallowing hard to keep from breaking down, "I am very sad. My wife and I are really suffering, but we have been talking. We know our little boy is in heaven with God, and we also know that if *we* died now, we would not go to heaven to be with him. We have decided that we want to ask Jesus to forgive us our sins and clean our hearts and make us His. We want to make sure if we die, we go to heaven to be with God and with our son. I want the elders to come up here and pray for my wife and I and then we are going to pray and ask God to save us."

You could have knocked me over with a feather. I stared and I am sure my mouth was hanging open. I suddenly realized they were waiting for me to get up and go up with the elders to pray for them. I was choked up as I prayed for them, remembering my own ongoing grief over the death of our little Mikeila, still a raw wound even after a few years. I wondered how in the world they had found the peace needed to go through this so soon. For a Yanomamö, to even be seen in public this soon after a loss is unheard of, and here, not only were they in church, but Sergio was talking openly about their son. My eyes filled with tears when, after the elders prayed for them, he prayed a simple prayer of repentance and asked God to save him. His wife then made her own public profession of faith.

After they finished, I sat there deep in my own thoughts. This work has grown increasingly difficult and, if I might say, less fun. Not that we are looking for fun and excitement, but up until this last couple of years I have always loved working with the Yanomamö and have enjoyed the time I have spent with them. Now, however, many of them have gotten into politics and, being the novices that they are, are extremely prone to manipulation and what not. Authorities in town, both military and civil, use many of these wannabe politicians to put pressure on us and have succeeded in making life very difficult. To be honest, there have been times when I have wondered why we stayed. In this political climate, it is easy to get discouraged and harder to keep our eyes focused on Him. But that morning, in spite of all our setbacks politically, God allowed us to witness a huge miracle. God showed us again that He will build His church and the gates of hell will not prevail against it.

◈▣◈▣◈

Speaking of the work getting less fun, this next incident proved to me again that working with the Yanomamö really is not about fun at all, but about the change that the Gospel of Jesus Christ makes in the hearts and minds of people. So many times we wonder: does the Gospel really work? Does it really have the power to change hearts? Even our Christian Yanomamö friends have not been immune to the power of hate and revenge that their traditional culture is based on. But going through this experience with our friends who have been so affected by death once again proved to us that yes, the Gospel of Jesus Christ is powerful enough to give our friends the grace to forgive a death even when it is caused by a brutal beating. Here is what happened.

As if malaria and snake bites are not enough to deal with, there are always the explosive situations that come about because of jealousy and infidelity. We had gone to bed concerned about Bautista, as he was very sick and I was afraid he might not make it through the night. At 3:30 a.m. we were jolted out of a deep sleep by a shrill wail right outside our house.

"Prepare yourselves! This morning is going to be terrible!" a man sobbed. I ran over to the side of the house to look out the window, but in the darkness I only saw a dark shadow. I knew it was about Bautista, but it made no sense. I walked back over to the bed.

"I have no idea who that was or what that was about, but there is no one wailing over in the direction of Bautista's house," I told Keila. We both laid back down, but because of our nervous tension found it impossible to sleep, so, after praying for Bautista, Keila got up to go ahead and get a start on her day. She is an early riser anyway, but I laid there in the night wondering what we had heard and what it meant.

Monday morning at 6:00 a.m., I went out to our Bible and prayer class, and on my way ran into a friend who was also on his way to the class. Lowering my voice, I asked him about the wailing I had heard. He told me that about 9:00 p.m., a young man sent his wife to find some *casave*, and because she was taking longer than he thought she should have, he started looking for her. She was on her way back, empty-handed. On her return, she ran into a young man she had had an affair with. Her husband found her just as she met the other young man on the trail. The husband threw a fit and tried to spear the boy, but the boy dodged, only getting a slight wound in his hand. The husband dragged his wife home. Her family told him to beat her and kept insisting that he beat her harder. Long story short, he beat her to death.

What a tragedy! Now, of course, her family—the same ones who insisted she be beaten—are beside themselves and are insisting that the husband kill the boy with whom she had had the affair.

Later on that day, my heart broke watching the father hold his little baby girl, sobbing his heart out while his family burned his wife's body. The girl's family refused to even come to the cremation, they were so angry. I think that by this time most of their anger was due to their own guilt, but that is hard for a Yanomamö to admit. So sad. Now, the other boy's family is expecting a revenge raid. We felt the forces of darkness arrayed against the work.

This tragic situation touched us all, but none more than Faith and Sharon. Jena, the young woman who was killed, had lived with them for two years. When she was little, she couldn't walk or talk, so her family said she was no good and didn't want her. They gave her to Faith and Sharon to raise. After a lot of TLC, it wasn't long before she was walking and talking up a storm. In fact, they couldn't keep her quiet at times! Her family returned two years later, saw what a pretty little girl she had become, and realized that she really did have value after all, so they took her back. Jena loved her mother and longed for her, so it was a good reunion. Of course, it was heartbreaking for Faith and Sharon in ways that the rest of us could hardly understand, but in this line of work there is always heartache. The joy they had was knowing that for the short time she was with them, she was loved and cared for.

Sharon wrote, "Yesterday was a time of grieving for all of us, but more for Faith and me … The horror in how she died … And yet, Jena had accepted the Lord at one of the seminars not too long before this and her life had changed. I so wanted to be angry with them all, especially her mother, but while weeping by the funeral fire at this unnecessary death, I could only feel compassion for them."

As a missionary, during these traumatic times, we don't have the privilege of just sitting and grieving, but instead have to be everywhere, trying to be the voice of reason. There are always many who counsel revenge and death, and so the few of us who try to speak up about what God says about this find ourselves, many times, not very accepted. Nevertheless, while things remain tense, it is also obvious that people are listening to the small, still voice of the Lord. I was able to meet today with headmen from the three families most involved and all of them asked us to keep praying for them; although this is an extremely difficult time, they want to do what God wants them to do.

Jena's body was cremated and her bones were gathered; at that point, the bones have to be buried. This potentially is the most stressful, dangerous time, as it is not uncommon for someone to go berserk in their grief—as I said, a very stressful time. Early the next morning, we went down to the house where they were going to bury Jena's bones. What a sad sight to see the mother, who by all accounts had been the leader of the mob demanding that the girl be severely punished. She was wailing the loudest, clutching the basket of her daughter's bones to her naked chest. I tried to be angry at her, but found myself only feeling sorry for her.

The hole in their hearth was finally deep enough for the little box Keila had made for them. The mourners' lamentations increased in intensity while the basket holding the bones was carefully untied and the bones gently placed into the box. After making sure the box was closed to his satisfaction, Vicinte, the father of the boy who had killed the girl, slowly stood up. Asking the mourners to quiet down, he said: "I was gone when this happened, but when I was told about this tragedy, all I wanted to do was avenge myself like our culture demands, but now I answer to a higher authority. God's Spirit is telling me that I need to forgive. My anger is of the devil and I have asked God to take it away from me. I don't want to live like the old way."

At his words, the old lady began to dance around in anger and began to berate him for being a coward and not avenging her daughter. She grabbed up his arrows and shook them violently, but everyone pretty much ignored her. After the box was put in the ground and the hole filled up, Vicinte asked me to read some verses. I did and then finished up with a prayer for them.

We walked back up to my house. Most of the men of the village were over in our cookhouse waiting. Without knowing which way Vicente might lash out, most had stayed away. Vicente and

I walked over and sat down. Timoteo, the father of the boy with whom the young lady was supposedly having the affair, started talking about how all the men sitting around there had all been little children or born after Dad came to their village. "We have all heard the message of love and forgiveness that our missionary brought us and that his sons are still teaching. Today, we all have to decide if this message is real or do we only mouth the words. For me, the message is real. God's word speaks of love, speaks of justice, and the wages of sin, but it also speaks of compassion. This is what we all need today. We need compassion. So, Vicinte, we don't want to yell and threaten and listen to you yell and threaten, I just want compassion. We have come too far to throw it all away now. A tree grows and puts its roots down deep. A big storm blows, but because the tree's roots are deep, it stands. We have had a lot of teaching. It is time we really stand, not just when things are going well, but when the storms come. This is a storm and I want to stand for God and what He teaches in His Word." The other heads of families said basically the same thing and then the meeting was over. I could not help but feel that so much of this entire affair seemed to be spiritual in nature and that the village had passed a huge test.

Then, a few days later, Keila was shocked to see that one of her orchid trees had literally disappeared from outside her kitchen window. I mean, it was just gone! She walked all over our yard wondering what could have happened to it, still hoping maybe a freak wind had picked it up and deposited it somewhere nearby. By the way, this "tree" was a trunk of a dead tree that was about six inches in diameter and probably twelve or fourteen feet long. Anyway, she could not find her tree, nor a trace of the beautiful white orchids that she had purposely kept close to the house because they were so lovely.

I, too, was mystified by the disappearance and joked to Keila not to accept any kids bringing orchids, as I could see them taking the tree, stripping the orchids off, and then, one at a time, bringing the orchids to swap for rice. Suddenly a light went on in my brain! "Keila, who brought most of those orchids?" I asked.

She thought for a moment. "It was Cojoima and her daughters and other kids from that family…" Her voice trailed off as she realized where I was going with my question.

Although we have no proof, we believe the tree was taken to be destroyed, as most of the orchids had been gotten from Jena, the girl who was killed. Her mother must have been reminded of the orchids when she came up to beg for a bag of rice, which we gave her; that is the only thing that makes sense. To the Yanomamö, everything that belonged to a dead person must be destroyed, as they don't want to be reminded of that person. We believe Cojoima came and took the orchid tree so she would not be reminded of her dead daughter. I just wish she had said something: we could have moved it from her sight.

◈ ▣ ◈ ▣ ◈

Death comes calling far too frequently in a Yanomamö village. Keila and I walked back up from Laban's house where they were having a funeral for his little three-year-old daughter. I could not help but be amazed at what an enormous change the Gospel of Jesus Christ makes in our lives!

Most of the time, only the pastor or one of us missionaries reads from the Word and tries to give words of comfort, but this time it was the family sharing. Laban's oldest brother spoke first. "We are very sad this morning, but one thing gives us strength and hope, that is, the knowledge that we have, that this is not the end. There is coming a day when we will all be in heaven. This little one has only gone on ahead of us. Now, while this brings me sadness, the fact that my father is already in heaven and other sisters and relatives are in heaven, knowing that this little girl who has gone on has family there to welcome her brings me much gladness. God is good to us. First because he sent missionaries to bring us the Good News and second, now, because of His Word, we have the assurance of where we are going. So, in spite of this sorrow, I say 'Thank you Lord!'"

I knew they would ask me to say a few words and I had some verses ready, like Matthew 19:14: *But Jesus said, 'Suffer little children, and forbid them not, to come unto me: for of such is the kingdom of heaven...'* But before it was my turn, someone else brought that verse, so I picked the precious verses in 1 Thessalonians 4 where it talks about how *we which are alive shall not precede them which are asleep*—and someone else beat me to that one, too.

My heart rejoiced that these precious brothers and sisters in Christ have truly been listening to all the years of teaching and God has made His Word real in their hearts to give them something to lean on during hard days. So many of the people who talked this morning told how thankful they were that someone had come to their village and had given them the hope that they have in Christ. This has been an incredibly difficult work, but on days like this, in deep humbleness, we rejoice at the spiritual growth we have seen and are thankful that God has allowed us to participate in this great job. How thankful we are for the wonderful team God has put in place for us to be able to continue working here.

◈▣◈▣◈

Some days, it is hard to remember all this when sickness and death stare you in the face. Kindra had been near death in a deep coma. No one expected her to come out of the coma, but she surprised everyone and did, in fact, not only come out of it, but also showed every indication that she was going to make a recovery. The believers met at her house every night to pray for her. They were spending every night singing and reading scripture to her and praying for her all night long for more than a week.

Then, she took a sudden turn for the worse and went unconscious again. Her sister, Cantana, was with her when she regained consciousness. Cantana told me: "My sister looked well when she regained consciousness. Her face was lively and she was animated. She asked me to call her children and she spoke to each one, calling each by name. Then she asked for her dad and spoke with him. She asked for her brothers, but when I told her they were down in Esmeralda she said 'OK.'"

"She looked at me intently. 'Sister, I am going home. Don't be sad for me, don't let anyone say it was some kind of a curse, God is calling me home. He has already showed me heaven and He has told me it is my time to come home. I am ready, sister. Don't mourn for me. I am going home.'"

With tears in her eyes, Cantana went on: "My heart sank when she told me she was leaving, because I was going to miss her so much. As you know, my sisters and I are very close. I started to cry and she told me, 'Don't cry, sister. We will see each other again.' She looked so well I could not believe she was telling me she was leaving, but she lay back down in her hammock and the next thing I knew, she had left me."

"So now, I wanted to tell you that while it is true I am grieving for my sister, in my heart, I am strong. I know I will see her again. What a precious gift God gave me by allowing her to get well enough to talk to me before she left." She told me, "You know, when someone you love dies, there is always a doubt about them, about their eternity. Well, today, because I had such a good talk with Kindra, I have no doubts. My heart is at rest. I am strong in my trust in God."

By the time she was finished, we all had tears running down our faces, but they were tears of joy. Then, if that were not enough, Kindra's husband, Alberto Perez, came to the house with Nando. Nando and I were able to lead him to the Lord. Actually, it was his wife's testimony and her dying words that broke his pride and allowed him to become a new creature in Christ.

These have been hard years. But with a testimony like Cantana's, and then watching Alberto accept Christ as his personal Savior… well, it just does not get much better than this. We can honestly say it has all been worth it and will truly be worth it all when we see Jesus!

This is why we have this hope! Praise Him!

3

EMBARRASSING MOMENTS

A posting on Fredericksburg.com on April, 26, 2105, read: "VILLAGERS' BENEFICIAL BACTERIA WOWS! In a remote part of the Venezuelan Amazon, scientists have discovered that members of a village isolated from the modern world have the most diverse colonies of bacteria ever reported living in and on the human body."

I could not help but smile while reading the article. I remembered one of our rare furloughs as kids, when our parents took us to the Camdenton Medical Center for our checkups and antiparasite treatments. As part of the routine, we all had to give samples (I won't go into further detail). What was funny was that the laboratory staff of the medical center called and asked my parents if they could get another sample from one of my brothers. They said his samples contained things they had never seen before, and they wanted enough of it for further study so they could start cataloging some of his biodiversity. We were joking about it the other day, saying we possibly could have gone into business and sold the stuff, but we were naïve and just gave it away.

◈ ▣ ◈ ▣ ◈

Back when we were kids, during furloughs from our work among the Yanomamö, we traveled all over the United States with Dad and Mom. We were shy kids and really did not care for all the times Dad insisted we get up and sing songs in Yanomamö or share a verse or testimony. During the entire ride to the church, we would plead and beg Dad not to make us get up. He would grin smugly and assure us that he would do what was best for us. Evidently, he figured what was best for us was that we get up and share! And share we did, practically coast to coast. One time in particular, Steve and Gary were called on to get up and sing. They briefly glared at Dad as they took their places on the stage and sang a gospel hymn in Yanomamö. When finished, they made their way back to their pew and sat down to applause from the congregation. A lady sitting near them reached across the aisle and handed them each a crisp new one-dollar bill. Grinning broadly, Steve looked over at Gary and said in a loud whisper heard by everyone in the church, "I'd of sang better if I would have known they were going to pay me!" Mom tried to melt into the pew. Good, good memories, despite our childish antics!

◈ ▣ ◈ ▣ ◈

As overseas missionaries, we don't visit with and get to know many of our relatives as much as we would like to and should. Case in point: One day Keila and I were invited for a brunch with some of Mom's family whom I had not seen in years. Of the four relatives, I knew one of Mom's sisters and her brother, but did not know her other two sisters very well at all. We walked into the restaurant where we were to meet and there were only two older ladies sitting at a table. They looked up smiling when Keila and I walked in. I had been expecting four people, but just assumed that the aunt and uncle whom I knew well had not showed up yet.

I looked around. "Well, not many people here yet," I told Keila.

"We are here. Go ahead and make yourselves at home," one of the gray-haired ladies told us. We sat down in the seats facing them across the table and tried to make small talk while waiting for the rest of the group. The conversation was stilted and forced and I couldn't figure out what was wrong. I expected the old ladies would at least have questions about my mom and dad still on the field … but nothing. I kept glancing at my watch, wondering where my other aunt and uncle were, prompting one of the ladies to ask if we were expecting someone else. I told her yes.

After about fifteen minutes of very forced, uncomfortable conversation, I was getting desperate. Just then, a door I hadn't noticed (into what I assumed another room) opened and one of my aunts stepped into the room. "Oh, here you are. We are all in this other room waiting for you," she told me, glancing at our table partners with a questioning look, waiting for us to introduce them. About that time, I realized the people we had been sitting with for the past fifteen minutes were not my relatives at all and were just as confused as we were! I at least had the sense to thank them for helping us pass the time, and followed my aunt into the adjoining room where the rest of the family were waiting.

◈ ▣ ◈ ▣ ◈

Sometimes, even in ministry I have displayed a knack for embarrassing myself, especially in the early days right after our missionary training ended and we returned to the field, thinking that because we had completed our training, we now knew it all. Thankfully, Bautista knew I did not know it all! He was a patient teacher and was not afraid to stand up and allow the Holy Spirit to speak through him. Looking back through a lifetime of lessons, one of the most memorable ones concerned my attempts to put the Gospel into Yanomamö chants. I detailed this story in my second book, *I Can See the Shore*, but here it is in a short version for those of you whom might not have read it.

While I was going to Bible school, I listened as seasoned missionaries from other fields told how, instead of translating Western music into native languages, they used the songs and chants of the native peoples, just putting Christian words to the tunes. Wow, I thought, this is great! I can try that. So, as soon as I returned to Cosh, I sat down with a few friends and we put Bible verses to the tunes of the chants I had learned as a kid. I couldn't wait for Sunday to wow the church with these new songs praising our Lord. *They will really appreciate this*, I remember thinking. *This will finally be their own expression of their love and praise for our Lord.*

Yacuwä and I, along with another person, got up and announced that we had translated some new songs that we wanted to teach them. They listened intently as we launched into the first chant, to which we had set John 3:16. As I watched their faces, my heart sank because instead of smiles, their faces showed gathering frowns. Thinking they might not have understood the gist of what we had done, we went right into the second chant, hoping to salvage a bad situation. To be honest, I couldn't understand why I wasn't seeing smiles. We had worked hard on this, and the words fit well. Why the frowns?

Bautista clued me in as he stopped me before I could start on the third chant. "What are you doing?" he asked me.

"I am giving you songs that you can sing that are really yours. This way you don't have to just sing our songs," I told him.

He shook his head. "No, you can't do that," he insisted.

"Bautista, listen to me. These songs will be yours. Do you only want to have something that we take from our country and bring to you? Why don't you understand what we are doing here?" I was frustrated and I am sure he could hear it in my voice.

Thankfully, Bautista had more patience than I did. "No, Maikiwä, you don't understand. Do you think just because you change the words that now it is OK to sing those old chants? Don't you know that not only do the words come from the *jecula*, but the entire chant is theirs? They even give the way it goes and sounds. Who do you think is smiling right now? I don't think it is God that is happy with hearing *jecula* songs in His house. But I will tell you, I believe that the *jecula* are enjoying this. Well, not in my church! We will never sing those songs in our worship services."

Quickly recovering, I realized what a mistake I had made. I promptly apologized, not only to Bautista but to the entire church family as well. It was a good lesson for me as a new missionary beginning to work—a lesson I really needed to learn.

The Yanomamö believers had a lot they could teach a green missionary, especially me. I needed to listen to these men. They knew an awful lot more about the spirit world than I did, and if I wanted to avoid a bunch of different pitfalls, I needed to listen. Praise God, I learned it right off! I can't tell you how many times I have been grateful that Bautista felt comfortable enough to stand up and correct me instead of just quietly going along. What a shame that would have been! Now, I am not making a statement or passing judgment on missionaries who have used native chants with their own tribes, but I am saying that one needs to exercise real wisdom, and have a clear understanding of the culture and beliefs of the peoples one is dealing with. I sure do know it did not work for us with the Yanomamö!

◈ ▣ ◈ ▣ ◈

The people with the best "embarrassing furlough story" have to be Gary and Marie. As is the norm, when returning from the mission field, you can't wait to get to the nearest Wal-Mart to look around. On one of their first excursions to the store, Marie was overjoyed to find a big five-pound bag of chicken jerky; knowing that Gary also loves it as much as she does, she bought two bags. Though she was a bit surprised to find it in such a large bag, she just figured it was Wal-Mart's marketing strategy to keep prices down.

They enjoyed their treat, and Marie even found the salty taste to be really good, although it was a bit dry, which prompted her to drink large quantities of water. After the first week, she was delighted to see she was even losing weight instead of gaining the "furlough flab" we usually have to put up with!

Well, losing weight while actually eating something you like is just too good to be true. The next time she was at Wal-Mart, she went back over to the jerky section and put ten of the five-pound bags in her cart, figuring she would pack some of it up and take it back to the field when they left. She waited for her daughter to finish shopping so they could check out. As they waited in the checkout line, Jeanie looked down at her mom's cart. "Mom, why are you buying so much dog food?" she asked.

"Dog food! What dog food? I don't have any dog food!" Marie replied.

"Yes, you do, Mom. This is dog food jerky," Jeannie patiently explained. "See, it says right here, 'Jerky for dogs.'" Well, all of a sudden those ten pounds of jerky they had already eaten didn't set so well! The moral of the story: If you have been overseas for a while and are afflicted with the effects of age, make sure you take your glasses and read the bag or carton before purchasing anything!

◈▣◈▣◈

Sometimes jungle-raised missionary kids who go on to become missionaries themselves find themselves in embarrassing situations, many times of their own making. Case in point is my brother Gary. He was in a high-end shoe store (he has to have good shoes because of an ankle injury). While in there, he decided to also get himself a pair of flip-flops, or what we always called *thongs*.

Gary, not realizing that through the years the word has undergone a transformation and is no longer used for something worn between your toes, innocently asked the young lady who was helping him if he could purchase a good pair of thongs. She looked at him like he was something that had just crawled out from under a rock, and her mouth opened and closed while she was thinking about what to say.

Luckily for both of them, Marie had overheard Gary's question and rushed up to help. "He's looking for a pair of flip-flops," she told the shaken young lady. After being shown to the correct store section, when they were once more alone, Marie told Gary what he had asked for in today's English. It was Gary's turn to stare with his mouth wide open.

◈ ▣ ◈ ▣ ◈

Sometimes it is good to hear your stories from a different perspective. In my book *Growing Up Yanomamö*, I told the following story about one of my best friends, Yacuwä.

"Let's go swimming," I said.

"No, I am too hungry. If you want me to go swimming with you, you need to bring me something to eat. I am so hungry I'll drown."

"I can't. The last time I brought you food I got a spanking, as we don't have enough to even feed ourselves, my mom told me," I replied.

"Just bring me some bananas," Yacuwä said.

"No, I'll get a spanking, can't you hear?" We argued back and forth. Finally, I compromised. "OK," I told him, "I'll go in and steal you one banana."

"No, I want enough to make a drink. If you bring one, I won't take it," he insisted.

"Look, if they catch me with one, I can say I was hungry. If I have a bunch, they will know I came in to take them to give away, and we just don't have enough. I'll be spanked again, and I refuse." I walked in and picked the largest banana I could find. He will be happy with this one, I thought. It is big enough we could both make a drink out of it. I took it out to him, but instead of a "thank you," Yacuwä looked for another banana. When he realized it was the only one coming, he threw it in disgust to the ground. Picking up a stick that was lying there, he beat it into a squishy pulp on the ground.

"Bei!" he said and walked away, the little tail of his loincloth bobbing along behind him.

Well, today we were all together laughing and swapping lies — I mean, stories — when someone asked me about that incident with the banana. Jaime, who used to be called Yacuwä, was there, so I said, "Tell them the story, Jaime, it was you after all who got me the spanking!"

He smiled really big and said, "Well, I was so hungry, I wanted Mike to bring me enough bananas to make myself a banana drink, but he was too selfish and only brought one. He kept making some lame excuse that he was afraid his mom would spank him, so I refused to eat it." He closed with a smile.

"So, you have been thinking all these years I was just too stingy?" I asked. "Well, let me tell you the rest of the story in case you don't remember it." My memory took me back, and because it had to go all the way back to a small boy about seven years old, it was a long way back. I remembered feeling guilty that I had stolen the banana. I had prayed the sinner's prayer not too long before that incident, so the weight of my sin was rapidly becoming too heavy for my skinny little seven-year-old shoulders. I found my oldest sister, Faith, and confessed to her that I had stolen a banana. Remember, we were barely keeping body and soul together ourselves, so stealing food was a serious offense that even a seven-year-old understood.

Anyway, I told Faith and she told me: "Listen, Mom is in there working and she is in a really good mood. You can hear her singing." Sure enough, my mom's beautiful voice was singing loudly as she swept the dirt floor in our house. "Go in right now and tell her what you did. She is in a good mood and you will probably get off with just a warning," Faith told me again. So, I hurried in. I remembered thinking that this way, I would have a clean conscience and possibly get away with it.

I stood beside my mom, made my face as contrite as I could, and slowly told my story: How, though I didn't want to disobey her, I had been forced to steal food again. I was surprised to see her face change, and she forcefully took me by the arm and led me to a bench. Laying me over her knee, she proceeded to give me the good spanking I probably deserved but had really hoped I could avoid.

"Easy for you to call me stingy, but it was me who had to endure getting spanked!" I finished up to laughs from the entire group.

Later on, Mom, Sharon, and Faith walked down to my house

and we were laughing about Jaime's version of the story. "Anyway, that is the last time I am taking your advice!" I told Faith. Mom laughed and said, "Well, you all read it wrong. If had been having a lousy day, I would have felt guilty spanking one of my kids, as I would think I was just taking my frustrations out on them. As it was, you caught me in such a good mood—so enjoying singing to my Lord—that I just knew I had to do my motherly duties and discipline you good! You know, 'spare the rod, spoil the child!'"

◈▣◈▣◈

In this country of constant and numerous scarcities, we have adjusted by trying to make things last as long as possible—possibly even longer than intended. For instance, I found out that if I wet the hairs on my lower arm, I could strop my razor on it when the blades get too dull to shave with, so I could get much more time out of a set of blades before changing. I have been using the set of blades currently on my razor for almost three months now and they are still going strong. I am wearing out the hairs on my arm, but the razor is shaving well.

I recently became aware, though, that possibly I was trying too hard. I have gotten to where I use and reuse coffee grounds, leaving the old grounds in the pot and just adding a small scoop of new grounds to the mix, and it has done well: the resulting coffee is not too bad. What I didn't realize was that others—if you can call insects "others"—were enjoying my coffee as well.

Keila decided she wanted a cup of coffee (she has about one cup a week). I asked her not to throw my grounds out, as I had only just put them in two days ago. Unlike me, before just dumping in some new coffee, she opened the pot and looked in. With a straight face she asked, "So this is how you like your coffee now?" I assured her it was not bad, and to just put a little fresh stuff on top. "And what do I do with this thing? Just settle a few grounds on him, too?" she demanded, thrusting the pot under my nose. I reared back in fright. There, calmly drinking from a leftover coffee puddle on top of the grounds, was a huge roach. GAG, GAG, GAG!

◈回◈回◈

We headed downriver and got to La Esmeralda about twenty minutes before the plane with our supplies was to land. As we unloaded it, the guard (this time a friendly guy) started going through all the bags, asking "What is this? Where is the receipt for that?," and so on. For each question, we dutifully looked through our handful of papers to find the proper one; so far, so good. Then we unloaded a large plastic bag with twelve large glass bottles in it. Our "friend" zeroed in on that one like a hawk on a mouse.

"What is this?" he demanded.

"Well, to be honest, I am not sure what it is, but if my brother sent it up, it is probably some kind of natural remedy, since most of the pharmacies are empty. Let me read the label."

He looked at me funny and repeated: "But what is it?"

Timoteo and Lanzo, the two guys who were with me, were also trying to come up with what it was or possibly could be. Timoteo was sure it was apple cider vinegar, which we use for almost everything, and he kept saying, "It is probably vinegar." Well, our guard was not buying the vinegar idea, so he finally told Lanzo to uncap one of the bottles and smell it.

Lanzo did, and his face screwed up at the smell. My heart sank. It is utterly against the law, on any number of levels, to bring any kind of liquid spirits into Indian territories. *This is it,* I thought, *I am going to get it now!* There was no way in this world I was going to convince this guard that I am a teetotaler and have never touched alcohol. We had been caught red-handed with not one, but *twelve* bottles of hard liquor, and we were going to do hard time for sure. We are under so many different investigations and whatnot, at all times, that there is always someone willing and ready to throw the book at us. *So here we are,* I thought.

Suddenly the pilot came running up. "No, wait, that is not supposed to be on this plane! The loaders must have made a mistake. This does not belong to you all." I think he must have thought we were going to claim his liquor and he was making sure we knew it was his—as if we wanted it. I was more than happy to have him claim it.

"See, I told you it was not ours. No wonder we did not know what it was," I told the guard. The pilot took his twelve-bottle bag and returned to the plane. Later on, I saw him give it to one of the guys who was out there waiting, so I am sure it was not a mistake that the stuff was on the plane—but it sure could have been a huge mistake for us! All the more reason we need our own air support.

◈ ▣ ◈ ▣ ◈

I have got to start watching what I say. My daughter Mia and I were heading to the river to run up a ways and retrieve a boat and motor of mine. Mia talks incessantly, and normally I only need to grunt and nod my head once in a while and she is happy. Today, however, she got my attention by asking, "Daddy, how big is a gnat's nose?"

"What?" I asked. "I don't know if a gnat even has a nose."

"Well, you said they did," she responded.

I sure don't remember ever saying that. Smiling, I asked her, "When did I say anything like that?"

"The other day, when you were talking about my dog, Olaf, you said he was so dumb that if his brain was dynamite it wouldn't be big enough to clean out a gnat's nose."

What could I say? The dog *is* dumb, but maybe I did exaggerate a bit.

When Keila set out a bunch of flytraps, I really didn't think much of it until one Sunday when I had the church leaders over. As we were discussing the church service, my arm straightened out a bit as I gestured or jerked slightly, and all of a sudden I felt it flop into something sticky. Horrified, I jerked my arm up, and yes! I was trapped in Keila's flytrap! Now, my question is: Should I be concerned? Is there something bigger behind her placement of these traps? She has been mumbling about how busy Sundays have become. She swears it was innocent, but the smirk on her face says something else.

In case you are wondering, it cost me a good amount of the hair and the outer layer of skin on my arm to remove it. Thank goodness, Keila doesn't set out bear traps, but perhaps I should reschedule Sunday afternoon meetings ... I'm just saying!

4
THEOLOGY YANOMAMÖ STYLE

One day, while I was taking the boat out for a trip, six-year-old Mia came up to me with her face full of concentration. "Dad, does God love the jungle, too?"

"Of course, honey! He created it and loves it as much as He loves any place."

"But Dad, God punished the Egyptians with gnats during Moses' plagues, then Moses prayed and God took the gnats away. Dad, we have an awful lot of gnats here. Who is getting punished?"

What could I say? She does have a very good point!

◈ ▣ ◈ ▣ ◈

Any of you who have read my books, *Growing Up Yanomamö* and *I Can See the Shore*, know that Yacuwä, now known as Jaime, is one of my best friends up here. He has a very close walk with the Lord and I love listening to his testimonies. Every Friday, we open the Bible class up to anyone who wants to share their testimonies. On one of those days, I had some paper available on which to take notes, so here is one of Yacuwä's testimonies speaking of the way Satan traps people, keeping them away from the love of God.

"Satan is a hunter," he said. "He is like we are on the trail of an armadillo. We follow the armadillo's tracks here and there, finally running it into a hole. The armadillo thinks it is safe now. But we hunters don't give up. We run around and find a termite nest. We place the termite nest to fit tightly into the burrow, then we carefully find and plug every other hole. Then we light the termite nest on fire, blowing the smoke down into the armadillo's hole, down into the deepest part of the hole where the armadillo is hiding.

"First the smoke is just an irritant, easily ignored, but it gets stronger and stronger, overpowering the poor animal. What does it do before it dies? It does not try to escape, but rather, for some reason, is drawn right to the termite nest that is producing all the smoke that is killing it. Smoke is not a strong force, we think. It does not have strong arms to pull, or a net to catch your feet and drag you. But the smoke is strong enough to draw the armadillo right up to the termite nest and there it dies with its little nose pressed right against the thing that killed it. All we hunters have to do is withdraw the termite nest plug, wait a minute for the smoke to clear, and there is the armadillo.

"My friends, this is what Satan desires to do to us. He lures us into thinking we are safe, but all the time he is plotting our death and destruction. We are already safe in Jesus, but Satan desires to lure our children away. Christ is the only One strong enough to remove the lures of Satan and allow us to live a true life with Him.

"My father and his father before him and his father before him were all shamans, steeped in the twisted evil dark world of the demons. All of my uncles, my fathers, and brothers were also shamans. As a small child I was told that I belonged to the demonic world, and that my destiny was to be a shaman. My father, being from another village, wanted to take my mother and go home, so in the compromise I was left as a small child with my grandfather.

"He was the acting headman of the village when Pepiwä and Milimi came to live here and teach us the Word of God. At a very early age, the demons began to come, trying to lay their claim on my life, but at that time Pepiwä and Milimi began to teach us about Christ. Oh, how I was drawn to this message of peace and love! The message from the demonic world was about hate, revenge, murder, and many women. One side was light and peace and love, living by the power of the Great Spirit. The other side was dark and evil, filled with hate and fear and a lust for power.

"When I was still a young boy, the power of the gospel of Jesus Christ saved me and the demons were told to leave and not come back, as I was now a child of God. I spent the last seven years as a missionary to my father's village. He has now gone on, as have all of his brothers. He got saved and some of his brothers, too. God was good to me in this time, as many of my relatives have now called on the name of the Lord. Oh, how I wanted to thank Joe and Millie for teaching me about Christ, but I did not get back here before my spiritual father and dear friend went to be with the Lord. But I have told Millie how much I love her and Joe for bringing me the greatest gift of all: the gift of Jesus Christ.

"I, Jaime Perez, stand here today a child of God, redeemed and clean because two people obeyed God and came to a dying, filthy village and showed us the love of God. Join me, my friends, in living for Christ!"

◈▣◈▣◈

Listening to and writing down his testimony reminded me of another time I had been so blessed by his faith. I had been wrestling with what to share on our Christmas cards one year and had not gotten very far trying to think of something "Christmas-y" to write about. This is not so easy when the outside temps are near 110 degrees. But then, during our time of sharing, my heart filled with joy listening to Jaime, and then even more joy as I realized he had given me exactly what I needed to share. Remember, the Yanomamö do not keep track of days or even months. We have two seasons here — a rainy season and a dry season — so when Jaime was giving his testimony, he was not thinking, "This is the Christmas season, so I will say..." but I felt he told the Christmas story in full.

Here is what he said. "Today, I want to thank God for giving us His Son. I was only a young boy and almost dead of malnutrition when the missionaries first came. They told me about a God who loved me so much that He gave His only Son that I might have life. When I heard this, I fell in love with the man who was God but left His power and became a man, not to live in riches as befits a king, but humbly, then died, so that I might have life abundantly. This amazes me! Every time I think about this, I am speechless. God loved me so much He gave His Son! This is good to think about. *God gave us His Son.* This makes me very happy! This is my testimony today."

I'll tell you, this testimony made my day! Not to mention that he gave me more than I needed for my Christmas card that year!

While listening to his testimony, I could not help but remember a day in April of 2006, when a young man in the village got into a fight with his wife. He beat her savagely, and when the wife's mother took up for her, he also beat his mother-in-law, actually taking a machete and chopping her twice in the head. The lady's husband (the boy's father-in-law) was Jaime, and we were over in church when this was going on. As soon as the service was over, people ran in to give him all the details. Jaime told Gary and me that he was just going to go get his wife and go home, that he had no desire to fight. But when Jaime did get to where his wife was, there was a large group of people all yelling at him to take his son-in-law in hand and show him that he could not get away with chopping his mother-in-law.

Jaime insisted that he did not want to fight and turned to go, but his son-in-law's family insisted he take care of the situation. He finally gave in and took the offered pole and hit his son-in-law a blow to the head; much to his surprise and to the shock of everyone in the place, his son-in-law fell unconscious and died a short time later. As you can imagine, the village went crazy. The very men who had insisted that Jaime take care of the situation by fighting now grabbed weapons to avenge the young man lying dead. We were called to the group and we stayed up all night praying and counseling, trying to find some way of diffusing the situation.

The next morning, Steve, Gary, and I were lonely guys standing between the opposing sides of the village. It was really ugly, with people urging the Rivas family, one of the largest families in Cosh, to just run over us and knock us out of the way. It seemed like we were staring death in the face. In my case, death's face was painted with black war paint and his eyes were angry and bitter. The headman of the entire Rivas family was a man by the name of Älawä. He had made a profession of faith years earlier, but his life had never shown a change.

As a mediator for the Yanomamö, as long as I am unarmed, I can stand in the way of, and hold onto, someone's weapon so he can't use it. He can try to wrench it away from me and push me, but culturally I am pretty safe. I stared into his hard eyes and gripped his spear harder as he tried to break my grip. I knew he and his son, Vinciente, who was standing shoulder to shoulder with him, were two of the main ones who had been urging Jaime to avenge his wife and show his son-in-law that the young man could not get away with that kind of behavior. Now they were insisting that Jaime had to die.

Things were tense. I doubted whether we could talk them out of the violence that threatened to sweep right over us. I was crying out to God to give us the words that would cut through the haze of hate that blinded and gripped them. While still holding on to Älawä's spear but talking to his nephew, Julio (the brother of the boy who was killed), I asked him, "Julio, is this what God's word tells us to do? Are your actions this morning going to bring your brother back?" I looked deep into Julio's eyes and saw his anger slowly turn to shame. "God's word says for us to forgive," I urged. With a barely perceived nod, Julio turned away and slowly made his way out of the front lines facing us and back to his house. Slowly, with God's help, another one, then another, turned to go home. Finally, it was just Älawä. He lowered his head and looked down at my hands still gripping his spear. I let go and he turned and walked on home, leaving Steve, Gary, and me standing there with the women who had gathered to watch and yell advice. To be honest, I was more afraid of the women than the men.

Suddenly we heard another commotion up by Timoteo's house. We ran up there and found another group taking an axe to Timoteo's door, because someone had heard that Jaime was hidden in there. Again, God intervened and we were able to talk them into going away. As soon as the crowd melted away, we started making plans to get Jaime out of the village.

We decided that we would move Jaime to my house as soon as we could, as we knew that one hot-head talking to the rest could easily get a crowd yelling for blood again—and that we might not be able to talk them out of something everyone would later on regret a third time. All that day, we hid Jaime in our house while secretly I got my boat and motor ready. We found a neutral driver to sneak the boat away from the village and wait for us upriver. That evening, we got Jaime out of the house and spirited him away, up to where the boat was hidden. I can't tell you how relieved we all were to have him safely out of the village.

He has been living in exile ever since that time, and has maintained a really good attitude about the whole affair. He never had intended to hurt his son-in-law and yet, at the same time, he knew the family had every right to demand his death. He has repeatedly asked if there might be some way that he could make restitution and has asked the family for forgiveness. He has spent the time since this happened working in the church up in Yajanamateli and, to be honest, the Lord has really used him up there. A part of the Rivas family who are strong believers have forgiven Jamie, and have urged the rest of the family to forgive him and allow him to return, but to no avail. It has been a closed subject.

After the situation had persisted for a number of years, unknown to most in the village, Marcos, Jaime's cousin, went up to Yajanamateli to get Jaime. Bautista, Jaime's uncle, had almost died, and the family was worried that he was going to pass away and not get to see Jaime again, so Marcos took matters into his own hands and left to go get Jaime. (As I said, most people in the village, Gary and me included, did not know anything was happening.) When Marcos and Jaime got to the village, things turned ugly really fast. To say we were worried would be a huge understatement.

Gary and I met with the believers in the Rivas family, and they too were really worried that they could not control the side of the family that was insisting on revenge. We prayed together, asking God to intervene and show Himself strong the next morning. Rumors were that they were going to attack Jaime at dawn. We asked our prayer partners to be much in prayer at dawn.

There was no attack at dawn, but the situation was not resolved. We knew it would only take the smallest incident to blow the entire village into some kind of war. This had been a black cloud over the village since the day it happened, and we have all recognized and spoken about the need to forgive and restore. So, for the past two months we had been meeting as a group of believers at 5:30 every morning, asking God to heal the village and give us a real revival. Honestly, looking at the last six years, this is where it does have to start, so my prayer is that this is God's timing and He is going to do a real work.

How we praised the Lord when the anger and pride of the Rivas family finally broke and they publicly accepted Jaime's request for compassion and publicly forgave him! What a blessing it has been to see Jaime and the Rivas family once again in good friendship and fellowshipping with each other. Only the power of the Gospel could do this. What a testimony of the power of the message of love of Jesus Christ!

◈▣◈▣◈

Another testimony was given after Nando's little daughter died. Nando stood up and shared how, in spite of the fact that he had much sadness, "our hearts remain strong and our comfort is in Christ. Even though my family is sad now, we know that our little girl is in heaven. This is our comfort. In Yanomamö villages without the gospel of Jesus Christ, they don't have this knowledge, and so when tragedy strikes them, they have nothing to fall back on. We Yanomamö believe that when someone dies, if he has been a generous person, he goes to live in thunder's land. But you know, down deep we had no comfort in that because we knew none of us were generous enough. But God is generous enough to cover for us, as He gave His Son.

"Now, because of His generosity, we are assured that when we die, and when our believing family members die, and when our little children die, we can rest in the fact that God's generosity is enough to assure us of heaven. Also, you know," he went on, "in spite of us saying we believed that our loved ones were OK because of their generosity, we knew they were not. How do I know this? Well, because of the fact that once a Yanomamö is dead, his name is never spoken again. Every evening, way into the night, family members cry and mourn for their loved ones. Our women take their tears and smear them on their faces, making a thick black crust of mourning on their cheeks. Why? Because they know they will never see our loved ones again. Here, on the other hand, you don't see many women with black on their faces. Not because we don't grieve: We grieve, but not like ones with no hope. We have hope. Our hope is Christ!"

◈ ▣ ◈ ▣ ◈

I have also been thinking a lot about another man's testimony yesterday. He told the story of Moses and how when God was talking with Moses that He told Moses that He was the God of Abraham, the God of Isaac, and the God of Jacob. The man said, "This really makes me feel glad and content to know that there is a God that not only loves us and has given so much to save us, but He is also a God who is personal. He knows me by name. I am so happy to serve our God and I know He knows my name." Hearing my friend bring out this so very simple truth really blessed me because way down, I know it to be true. God loves me with a personal love and He knows my name.

◈ ▣ ◈ ▣ ◈

Although it is true that we don't know what the future holds here in Venezuela, we do know who holds the future. We struggle to find the most basic of items, like milk, sugar, coffee, any kind of soap or shampoo, and even bathroom tissue, not to mention bottled gas for cooking, gasoline for our outboards, and diesel for our generator. But in spite of this, we continue to see Christ building His Church as He promised. During one of our early morning prayer and Bible study times, we opened up the meeting for general sharing. I was surprised to see Freddy stand up. As a matter of fact, when Freddy started coming to the class, about a month earlier, I could not believe my eyes.

This is a man who, although he had grown up in Cosh under the influence of the Gospel his whole life, had never showed any interest in spiritual things at all. When he was a teenager, he had been bitten by a large bushmaster [snake] and almost died. My sisters worked with him for months, doctoring his leg and never giving up even when it seemed his leg would have to come off because it was so infected. His leg stank so badly that it was difficult even to be near him, let alone work on him, but God healed him. Although he lost some toes, he regained full use of his leg—and yet he still wanted nothing to do with the God who had healed him.

That's why I was so surprised to see him stand up, and even more surprised when he quietly gave his heart and life to the Lord. He told how, in spite of all his resistance, God had continued to work in his heart and he was finally giving his life to Him. He asked us all to pray for him so that he would truly live for the Lord. He was someone I never thought would become a Christian. Praise the Lord with us!

◈▣◈▣◈

A while ago, we received word via radio from Shijobuwei, a village way up the Ocamo and then the Iyowei Rivers. One of our friends who is related to many people here in our village was badly mauled by a jaguar. We were told that Onesimo had gone night hunting and had not returned home. The search parties that were sent out found a dead jaguar and then, just up the trail a ways, an unconscious Onesimo.

We were scared for him, as we know a jaguar's teeth and claws are full of infection, so we knew poor Onesimo was in for a long, rough road to recovery. We prayed intensely for him and tried to get more information on his condition. They said he had been carried back to the village and was not doing well. The river was too low to get a boat and motor up there even if we had had enough gasoline to drive it. So, we continued praying for him.

Imagine my surprise when, a short time later, Onesimo showed up, looking to be in better health than I am! Figuring our prayers had been answered beyond our wildest hopes, we greeted him with excitement, only to be met by his utter bewilderment. Onesimo knew nothing of a jaguar, nor of being mauled. Now, we were almost angry at him: We had wasted a lot of prayers on him, after all! He assured us that he had not heard the story until he got to our class, and could not be held responsible for it. "You should be happy I am well; in a sense, your prayers are answered. You wanted me well, OK, I am well! Let's all be happy!" he encouraged us with unabashed Yanomamö logic … something we finally agreed to, though a bit reluctantly. We still don't know why and how the story got started or what the purpose was.

◈ ▣ ◈ ▣ ◈

We were getting ready for another trip when it started pouring rain. Tropical downpours are no joke. After the rain stopped, we took off—much later than we had anticipated, but because the boat had places to hang hammocks, we were in fine spirits. After about sixteen hours of running time, we were passing the village of Majecototeli, and a guy waved us to stop. Everybody wants you to stop at their village, just to hear the latest news, if for no other reason. But it was already 2:00 p.m. and the village I had promised we would sleep at, so that we could show the Jesus/Passion movie, was still more than four hours upriver. I stood up and yelled at the guy motioning us in. "We will stop on our way downriver. I promised to sleep in Cashola." I waved and we continued on up the river. The last I saw the guy, he was sprinting up the bank to his village. That's funny, I wonder why he was running so hard, we all said to each other.

About ten or fifteen minutes later, a speedboat came roaring around the bend in hot pursuit of our slow boat. By this time, we could see that the six heavily armed guys in the boat were all painted black. This is not a good color with the Yanomamö! They roared past us and disappeared around the bend. *Boy, I wonder where those guys are going,* I remembered asking myself. I shouldn't worried, because as we went around the same bend, there they were! We had to panic-stop to keep from hitting them. They motioned us to pull over beside their speedboat. Since they had the weapons, we figured it was a good idea. They were armed with bows and arrows and one guy had a 12-gauge shotgun. We stopped!

I was glad I recognized some of the guys, and one especially was a good friend. "Hey, if I would have known it was that important for us to stop, we would have made time," I tried to joke, but they were serious. As we pulled alongside, they grabbed our boat.

"Oh, it is you!" The head guy finally had slowed down enough to recognize me.

"Yes, friend, it is me," I told him, glad that he had finally acknowledged that he knew me.

"We thought you were someone else. If you would have been that person, you would be floating face down in the river by now! But you are my friend! You may continue your trip! But you should know when I am really angry, you should stop and tell me where you are going. This way, I don't chase you down!"

"Friend," I told him in all sincerity, "if I would have had the slightest idea that you were this touchy up here, I would most surely have stopped! I planned to stop and visit with you on our way back down. I yelled telling the guy waving at us that we had to sleep in Cashola tonight, but would visit on the way down."

He nodded. Finally, I saw him relax, so we visited for a bit. Telling him what day we would be heading back down, I pushed away from their boat and waved at my guy to start our engine.

We continued our trip and finally made it to the village of Cashola. This was a Sunday evening. We had been traveling for a bit over twenty hours just in travel time. By that time, we were way up the Orinoco River, it was late, and I had promised the Cashola residents that we would show them *The Jesus Movie*, so we got everything ready and started the movie. While showing the Passion part of the movie, a lady started wailing as if she were wailing for a family member who had died. She refused to be comforted or silenced. She was deeply affected by the movie. Hearing her wails, I planned on trying to speak with her and her husband after the movie, but they disappeared into the night while I was talking with someone else. By that time, it was 11:30 p.m., so, telling myself I would try and speak with them in the morning, we went to bed. Sadly, I did not see them the next morning. We prayed that the Holy Spirit would continue to work in her heart and draw her to Himself.

While talking with the people of Cashola, we mentioned the village we were ultimately heading for. I was carrying some letters from a major news organization to see if the village would sign an invitation for them to be able to come to the village. It was this organization that had purchased the fuel that was allowing us to get all the way up here. But when we mentioned that village, the Cashola men were pretty emphatic: "They are not home, the village is empty. They left on trek long ago. Their gardens are empty so they are just on *wayumi*, on trek." It is always so interesting how these peoples who live miles apart somehow know what is going on in the other areas. Even with an outboard motor, it was going to take us almost five hours to get there from this village, but they knew despite their lack of modern communications. Anyway, this was a big problem for us. I felt responsible to at least deliver and read the letters to them, but now they were supposedly not home.

"Who knows where they go when they go on *wayumi*?" I asked. A couple of guys stepped up. "Do you all want to come with me, so in case they are not home, you can find them for us?" They were exuberant.

"Yes! We will come," they told me. We took off, heading back up the Orinoco River. At 10:00 a.m. we got to the rapids and pulled in to walk along the shore through the jungle to try and find the best way to get our boat through there. It can be a nasty portage, especially as the boat we were using was a bit larger than we normally travel in, so I wanted to walk the whole thing to make sure there were going to be no surprises.

We figured out the best way through, and tying the twenty-five meter rope to the prow of the boat, we started pulling it along the shore. I stayed back at the motor and used it to help propel the boat over hard points where the guys pulling were not able to make headway. We were making good time, but we got to a place where even with everyone pulling and the motor screaming full power, we just stopped. We worked as hard as we could, but it became obvious that the boat was not going to get over this hump. We were stopped. Then we had to back the boat back down, which is quite a bit harder to do than to tell about it, I must say. But we finally did make it back down, and then the question was: Where to go?

We were pushing the boat with a small 15-hp outboard and I was not sure if it would be enough if we just tried to run it through the main channel. The current was strong, but we really didn't have many other options. So, we pushed out into the current of the Calabä Rapids to try again. There were a few tense minutes when we came to a place where the boat just stopped and we were not sure we were going to make it through, but we moved a bit to the right, got behind some big rocks where the current was less, built up a bit of speed and pushed on through it. All good, except for the extra grey hair.

At 2:00 p.m. we arrived at Ilocai's port. It was obvious from the lack of fresh tracks that the village was in fact deserted, and had been for a while. We walked on up to the village and it was empty. An empty Yanomamö village is eerie, hauntingly so. You find yourself speaking in whispers. Two of the guys who had come with us assured us that they could find the missing villagers and took off running into the jungle. We continued to look around the village that at first glance had appeared deserted, and it became obvious it was anything but when I looked down at my pants, which were literally crawling with fleas! The ground appeared to be moving!

Fleas were everywhere. Count stars? Sand? Abraham would have had a shorter time counting the stars or the sands of the seashores than trying to count the fleas in that village, I'll tell you! Mercy!

After the runners left to try and find the missing villagers, we quickly decided that with the massive number of fleas crawling everywhere, staying at the deserted village was not a wise option. We made our way back to the river bank and our boat. Coffee is always good, so we boiled up a pot and sat around trying to list our options if the runners could not find the villagers of Ilokai. We had thought we would sleep in the village, but it was pretty unanimous that with the fleas, we would just stay on the river bank. Well, we might just as well have taken on the fleas, because as darkness fell, the mosquitoes rose out of the jungle around us and we were quickly engulfed in a fight for our lives. I am not sure how many pints of blood one can lose and still live, but I am willing to bet those mosquitoes came close to getting that amount from us. We had already swatted—and if we would have been lesser men, I would say we swatted and swore, but I never heard a word except grunts of pain and wails of misery from my companions.

Then one of the guys from Cashola who had come with us arrived, saying he had seen smoke rising from right outside the village. He was so convinced in his mind that it was enemy *oca* (black magic raiders) that he wanted to move away from that area. We tried to talk him out of it, but figuring that the mosquitoes could not be that bad everywhere, we got in the boat and moved across the river. If you are being swarmed, maybe one or two million less is hardly worth writing about, but to be honest, I think the mosquitoes were worse where we moved to. At first light, we moved back over to the village's port. We had no way of knowing if the guys searching for the villagers would even find them, so we were pleasantly surprised when at 8:00 a.m. a young guy came in, barely panting from his early morning run.

He assured us that the people were behind him and would be arriving shortly. By 8:30 they were all there. I read the letter to them and they were enthusiastic in their endorsement of the project. We finished up our business and I asked them how they were going to sleep in the village with all the fleas.

"What? No, we are leaving right after you show us the moving pictures you showed to Cashola," they told me. I tried to explain that with a video projector it has to be dark, and it would be impossible to show the movie to them during the day. They did not understand, so we decided to just set it up and let them see for themselves. They really wanted to see the pictures! It seems the runners we had sent to find them had spent most of the night telling them about the man who was beaten and did not try and defend Himself. We set it up and we were right: It was way too bright in the *shabono*, a structure that has a round circular roof with an open center, so there was no "room" to darken. One of the guys with me reminded me about a large tarp we had with us. We moved the projector to a section of the *shabono* where we could wrap the tarp around it and it was not bad! The movie showed up way better than I had thought it would, so we started it.

You could not hear a peep out of them as they watched the Greatest Story Ever Told! I kept being distracted by the fleas, which were not only walking up my pants leg, but actually making my skin crawl as they marched rank by rank up my legs *inside* my pants. There was no stopping them! I finally gave up. How in the world the naked people watching the movie could just sit on the floor and act like there wasn't a flea within a hundred miles is beyond me.

I love *The Jesus Movie* showing the Passion that we have translated into Yanomamö and have shown it hundreds of times, which means I have watched it hundreds of times. But honestly, this time it felt like it was just endless. When it was finally over, the people got up and melted away into the trackless jungle, with hardly a word. They had a long walk back to where they were living in the jungle. I wished we could have talked them into staying a bit longer, but they left because there was no food and the fleas were terrible. Boy, didn't I know it! I prayed God's Spirit brings the Gospel they saw and heard back to their minds. As soon as they departed, as there was nothing left there but the fleas, we made our own hurried departure.

We headed back downriver at 12:00 noon and traveled until it was too dark to see. We were awakened at 3:00 a.m. by a fierce storm. We hurriedly took our hammocks down and moved back to the boat. Finally, at about 10:00 a.m., it settled down to a drizzle so we continued back downriver. We arrived home at 6:00 p.m., tired but glad to be home. Did I mention we scratched all the way home? Then, to make matters worse, the next day I started feeling the pinpricks of pain that signal the presence of *niguas*, flea eggs. Keila was kind enough to get her medical kit and go to work. All in all, she dug eight out of my feet and one from under they pinkie on my right hand! Mercy! Good to be home!

◈ ▣ ◈ ▣ ◈

The results of the 2013 election in Venezuela left us devastated, as the candidate we were hoping would win was defeated. We figured that now there was every chance that the government would order us out—or worse, come up and arrest us. To be honest, I just did not know how to take this setback. We had prayed intensely for divine intervention.

So, I was very subdued when heading over to my Bible class the morning after the election. As I said, humanly speaking, this was a huge disappointment. After class, while I was speaking with my good friend Nando, he commented, "I am not sad over the [election] outcome."

Sure, I thought to myself, *what have you lost? Nothing really changes for you.* But his next words felled me. "My confidence is in God, I am happy in Him."

Wow! Amen! Our confidence is in Him! Philippians 4:4 comes to mind: *Rejoice in the Lord alway: and again I say, Rejoice.*

5

BAUTISTA AND POKÉMON

"Hi Michael, I don't expect you to remember me, but my dad and I stayed with you all with Don Shire back in 2003. Random question, can you refresh my memory on what Bautista said about Pokémon? I remember him describing them as little demons. Crazy thing is they are everywhere up here and I share his testimony with others, it's not believed. Do you have that testimony written anywhere so I can share it? Random, I know. Stay strong in the Lord my friend."

Landon

◇ ▣ ◇ ▣ ◇

I stared at my screen. It was almost 7:00 p.m. of a very long day. Bautista had been sick and was failing rapidly. I had notified Gary that I was canceling my flight out, as I did not think it right to be gone from the village when I knew Bautista's days were numbered. Gary agreed, but because the flight was already scheduled and the necessary permits issued, instead of canceling the flight, Gary would fly up to see Bautista. I had gotten up early to make the 104-mile round trip by boat from Cosh to La Esmeralda to pick up Gary. Sharon went down to check on Bautista after I left and told him that I had gone downriver to pick up Gary.

"That is good, he needs to hurry," Bautista told her. "I am getting so tired." After the plane landed and we went through all the inspections and whatnot, we headed upriver and arrived back in the village about 1:00 p.m. We walked right on down to Bautista's house. I have always envied Gary's bedside style. He has such a gift! I always stand stiffly and fidget and never can put into words what I feel—but not Gary. He got right down on the floor beside the low-hanging hammock and hugged Bautista's wasted frame to himself. "I am here, Bautista, I am finally here," he kept repeating.

Bautista's granddaughter was sitting on the other side of the hammock. She put her mouth right against his ear and said, "Grandfather, can you hear me? Gary is here. He is asking about you." Finally, after repeated tries, the old man slowly opened his eyes. It finally registered who his guest was and he hugged Gary's arm to him with a strength none of us realized he still had.

"Is this you, Galiwä?" he whispered. "Is this really you?"

"Yes, I am here. It is me," Gary told him.

Bautista hugged his arm harder and said, with a bit stronger voice, "Gary, don't stop teaching my children. Keep teaching my children about Jesus. Love my children."

"I will," Gary promised. By this time, there was not a dry eye in the place, and some people were sobbing loudly, as we all knew we were witnessing an old man say goodbye to someone he loved.

"Galiwä, I am going to be leaving you soon," the old man whispered, in a voice so low that I could barely hear him.

"Yes, father, you are going to be leaving us soon. You are going on, but we won't be far behind you," Gary told him. "*Cujamö a da cobojälö* [Go on home ahead of me]," Gary told him.

"Yes, I am going on, but you are going to stay here and teach my children," the old man repeated. With those words he seemed to fall into a sleep. So, assuring the family that we would come back in a bit, we said our goodbyes and left. Not even an hour later, Mia, who had been up at my sister's house, came down and told us Bautista had died. Though it is impossible to grieve for someone who is standing in the very presence of God and reunited with so many of his own people who have gone before, we share the sadness of the village and the family. Our lives have been so blessed by our friendship with Bautista and by his trust in the Lord.

The village of Cosh is not going to feel the same. Still, we praised the Lord for the hope we have because of the resurrection of our Lord, Jesus Christ. The next days were difficult, but in spite of the sorrow of losing such a leader as Bautista, the village rejoiced in the fact that they knew he had gone to a better place and is with Jesus, whom he loved so much, and with my dad, who was closer to him than any brother.

That same day, I received a message from someone with whom I had had no contact with since 2003, asking me about Bautista and his comments on Pokémon. I sent him this note a few minutes later:

> *Hi again, Landon. Here is the link. I published it to my I Can See the Shore page a while ago as someone had asked me about it. By the way, Bautista was promoted to glory today at 3 p.m. I know the family and the village would appreciate your prayers.*

Adding the write-up on Pokémon as an attachment, I clicked the "send" button. Here is the article which has garnered such interest.

> As missionaries working with the Yanomamö, I am constantly reminded that when it comes to spiritual matters, I am not the expert. Bautista was an ex-witchdoctor or shaman. He

accepted the Gospel of Jesus Christ many years ago when my parents first started working with his tribe back in the early 50s. Although still a young man when they arrived to his village, he was a witchdoctor of considerable fame. He had already attained the highest level, known as *ijiluwalewä*, or childeater, because he could attack other villages in the spirit world, stealing the soul of a child there and causing the child to die. These souls were given to the many cannibal spirits who were his accomplices in this "murder." The soul would then be eaten by these demon cannibal spirits. Although having attained the highest level he could go, by his own admission, he was being overwhelmed by the bondage he was under even before he heard about the saving power of the Gospel. So once he clearly understood that Christ was the only way to be freed from this bondage, he accepted Christ's claim on his life and his life has never been the same.

One of the times I was reminded of how much more the expert he is in spiritual matters happened one day a number of years ago. We had been in the jungle many long weeks with no mail from home when the plane landed bringing us a package. I was excited as I took it home. "Look, hon, a package from a church back home." I gave her the package and she opened it immediately as she was as excited as I was. But, instead of something really interesting, like a box of chocolate or something, enclosed was a book. Now that in itself was a big enough disappointment, because I wanted some "real mail," but when I saw the cover, I was even more disappointed. It was a book on the Pokémon cartoon characters. I am old school on cartoons (Bugs Bunny, Road Runner, and their friends) and really don't get into any of the new ones, especially ones that look as ugly as these did. Then we noticed there was also a letter enclosed with the book and we read it together. "Dear Mike," it said, "it seems the church was having a discussion about Pokémon, with the church divided about this 'toy.'" So, they were sending this book of all the Pokémon characters and their attributes to me asking me to have Bautista look at it and see what he thought about the characters.

Well, that was more interesting than just having a book of ugly cartoons for the boys; but to be honest, this was pretty low priority for me. We are extremely busy in the jungle and I did not see any sense in this book. Keila reminded me that she had been telling me about this very cartoon. My sister had sent Stephen a tape of them and Keila had been telling me for weeks that she did not like what this cartoon was doing to our gentle son. She wanted me to watch it with him to see exactly what it was, but like I said, we are busy and I had not gotten to it yet. So, one day while I was talking with Bautista, Keila remembered the book and ran upstairs to get it. Bringing it back down, she handed the book to me. Just opening the book at random, showing him a picture, I asked, "What do you think of this, Bautista?"

He looked at it, and said, "Oh, I know this one." He suddenly had my attention! Looking closer at the picture, he went on, "Oh, this is a nasty little demon. It is always underfoot, bites, scratches, screeches, and what not." I looked at the page and on the list of attributes, and it said, "bites, scratches, screeches, claws..." and I forget what else. It was as if Bautista were reading the page, but he does not read or speak one word of English. I figured that the first one could have been just a lucky guess, so I flipped the page to another picture and asked him about that one, and again, he told me exactly what its attributes were. He did that over and over. There were some he did not recognize, and he said: "There are so many *jecula* (demons), it is impossible for any one person to know them all." So, he made a believer out of me.

Looking over my shoulder, Keila suddenly turned and ran up the stairs. She came back down a few minutes later leading our youngest son, Stephen. He did like Pokémon cartoons and from the look on his face, it was obvious he was not wanting to listen to anything anyone had to say against his cartoons.

Without saying anything to him, I flipped the page again for Bautista. Again, Bautista told us the name and the attributes of the demon cartoon. The list of attributes listed on the page was a direct translation of the name and attributes Bautista was telling us from his own experience with these ugly demons. Again, he did this over and over. Even someone as skeptical and defensive as Stephen finally had to admit that Bautista knew what he was talking about. He walked back upstairs and came back down with his VHS tape in his hand. Keila helped him destroy it.

Bautista looked on with curiosity. I explained that the tape held stories about these cartoons and that after listening to him tell about them being spirits from the demonic world, our son realized these things were not a toy and he did not want to have them any longer.

It was then I gave Bautista the history of the book and who had sent it to us. I explained that these cartoons were all the craze back in the United States and since many of the people in this church had heard him speak and respected him, they had sent this book to ask him if this was something they should be careful of, or did he think it was just a harmless toy.

"These are spirits and they are violent beings. They are always underfoot in the spirit world. These are the ones who entice the children into the spirit world." Then he added, "Tell the people from your churches that if there are things that make them feel uncomfortable, it is probably not good. This uncomfortable feeling is God's Spirit getting your attention. God's Spirit will speak to them about what is right and wrong."

As I was writing this chapter, I was thinking about Bautista and about his knowledge and spiritual discernment. I remembered again how I had thought the book the church had sent me was a waste of my precious time—but then, how much I had learned from the experience listening to Bautista. I had, of course, sent a writeup back to the church. As a matter of fact, once I saw how knowledgeable Bautista was on the subject, I had even gotten my video camera and set it up to record his comments. I translated the video with subtitles and even mailed the tape to the church. That was the last I had thought about it for a while. These things come in crazes, it seems, so then (it must have been around 2010 sometime) the question was once again asked about this cartoon. It was after that question that I went back, found my writeup, edited it down for a Facebook post, and posted it to my *I Can See the Shore* book page.

To be honest, I was surprised at the amount of pushback I received from it, especially from church youth workers. I found myself answering comments and questions, many of the comments rude.

In one of my responses, I tried again to tell people I did not consider myself any kind of an expert. I was not trying to make this about me. Here is one of my posts.

Hi all, my name is Michael Dawson and I guess you can say I am responsible for this thread by writing down and posting the article. I am not one who sees a demon under every rock and behind every bush, but having been born and raised with the Yanomamö in the

Amazon rain forest, I feel I can view this whole Pokémon thing from a bit different angle.

The Yanomamö are a tribe who, for who knows how many thousands of years, have been in bondage and worship Satan and his demons. Bautista, as a former witchdoctor, has a knowledge of the spirit world that I will never have. So when I asked him about the Pokémon craze by showing him a book on them and he started naming them, he had my attention. So, now, it has been extremely interesting to read all the comments and especially, to note the defensiveness of some of the comments. It reminds me of the last verse in the book of Judges, verse 21:25: In those days there was no king in Israel and every man did that which was right in his own eyes." It seems the major theme I am reading is "it might be wrong for you, but for me, I don't see anything wrong with it, so it is fine for me." That is an interesting view.

I had no idea this was going to be so widely read and basically just wrote it up as Bautista was talking. One thing I did not make really clear was that, to Bautista, these characters did not just remind him of demons, he knew them by name. He recognized that they were drawings of real beings that he had seen and known. He knew each of them by name, at least the ones he recognized. He not only knew them by name, but accurately told what their attributes were, and every attribute that he attributed to that particular character, the page on that character also had that same attribute listed. There were some in the book that he did not recognize and he admitted that it would be impossible for one shaman to have met them all. There was absolutely no doubt in my wife's mind, nor in my mind, nor in our son Stephen's mind, after he reluctantly started listening, that Bautista knew what he was talking about.

As I said, I am in no way considering myself to be an expert in either demons or Pokémon. I do work with a culture which has been demon worshipers for who knows how many thousands of years. Personally, the only contact I have had with Pokémon was the book the church sent me asking me to ask Bautista, an ex-shaman, who had had the opportunity to go to the USA and speak in some churches back there. The people in this church had heard him speak and respected his opinion on this matter, so they sent this book to get his "take" on Pokémon.

Personally, I could not have cared less about it, but when I showed him the first picture, just opening the book at random, he said, "Oh, I know this one, this is," and he named the demon. This is a nasty little thing, always underfoot, bites, scratches, screeches, claws…" I was also looking at the page and it said, "bites, scratches, screeches, claws…" and remember, Bautista could not read one word of or speak one word of English. He did this over and over… enough times that he totally made a believer out of me. He knew what he was talking about. Personally, I think the verses you all should be looking at are found in Ephesians where we are told we wrestle not against flesh and blood, but against principalities and powers… wickedness in high places and then goes on to tell us to put on the whole armor of GOD. I don't believe this is an issue of someone being a weaker brother.

A snake lying in the trail can bite a strong brother or a weak brother, they only have to not see the snake, be too slow to move away from the snake, or ignore the snake; either way, the snake is the danger. And if I saw a snake in the trail, I would warn people coming behind me about the danger. The article was written as a warning.

In your comments, I read a lot of your opinions, "not evil, no monsters in the game, etc.," but in this case, I am going to go with the expert. He recognized something about the way those cartoons were drawn to identify those creatures, not only enough to name them, but to tell their attributes. Trust me, if you would have heard him, I don't think you would be talking about "weaker brothers and strong brothers able to eat meat offered to idols" but would instead be saying, "I want to keep this as far away from my family, my church, and especially my kids as I possibly can! I am not going to give any kind of an open door to Satan in my house." This was my conclusion, and remember, I was probably even more skeptical than you all are.

There were many, many comments on this post on Facebook. I won't list them all, but would like to list a few of the questions from a youth leader posted to my *I Can See the Shore* page. These questions were fairly typical of the questions I got on this page.

1. Where is the Biblical proof for this? Yes, it's a personal experience but there is no Scripture to back it up. None of these creatures or abilities are laid out in the Bible.

The Biblical proof is found in too many verses to try and quote here. I have already used Ephesians 6, where it talks about principalities, powers, rulers of the darkness of this world, and spiritual wickedness in high places. As far as Bautista being aware of the demonic world he had come out of, I believe God had given him the ability to really discern things, of which the "gift of discernment" is one of the gifts of the Holy Spirit as detailed in 1 Corinthians 12:4–11.

2. Where is the corroborating evidence from other believers? Did God give such a damning revelation to one person only? Typically, God gives grand revelation through Scripture or to groups. One man's testimony does not a case make.

I don't know how many people have written me since I first posted this article in 2010 about this, saying. 'I always felt troubled in my spirit when around this,' or, 'Our kids started playing with these toys and started having all kinds of nightmares. After reading your note we read it to our kids and decided to remove them, now, no more nightmares," and the testimonies go on and on. I know this is anecdotal, but this could be listed as corroborating evidence of a sort. Another thing that is a bit telling to me is the amount of pushback received. I think this really has struck a nerve. We always defend what we know we should get rid of but we really want to keep.

> *3. Does anyone find it suspect that the English names were given for the demons even though the game was originally Japanese and the names don't have a direct translation or sound the same in each language?*

Sorry, I did not make that clear. Bautista never spoke a word of English. He gave me their names in Yanomamö, just like he gave me their attributes in Yanomamö. He said *"suwäyäö, dicocaö, silalamou, yacöcaö, ... "*—you get the picture. But if I would have only written what he said (in Yanomamö), instead of translating it, you would not have known that in English he was saying, "bites, scratches, screeches, claws ..." What was so telling to me was that in the book, the attributes were the same.

> *4. Is anyone familiar with cold reading? As a practicing magician (illusion not spiritual) there are some methods to the story that seem like basic mentalism 101.*

I am not sure what you are trying to say with your question. But if you think I somehow set the whole thing up to get the answers I wanted, sorry, that did not happen in this case. Personally, I had no prior knowledge of Pokémon before the church sent the book. I thought it was childish and stupid for the church to want to take my time and waste it over such nonsense. I gave Bautista no background. Just opened the book to a random page and asked him what he thought of it. I did not know what I expected him to say. But I was blown away by his obvious prior knowledge of them. By the way, I live about 300 miles away from the nearest city in the Amazon jungles, if you are wondering how is it possible for someone to live and not know about Pokémon.

5. Yes, the creator of Pokémon could have lied in the interview. But so could the man who created this post. Most of us lacked a front row seat to each. Anyone can say anything in the church body or out of it. Lying is not new. I don't want to accuse anyone of it but it's not right to say one person is lying without thinking the other might be as well.

I won't answer anything about the creator of Pokémon, as I don't know the man, and honestly, could not care less what his reasons were for creating it. I can assure you, I am not lying but am giving an accurate accounting of a first-person account of what happened. Take it or leave it.

6. Lastly, it's too easy to lay everything at Satan's feet. We want to find the devil behind every bush. Is he behind some? Certainly. But if we label him behind so many, we become ineffective at identifying him.

I guess you have to answer that one. I find it interesting that when the people mentioned in Acts 19 were confronted with the truth about demons, read the story prior to verse 18 and 19, and there was pretty convincing proof. The Bible says: *And many who had believed came confessing and telling their deeds. Also, many of those who had practiced magic brought their books together and burned them in the sight of all. And they counted up the value of them, and it totaled fifty thousand pieces of silver.* And you know what, I will bet you that even after seeing what had happened in this instance, I will bet there were still people saying, "Oh, come now! Stop seeing demons behind every bush!" Again, *you* have to decide for yourself. It makes no difference to me what you ultimately decide about this. We each have to answer for our own actions and decisions. I think I was shown a little bit of light on this subject. I would be in error not to sound a warning. Remember, this happened years before this current craze.

None of my points are full proof, but they're also not baseless. It all comes down to prayer and thought. If you come to the conclusion that it's wrong for you, so be it. But be careful making broad sweeping generalizations.

I would add, I think it comes down to what the Bible teaches on the subject, not to prayer and thought. We can be misled too easily otherwise. The Bible teaches enough on the subject that we know we are to be ever on our guard. We are to have the whole armor of God. We are to stand. If, after you study it out with Scripture and you can still play, go for it. I see so many instances of the Jewish nation turning back to idol worship in the Old Testament and forsaking God. I don't think it happened—boom!—all at once. I think it was a subtle thing, a thing where some people felt it was wrong but were finally slowly convinced it was "OK, nothing wrong" when, finally, the entire nation had been led into idol worship, which is only another name for demon worship. So, you are right. Care should be given. MUCH CARE. May God's Spirit guide you as you search.

I would like to make one further comment and then leave the matter alone (I think we have pretty much beaten this to death anyway). My example of a snake in the trail is still a good one. If I see a poisonous snake, it is not legalism that makes me give warning—but each person hearing the warning has to decide for himself or herself whether to heed the warning. I have no axe to grind here and have never thought of myself as a legalistic person.

I will say again, Bautista was the expert. I learned a lot from him. I still remember him telling me about the time he was taken through a haunted house. This happened while on a book tour for Mark Ritchie's book, *Spirit of the Rainforest*. Here is his story.

I am known as Shoefoot in your country, but, as do most Yanomamö, I have many names or rather nicknames, as we Yanomamö guard our real names closely. One of my favorite names was Cajicuwä, "He has a mouth" and now that God has given me much opportunity to speak for Him, I think it is the best one for me. It was funny how I got this name; shortly after Pepiwä [Joe Dawson] came to work in my village, my brothers, along with other men, started working for him. He and Milimi, his wife, always wrote our names down on little white pieces of stuff that looked like bark, but was much thinner. They always wanted a name for each of us. Milimi asked my brother what my name was and my brother did not want to tell her, so he said, "He's got a mouth, ask him." She wrote down Cajicuwä and when it was time to get paid, Pepiwä called out, "Here is the pay for Cajicuwä." We all looked at each other, then my brother remembered what had happened, and pushed me forward to collect my pay. From that day on, for years I was called "He's got a mouth": in my language, Cajicuwä. But in my village now, most people call me Bautista.

My friend Maikiwä asked me to tell him the story of what happened on one of our trips with my good friend, Mark Ritchie, who helped us Yanomamö tell our story in his book, *Spirit of the Rainforest*. We were going around telling stories of how much my people suffer in bondage to the spirits, and in one place, I forget exactly where it was, but it was in the state called Michigan, we were speaking to many students. My friend, Gary, was telling my words in the *nabä* [non-Yanomamö] language for me. After we finished one talk time, we were told that the people had made a house to scare others with and they wanted Gary and me to go in there and see it. I had no desire to go in a house just to be scared. I have known enough fear and now that I don't have to live in fear, I have no desire to put myself through that for anything. Gary also did not want to go in, but he and Mark thought it would look badly, it would look rude, if we did not humor the young people who had worked on this house. So, we went in.

After Bautista told me this story, I later asked Gary what had really happened, as I thought maybe Bautista had just gotten the wrong impression about something and read more into it than had really been there. But Gary remembered the incident pretty much like Bautista had. Here is Gary's side of the story: He agreed with Bautista's account of going through the haunted house with the students.

We were introduced to the two young college students that had invited us to speak. Once again, talking to the student body, as he always did, Bautista held the entire room captivated with his stories from the jungles, the violence of his culture, and the peace that he now lived in. Someone always asked him, "What brought change to your people?" and he was always able, without being offensive, to declare to them the glorious news of the Gospel of Jesus Christ, the Lord of Peace.

After our talk the two young men invited us to go to a haunted house that they had built to raise money for their campus during Halloween, which was just around the corner. I was getting ready to decline, as I had no desire to go through anything that glorified horror and death, but before I could say anything, the one in charge of our group said, "Yes, we would love to go." The next thing I knew, we got into our cars and headed through town until we arrived at this dark, dismal looking building. Marie and the other lady were ahead of us and Mark was in the lead with the two students.

When Bautista and I entered the building, he tensed up and came to a dead stop. I said to him, "*Jabe, wedicätä?* [Father, what is it?]" He turned to me and told me this, "I have been here before." I laughed and told him that was impossible as I had never even been here before. Solemnly he said to me, "This is 'evil spirit of darkness" house. It is only a physical replica, but this is the place that I was initiated into the demonic world." Now the hair on the back of my neck was standing up. Those in the lead came back to where we were talking as they sensed something was holding us back. They asked what was going on, so I told them what Bautista was saying. Now remember, we are still back by the entrance, we have actually seen nothing so far. Bautista spoke up and began to describe in detail the room we are about to go into.

Bautista picked up his story again. "Imagine my surprise when we went in and I immediately recognized a demon's house that I had gone through as a novice witchdoctor so many years ago in the rainforest. This was part of my training and initiation and I had spent much time in this particular demon's house. I turned to Gary and told him, 'Oh, I have been here, this is, and I told him the name of the demon, house.'

"At first Gary did not believe me. He said, 'Bautista, this was just made up to scare kids and make money. Stop it already, let's just get through it as fast as we can.'

Bautista continued: "No," I told him, "this is his house." By this time, we had been rejoined by everyone who had come in. When we had stopped, they came back to see what was wrong, why had we stopped. So, I told them, "From here we will go into a long room. Trapped in the walls will be people's faces, frozen in terror, shrieking in pain." Sure enough, from that room we went into a long narrow room, and it was just like I told him. Of course, in this house, it was just a replica, not the real demon's house. The faces were just masks and the screams were just coming from a box that traps people's voices, but it looked enough like what I had seen for me to know beyond a shadow of a doubt that this was patterned after the spirit's house I had seen.

"We continued on, going into seven or eight rooms. Before walking into the next room, I told Gary what we would see there. By this time, Gary was translating for the young people who were supposed to be helping us get scared, but instead of us being scared, our guides were turning even whiter than they had been when we started on this game to scare us."

I looked at the students and their faces were sort of a pasty white as they heard my translations of what Bautista was saying. We decided to continue, and I heard Bautista quietly pray for God to protect us as we walked through that place. He then kept up a running narrative from room to room describing in detail the bodies, the faces grimacing in agony protruding from the walls, the ones dangling from the ceilings in chains, the vampire bats with blood on their faces. Wow! Was I ever glad to get out of that place. When we exited the other side, we were a very subdued group. The young guys looked like they had seen a ghost. Bautista proceeded to tell us that if it had been the real house of the spirit, that the horror and the suffering and the agony would have been real, and that we would have fled in terror.

Then he addressed the young guys. This is what he asked them: "How were you two able to duplicate the home of a wicked and very evil spirit? How were you able to replicate the home of the spirit of darkness and bondage? You are both dabbling with someone who is far more powerful than you can imagine. If he ever gets you in his grasp you will never be able to break his bondage. I have been there, in the real house. I have been in bondage to him and I still would be except that Jesus set me free!"

"We had no idea," they told Gary and Mark. "We got the plans for this house from the place of many books [library].

Listening to their agitated talk, I thought again of how my people say that after *omawä* (Satan) taught my people, he left them with the demons and went to the land of the *nabäs* to teach them about himself. "Maikiwä," he finished, "it is so sad that your people are really turning from the Lord and learning about *omawä*. Do they really think that they can turn their backs on the Living God and escape the life that I had and for the most part, my people still have?"

6
SHOCK AND LIVE

Today, here in the village of Cosh, if anyone gets a snake bite, we want to be shocked! We have not used any antivenin medication here since that time so long ago in 1986 when Rolland Trempert told us about how his dad used shock therapy for snake bites. That information has saved a lot of lives down here.

◈▣◈▣◈

It was February of 1986 and we were tired and sunburned after spending eight days hunting and two days on the river heading home from our conference hunt. Spirits were high, as we had had a hugely successful *jeniomö* (extended hunt). Along with fifteen wild pigs, we had numerous turkeys, alligators, *lapas* (agouti paca), more fish than I bothered to count, and two tapirs. The day was almost gone by the time the motor slowed down to dock at the port. Suddenly, we were chilled by the somber mood of everyone standing on the bank. Something was obviously very wrong, and everyone searched the crowd for their own loved ones because everyone knows how fast death can strike in the jungle.

Silently we docked the boat and began to gather our own personal belongings to disembark. As hunters, our efforts ended with getting the meat to the village. We left the transfer and distribution of our huge packages of meat to someone who had stayed home to worry about. One of the elders of the village came up to me and, in the urgent whisper the Yanomamö use to convey bad news, told me that Manuel had been bitten earlier that evening by a huge poisonous snake. The snake was so large that the bite was high up on his thigh, and Manuel was not doing well.

We rushed up to the house and were told that the pilot out in town had already been informed and a flight was scheduled for first light in the morning. The antivenin had already been given, but did not look like it had done much. Manuel steadily became worse. Finally, at about 3:00 a.m., he lost his fight and went on ahead of us to meet his Maker. How we wished we could do more for him! But no flights are allowed in the jungle at night, so there was nothing to do but wait, and in this case he could not hold on long enough. He was gone.

The next day, Rolland Trempert, our pilot with Missionary Aviation Fellowship (MAF), flew in. We had already told him the patient was gone, but because there was cargo to be delivered in the area, he dropped in to see how we were doing. During the course of his visit, we went over in detail how devastated the village was. Rolland asked us if we had ever heard of using shock treatment for snake bites. We answered in the negative. He went on to describe how it worked. His dad had been a medical missionary in Ecuador and had used shock treatment on snake bites many times. He told us, "It has to be DC current, very low amperage, but extremely high voltage. Something like the current you get off the electrical system of a car or outboard motor." He also assured us that his dad had had a very high success rate with this treatment.

I couldn't believe it could be that easy. I had seen many snake bite victims die in mere hours and when people were not killed quickly, I had seen them suffer for weeks and sometimes even months as gangrene set in. I watched my brother Gary and sisters amputate toes and fingers and even whole portions of a foot when the gangrene became too much for the antibiotic, and it was either lose the toe, part of foot, fingers, or what have you, or die.

So, as I said, I did not think curing a snake bite could be that easy.

It didn't take long to have our first test case. Somebody came running into the village and told us that Marcino, while far out in the jungle, had been bitten by a snake and they were bringing him home. He was still hours away and the concern was that he might not make the trip. Steve, Gary, and I, along with some friends, grabbed the portion of the electric fence that actually produces the shock. It was the smallest thing we could carry, as trying to lug any kind of an engine out there would have been too difficult. This electric shocker was only about six inches high by maybe about four inches deep and about ten inches long, and probably weighed ten pounds. The only thing that worried me was that it might be too powerful. If memory serves me, according to the little plaque on the side, it produced about 250,000 volts but very low amperage. I remembered Rolland saying it had to be high voltage and pulsating DC current, but I was not sure he had meant 250,000 volts high! I wondered if that might not be a bit excessive! But we grabbed it and ran down to the port, where we jumped into our boat to run up to the trail where Marcino's friends and family were making their slow way home.

We started down the trail running. After a bit more than an hour, we could hear them making their way down the trail. Actually, we could hear his mother-in-law crying for him. Fearing the worst, we quickened our pace and soon met them. Marcino was in a bad way. My brother examined the bite area and was shocked to see that his leg had already swelled to the point that the skin could no longer stretch anymore and had split, leaving a huge area of raw ugly flesh exposed on his lower leg. His leg and torso were covered with huge deep purplish bruises, indicating that he was beginning to bleed internally from the breakdown of his blood vessels. I knew we did not have much time with him and honestly doubted whether a silly electric box could make much difference to him at this point.

We connected the wires. I hate electric shocks and had to clench my teeth as the two wires were positioned near the bite. My brother held the wires while I turned it on. Marcino's body jerked from the force of the current hitting him. I don't remember how many times Gary shocked him, but although it was hard to watch Marcino jerking, it was also obvious that the treatment was doing something. It is hard to describe, but the truth of the matter was we were actually watching the swelling going down! Marcino was breathing easier and had stopped thrashing around from the pain. Gary asked him if he felt good enough to start his trip again and he nodded. During the course of that night, he called us a couple of times to re-shock him, and every time he assured us he was feeling better. In a few days, he was up and around, none the worse for his long ordeal.

One of our next test cases was Yupa. He was bitten by a very large snake while out alone in the jungle. Knowing he would possibly be incapacitated shortly, he ran as hard as he could to get to a more frequented part of the jungle, where he was hoping to find someone who could help him home. By the time he did get home, he was bleeding from his gums, the corners of his eyes, and his ears.

Now, I am not medical—never have been, and have no desire to be—however, when I see someone brought in bleeding from his ears, eyes, and mouth I don't leap to optimistic conclusions. It is almost always late in the day when someone with a snake bite gets home. I remember thinking, "This guy will never make it through the night, so we could get a plane up here to get him out." But again, we grabbed the trusty electric fence and started shocking him, first around the bite area, and then following up his leg at each joint, ankle, knee, etc., until we got to the top of the swelling.

Again, I knew we were watching a miracle, as I could actually see the skin that had been stretched so tight began to get wrinkles again. It was unbelievable! This was on a Saturday and the next day, Sunday, Yupa was up in front of the congregation, giving praise to the Lord for another day the Lord had given him.

We have since shocked many people for snake bites, spider bites, stinger ray stings, big ant bites and stings … as a matter of fact, just about anything that can bite or sting in the jungle, we have shocked for it with great results. Each time the person who was shocked has responded in a grateful and thankful manner befitting someone who, in all probability, had just had their life saved. I can still remember the exception to this, however!

It had been raining all day and the ground was waterlogged with more rain than the ground could absorb. There were visitors from the village of Aweiteli and they were still very primitive, meaning that they did not wear clothes. Anyway, on that day, at about 5:00 p.m., some of my friends brought in a visitor lady who had been out getting firewood and had gotten a snake bite. She was frantic with pain. We quickly got the fence ready, which was easier than it had been because by that time, the fence had been moved to just behind my house. It was easier to take the person to the fence and just shock them out there than it was to disconnect everything and bring it in. So we took the lady out to the fence.

Looking back with the aid of the corrective lenses of time, I realize there were many things I could have done to make the lady's "shocking" experience a better time for her. The first thing would have been to bring her a chair. Remember, the ground was wet and waterlogged, our patient was not wearing a stitch of clothing, and she was sitting on the wet ground. In other words, she was about as well-grounded as you could possibly get someone without actually putting metal probes on her.

I started toward her with the wire leads, but before I was even close enough to position them carefully, a long, blue spark zapped through the air and nailed the poor lady. She shrieked and immediately levitated straight up. I did not measure how high she bounced up, but I will tell you, she was one angry lady when she came back down! I'll tell you another thing: It does not matter how bad you feel, it is extremely difficult to keep a straight face while being bawled out by a naked lady whom you have just about electrocuted.

I did regain my wits enough to ask the lady, when she finally stopped for a breath, if her snake bite felt better. Well, that set her off again! The interesting thing was, though she walked home still yelling and screaming at me, she was not limping and no longer crying from snake-bite pain! So, in spite of how badly she thought it turned out, as far as I was concerned, I chalk that one up as a success as well.

Another night, we were sitting around talking with some pastors and doctors from a Korean church who were visiting in the area, sharing the joys and sorrows of working with the Yanomamö. Suddenly there was a commotion at the door and a couple of guys from the village of Seducudawä came in. From the look on their faces, I could tell it was something serious. "Come quick," they begged, "our mom has been bitten by a large snake!"

"OK, let me grab some things," I told them.

Returning to our guests, I explained what was happening. "We have to go up there," I told them. The very fact that we had doctors present in the room and we were not running up to them asking for help was perhaps the greatest testimony to the viability of the shock treatment program that I can imagine. Before we had heard about the shocking method, I would not even have wanted to go, let alone contemplate running up to a different village without inviting visiting doctors to help. But such was our confidence in this method that we no longer even stocked antivenin on the base any longer.

The Koreans talked among themselves for a few seconds and then one of the doctors approached me. "We would like to go with you if you need our assistance. We also have the latest in antivenin available," he told me. I explained that we used an electric shock for snake bites and did not even bother with the antivenin, but they were welcome to come along. He looked at me quizzically, as if not understanding what I was trying to tell him, but slowly nodded, saying "Two of us doctors would still like to go." I nodded and rushed off to get gas and our trusty electric fence, which by this time no longer even did duty as an actual fence, but was on 100% duty for snake bites.

We drove up to the village of Seducudawä and in between paying attention to the river for rocks, floating logs, and whatnot, I tried to fill the doctors in on what we had found out about using shock therapy on snake bites.

About an hour later, we arrived at the village and made our way up the house of the lady who had the snake bite. Even from a distance we could make out her groans and cries of pain. We quickly went inside and set up our appliance. The lady's leg and foot were hugely swollen and again, I saw the ugly, purplish bruises all up her leg and torso. By this time, I was comfortable shocking someone, realizing that the short-term discomfort from the pain of the shock was well worth the long-term gain, so without further ado we began to ply our trade.

The visiting doctors watched silently, and seemingly with a huge dose of skepticism, but they did not say anything. Finishing the treatment, we helped the lady back into her hammock. By this time, she had already started settling down. We were called to come treat some sick kid for something and I was glad for the doctors who were with us. We finished up there and returned to the snake-bite victim. The lady was sound asleep! We looked at her foot and leg and the swelling was down by a good 50% or more! We packed up our stuff and headed back into the night.

The next morning, after breakfast, the two doctors who had gone with us asked if there were any possible way that we could take them back up there to check the patient. "Well, I don't feel it is necessary, but if you want to go up, we can do so," I told them.

The doctors were amazed at the rocks as we roared up the river. "Is this the same way we came last night?" they asked with their mouths open.

I nodded. "On well-traveled rivers, we worry more about floating logs and such than rocks, the rocks never move," I explained to them. So anyway, we got to Sedu and walked up to the house of the lady. The doctors were surprised to see her calmly sitting by her fire preparing breakfast for her family. They were incredibly impressed!

In the years since then, we have shocked a huge number of different people. Most of those treatments have been tremendous successes, but the one we didn't save was such a bitter loss that the pain of it is still with me—and it has been almost twenty-four years since we lost that little girl. Her brother came down and called us at about four o'clock in the afternoon. He was extremely concerned as he told us that his little seven-year-old sister had been bitten early that morning by a huge snake.

We loaded up and rushed up to his village. By this time, I was full of confidence in our method. Still, we did pray as we thought of how bad the little girl might be since it had taken her brother so long to get down to get us. We roared into port and raced up to the house. The entire village was present and most of the women were wailing, though they quieted down when we went inside. The inside of the house was so dark I could barely see anything. As we set up, I was surprised to see from the wound that there was about a four-inch gap between the snake's teeth. I knew this was possibly one of the largest snakes I had ever shocked for.

I continued examining the bite and as my eyes adjusted to the light (or lack of it) I noticed something on the girl's foot and all the way up her leg to her little thigh. I could not see well enough, but it felt as if the leg were charred. I was perplexed, as I had never seen anything like this. Not wanting to delay any longer, I started shocking her. There was no response from the girl.

My equipment is not working, I frantically thought. I checked the leads for tightness and tried it again. Nothing! Frantically I looked around for someone to test it on. Not having anyone closer than myself, I touched the lead to my own hand and almost wet myself from the force of the shock! It *was* working! So, what was wrong? At this time someone came in with a flashlight, and I began examining the girl's foot and leg. Now that I could see better, it *did* look like the leg was charred! I asked her brother, who was standing there, what had happened. "Her leg turned like that shortly after being bit!" he told me.

By this time, we had verified that the leg was dead to shocking all the way up to her thigh, and I realized there was nothing we could do for her there. We had to try and get her out to a hospital! I called the parents over and told them there was nothing else we could do. Explaining that I was afraid all blood to her leg had been cut off, somehow I convinced them that we needed to take her out that evening and would call for the airplane to evacuate her early the next day. Tearfully, they agreed. While they were getting their daughter ready, Keila and I ran down to the port to set up a bed in the boat to make the little girl more comfortable.

Before we could get back up to the house, we suddenly heard the death wail keen through the village. The little girl was gone! Keila and I were both devastated. Keila was new to the work; as a matter of fact, we had only been married a few short months, and this death hit her hard. To date, this little girl has been the only person we have lost to snake bites since we started shock therapy, and to be honest, I have no explanation for the condition of the little girl's leg.

◆回◆回◆

Speaking of shock therapy, I might add, the *one* thing that I *am* petrified of—yes, I am afraid of being bitten by a snake—but what *terrifies* me is to have to have Keila shock me. This was brought home to me one morning a few years ago. I had been traveling most of the night and got up to check our batteries. We use solar panels and an inverter for power, but the batteries have to be monitored. Still wiping the sleep from my eyes after a long trip to La Esmeralda, I went to the little meter that shows the charged condition of our battery bank and the amount of charge coming in from the solar panels. I noticed with irritation that someone, probably Keila, had draped and wrapped a rope off the meter. Due to the aforementioned lack of sleep (I am sure age has absolutely nothing to do with it), I had to get extra close to focus on the dim numbers.

All of a sudden, my eyes did focus on the end of the rope, which, oddly enough, seemed to have a life of its own and was waving back and forth in a most interesting manner. The shock slammed my eyes into focus and I stood out there quivering for a brief moment. I was literally eye to eye with a snake!

The ensuing battle was fierce but brief, and since I am the one writing about it, it goes without saying that I was the winner! Now, Keila would want you to believe that she was actually the winner, as she stepped in and with a well-placed jab with a shovel delivered the *coup de grace*, but this was after I had already chased the snake outside. To be honest, if I had not been there flailing violently with my broom handle, she would never even have gotten close to it.

I tell you, I am extremely thankful I was not bitten in the forehead right between the eyes that morning, for a couple of reasons. The first is I am sure it would have hurt; the second reason is, as I said, that we use the electric shock treatment for snake bites here, and getting whammed right between the eyes with more than 40,000 volts is not my idea of how to start my day, I don't care how small the amperage is! Actually, there is even another reason I am happy: Keila would have way too much fun shocking me.

7

JEMOSHAWÄ

It is funny how things seem to happen randomly, and yet, when you really start looking at the whole story, you realize there was nothing random about it. Take this next story for example.

Ruth Ann wrote:

> As the cold winter winds gave way to warm, soft breezes in March of 2016, we were in the doldrums of school and my young one was struggling to stay engaged. What to do to motivate him? At 10 years old, Devon still loved snuggling on the couch and being read to, so this teacher decided beginning the school day with a good story may be the answer. His love for all things missionary-related inspired me to look for that kind of book to read to him. Searching on Amazon yielded many suggestions and after careful consideration, I chose one that had good reviews and sounded exciting. Little did we know the destiny of one soul was set in motion the day we chose that book, but God knew, and His hand had already begun to pen a story so amazing one can only fall in worship to Him.
>
> Upon the book's arrival we immediately began reading it, every morning and sometimes in the evening as well. The story was incredibly captivating and it was impossible to read only one chapter, so frequently we read two and three at a time. We laughed and we cried as our hearts

began to feel a deep attachment to not only the missionaries but also certain of the Yanomamö, which is what the natives are called. *Growing Up Yanomamö* is a beautifully written story of a missionary family living in the heart of the Amazon rainforest in Venezuela that ministers to the indigenous tribes in that region.

Have you ever felt like you knew someone simply from reading a book? That is what we felt by the time the last chapter was read. The entire book was such a powerful story of faith in God that when we finished, I was moved to search for this missionary online to see if they are still living in Venezuela. Not only were we able to find an update on the work there, we discovered the missionary had a Facebook account! I immediately messaged him telling him what a profound effect his book had on Devon and that we laughed at the funny stories he related and cried when we read about the incredible difficulties they endured. In the course of communication, Michael Dawson, missionary and author of the book, informed us he wrote another book which he sent as a complimentary gift. It was equally interesting and captivating.

Michael was one of ten children born in the jungle to parents Joe and Millie Dawson. He grew up with the Yanomamö children, hunting and fishing with them, some of whom became his best friends. When Michael was twelve years old, he formed a strong bond with a lad by the name of Jemoshawä who was visiting from another village and ended up staying in the village where the Dawsons lived for an extended period of time.

One day Jemoshawä announced to Michael that his dad had sent the *jecula* (evil spirits) to summon him and that he must go because it was time for him to become a witchdoctor.

Every night for two weeks, he would go running through the jungle and when the Dawsons would finally catch up to him, he would scream that he was on fire. They pleaded with him to call on the name of Jesus to save him from these assaults, but he refused ... it was clear the evil spirits already had a powerful effect on him. Finally, he gave up fighting his father's evil spirits and stated he was going home to his village.

The following morning Michael said goodbye to his young, childhood friend as he shoved off the banks of the river in his canoe for the long journey home.

Over the next few years, the stories that kept coming back to Michael about his friend Jemoshawă were so gruesome, it is a miracle he survived. The atrocities that occur to initiate a young boy into becoming a witch doctor is too evil for a mind to comprehend. It was told to Michael that his friend had received one of the most evil spirits there are, a deer spirit. This meant that no missionary would ever be able to see or talk with him again because he startles like a deer at every noise and could also run like a deer, totally held captive by extreme fright, causing him to flee when any of the Dawsons came close to his village. They attempted numerous times over the ensuing forty years to establish communication but he always left the village before they arrived.

Fast forward to 2010, Michael Dawson who is now in his fifties, and still living in the same village his parents raised him in, writes a book, including a full chapter on the story of Jemoshawă. Six years later in the spring of 2016, Devon and I are reading this story and we are so deeply touched by the brutality this young boy endured at the hands of his father and the chains of evil that bound him all his life, we begin to earnestly pray for his salvation.

By now, Jemoshawä is a grown man, in his fifties. I messaged Michael of the burden God gave us to see him set free and of Devon's steadfast declaration he is going to pray for him by name every day.

In September of 2016, Michael sent a message saying he and his wife were coming to the United States on furlough and they would like to stop at our house to meet the young prayer warrior. You talk about excitement going through the roof!! Top priority was for Devon to make a card for the witchdoctor to send along back to the jungle.

But wait, how could Michael GIVE the card to Jemoshawä when he hasn't seen him in forty-five years? I can testify that the enemy tried to throw every obstacle in our path to keep that card from being made! But... the problem of how to get the card in Jemoshawä's hands was one for God Almighty and so we were not deterred by some cruel doubts thrown at us from the enemy! We only knew God is asking us to do it so Devon set to the task.

We had sweet fellowship with the missionary and his son, Ryan, who is a bush pilot. How amazing to meet a "stranger" only to be in awe of a beautiful bond because the Holy Spirit of God makes us one. Michael presented the Warrior with a delightful gift; a beautifully hand-carved, wooden paddle, fashioned around a camp fire by none other than the Yanomamö. The faint scent of smoke still lingered on the smooth, sleek paddle. What a fine specimen straight from the Amazon rainforest!

We carefully sealed the card in a Ziplock bag and gave it to Michael. He promised he would do his best to deliver it to the witchdoctor.

I was happy as I read in Ruth Ann's account that they loved the paddle that had been created for them. I continued to work with the Yanomamö with the three boys. I made many trips to the headwaters of the Padamo River, stopping often at the village of Maweni where Jemoshawä was now the head witchdoctor and making many attempts to see him, but it always proved impossible. Our work had settled down and matured to the point where, on our outreach trips, it was not just me teaching and preaching, but us going out in teams. I left most of the teaching to the Yanomamö we had been discipling in our work. Even for our guys, getting in to see Jemoshawä had proved to be impossible. Anyone nearing the village with God's Spirit would send him into a panic and he would flee the village before they even got there.

In 2009, I made the hard trip up through the white water and rapids to Maweni, Jemoshawä's village. Our team was my son Joshua, who was here helping out with his family for some months, Abraham, Alberto, and myself. Our main purpose in going was to try and encourage our good friend Paquito Rivas. He was one of our seminar students and we had heard he was going through a hard time. I knew he was married to the granddaughter of the main witchdoctor in his village and in the entire area: Jemoshawä.

We were finally able to get together enough gasoline to make the trip. It was good to get out and visit with Paquito. We had a good meeting with him the first night we were there and then again the following morning. I think he was encouraged by our visit. Paquito is a good guy and loves the Lord and wants to live for Him. He asked me to remember to pray for him and his family. He told me, "We live in a village where there are many witchdoctors and it is really hard to serve the Lord, but I truly want my life to honor Him." I nodded, knowing what he was telling me was true.

Alberto, one of the guys with us on the team, is Jemoshawä's brother-in-law. While we were still hanging our hammocks, Alberto left to head across the village to see if his brother-in-law was still there. Paquito had made us supper and he came to call us for dinner. As we were leaving, Alberto came back in, saying that his brother-in-law *was* there and had agreed to see me! I was excited, but we decided it would be better to wait until the village had quieted down and there would not be that many people around, so we went to eat first.

Even though Jemoshawä and I had been best friends when I was about ten or twelve years old, I had not seen him since. Every time I had ever visited his village, he knew beforehand we were coming and got agitated and left before we arrived. When I heard he was still in the village and had agreed to see me, I was excited and prayed for God to give me the words that would penetrate the bondage that he is held in, that he might clearly hear the saving Gospel of Jesus Christ. After eating, we made our way over to Jemoshawä's house; I was tense as we walked into the dark structure.

We paused inside the opening, letting our eyes grow accustomed to the darkness. The shadows of the swinging hammocks, grotesquely exaggerated by the flickering light provided by a small diesel fuel flare, provided a fitting backdrop for the tenseness I felt as I waited to be shown to Jemoshawä's hearth. As I had never been in his house, I had no idea which the five different hearths was his, so I assumed, when Alberto made his way to a lone hammock swinging in the center, that we were approaching Jemoshawä's hammock, although I did find it strange that he would be in the center. Well, in fact it was not his: Alberto was only asking the young man in the hammock where his brother-in-law was.

I was disappointed to hear that Jemoshawä was gone and knew that once again we had missed him. His wife assured us that he had only just stepped out and we should wait. We not only waited, but sent a kid to find him and let him know we were there waiting for him. After a long wait, the kid came back in saying he could not find Jemoshawä anywhere. We returned, disappointed, to the little house where we had hung our hammocks for the night. The next morning at first light, Jemoshawä's brother, Cojolomöshicö walewä [fishing worm eater (hey, I don't name these guys!)], came to the house with a message from his brother. He said, "I am telling you that my brother was overcome by deer spirit and fled while it was still dark. He will not be back as long as you are in the village, but he did leave a message for you and asked me to tell you that anything you were going to tell my brother, tell me and I will give it to him 'with the words that you tell me.'"

I felt confident that Cojolomöshicö walewä would give the message to his brother. I spent a long time giving him the salvation message. I started with what the witchdoctors know about heaven, hell, the Supreme Being, and His beautiful land. Then, using what the Bible tells us, I filled in the blanks of how we can truly know that He is not the enemy god, but a God who loves them so much that He sent His only Son so that He could live a sinless life, and be put to death to provide the sacrifice for our sins. He rose from the dead to show us that He truly had conquered Satan!

Cojolomöshicö walewä listened very attentively and assured me he would tell it to his brother just as I gave it. Sometimes the Yanomamö are amazing in how they can give back something verbatim almost as well as a tape recorder. I pray he does so this time and, with God's Holy Spirit calling, that not only Jemoshawä will be saved but that Cojolomöshicö walewä will accept Christ as his Savior as well.

Later on, my brother Gary made a trip up to Jemoshawä's village. Gary normally doesn't get up there much, as he hates the rapids and white water. This is probably because he was old enough, back when our parents were going down through them broadside, to have been traumatized, whereas I don't remember any of it, and so am relatively normal. Anyway, Gary came back excited because they had had a very profitable time with the people in the village. Although he was not able to visit with or even see Jemoshawä, both of Jemoshawä's wives were two of the fourteen people who prayed for salvation and then asked to follow the Lord in believer's baptism.

Jemoshawä's wives both shared with Gary that their husband is really interested in hearing more about God. "It is true," Jemoshawä told his wives, "Jesus is returning soon. My *jecula* [demons] know this and are scared to death of that day. Go listen to Gary, believe, and do what they tell you to do. After you do this, you can tell me how to get rid of this heavy burden I am carrying." The women did as they were told and returned afterward to tell Jemoshawä.

Gary was overjoyed that Jemoshawä's wives and his son and daughters all were saved and baptized. Gary said both wives cried out to God for mercy for their husband and asked God to save him from his demons and to bring him to Christ. Gary also shared with me that as he got out of the boat and started up the bank, a wave of darkness just seemed to engulf him.

"I felt a presence of hate and anger like never before," Gary told me. "I could hear a kind of hissing voice telling me I was not welcome and to go home. I began to cry to God to remove this spirit of darkness from the village and I began to walk forward claiming the village for Christ. As I started advancing, claiming ground, the darkness began to fade away and for the remainder of the time I did not feel that presence any longer."

So, while it is true "we wrestle not against flesh and blood, but against principalities and powers and wickedness in high places," we serve a great and powerful God who goes before us and prepares our way, guiding our steps, and one person at a time builds His church.

In our debriefing of the teams that went out, I was thrilled to hear the excitement in the faces and voices of the various ones sharing their experiences. One thing that really impressed me was that our team members, along with the believers in Maweni, decided to go to Jemoshawä's house and hold a praise and prayer service. They asked God to intervene and grant him liberty from the bondage that he was suffering. One of our team members and also an elder in our church here, Lanzo, stated with a smile that "we even prayed holding his hammock and asked God to grant him peace to be able to hear the Gospel clearly."

A short time after Gary's trip up to Maweni, we decided another effort should be made to talk with the old witchdoctor. So, Abraham and Timoteo headed back up there to try and see him again. When they got back to our village, they were so excited they could not contain themselves: They had actually been able to talk with Jemoshawä, for about thirty minutes! Then he began to get agitated and said that was all he could handle. Timoteo said they gave him the Gospel and he did listen really well. He did not make a commitment, but did ask them to come back.

Their trip to the village was marred by one incident on their way back down through the rapids. Their boat hit a really big wave and was slammed down, throwing off the bonnet of Abraham's motor. It was lost in the rapids. Despite this, they did not allow it to take away their excitement that they had been able to share the Gospel with old Jemoshawä. Abraham told me that although he was sad and disappointed that he had lost the bonnet of his motor, "it would be a small price to pay for Jemoshawä's salvation."

A few months later, I had the opportunity to make the trip to Maweni. Due to meetings in Cuwa, we decided to sleep there. We left Cuwa at first light, as I wanted to get to Maweni early so as to have a better chance of catching Jemoshawä in his village, but I was disappointed to find out he was already gone when we got there. Disappointed, but not surprised, as this was been the same result I have gotten for the past thirty-six years.

From here, I will allow RuthAnn to tell Jemoshawä's story from her perspective:

> After a few more months in the US, Michael, his wife Keila, and daughter Mia flew back to Venezuela in November. Due to fuel shortages in their village, we knew it may be a couple of months before the missionary team could make the trip upriver to the remote village where Jemoshawä lived. One evening in March of the following year (2017), Michael messaged us that they were packing up and heading out the following morning with hopes to be in Jemoshawä's village by late evening. The card was still safely sealed in the Ziplock bag and carefully stashed so as to stay dry in the trek upriver. Six long months after the card was made, and many prayers later, it would finally be delivered!! Or would it?? We did not know. Our faith felt so small. Yet we knew faith as small as a mustard seed is big enough to move mountains. We chose to place our hope in a very powerful God who desires that all men be saved, and whether or not Jemoshawä gets the card was up to Him. But how we desired and prayed Michael would finally be able to talk with the witchdoctor and hand him the expression of love from Devon.

A few days later, upon the missionaries' return from the village, we finally got the highly-anticipated report! Here, in part, is the account Michael emailed:

"We stood around talking to others in the village and in about ten minutes or so, I was surprised to see Jemoshawä coming up the trail. Although I had not seen him for over forty-five years, I knew it was him. We waited respectfully for him to get settled in his house before we went in. He was standing there to greet us and he had a big smile on his face. I was overjoyed to finally get a chance to see the friend I have not seen for so many years. Not knowing how long I was going to have with him, I went right into my reason for wanting to see him. 'My friend, I have thought about you ever since you left Cosh so long ago and we had never seen each other again. You know I represent *Yai Bada*, the Supreme Being.

'I want to tell you again that He loves you so much. He loved you so much that He sent His only Son and He was willing to lay down His own life for each of us. He paid the full price for all our sin. He became the trail for us to get to His land. He told the people listening to Him: "I am the Way, the Truth and the Life. No man comes to the Father except through me." Then, starting back with Adam and Eve in the garden, their fall and God's provision for their sin and His promise of sending a Savior, I fully shared the Gospel with him.

'We spoke together for about half an hour, and I could see he was getting more and more agitated and antsy. Finally, he said, "I have heard you, my friend, but now, I have to go, you understand?"

'I told him, "Yes, my friend, I understand." I then pulled out the card Devon made. "Let me give you this paper from a young man in my country who prays for you every day. He has never met you, but he is asking *Yai Bada* to open your heart to Him, so that you might be freed from your bondage."

"'But I can't read," he protested.

'I answered, "That is OK, I will read it to you. This is what his words say to you although he is far away. He sent his words." I then read the card to him and gave him the card. He asked for the Ziplock bag the card was in so I gave him the bag also. His face had a panicked look to it.

"'I have to go!" he repeated.

"'OK, my friend," I said. I then decided to push my luck. Stepping up to his side, I asked him, "May I pray to *Yai Bada* for you?" His eyes widened, but he nodded his head. Really pushing my luck, I put my arm around him and asked God to show Himself real to him and to set him free from his bondage. Finishing up, I stepped back. He nodded his head at me and was gone."

Tell me, what cannot be accomplished through prayer? The answer is NOTHING!! God delights to demonstrate His awesome power when we trust Him, when our hope is Him. After forty-five years, God bound the awful demons in Jemoshawä, giving Michael the opportunity to talk with his childhood friend and share the Gospel with him one more time. There are no words that define our awesome God! Our hearts were full and overflowing in gratefulness to Him. I thanked God He honored the Warrior's prayers and also allowed him to see the power of a sovereign God so effectively displayed against the enemy!

In the many months that followed, I had doubts Devon prayed for the witchdoctor everyday but each time I asked him, he assured me he always prays for him at night before falling asleep. I do not understand entirely how the Spirit works. I do know He is like the wind; you see His influence but what He speaks to the heart of a child may be too divine for human understanding. Why did He give Devon a burden to intercede for a man enslaved in demonic chains for years? Was it for the salvation of the witch doctor or was it for Devon to gain greater understanding of who God is? I don't know.

For twelve long months there was no word on the witch doctor. Then finally, on a Friday morning, there was an update from Michael on Jemoshawä and here it is:

"We just received word that old Jemoshawä is dying. Before going unconscious, he said his *jecula*, or demons, are killing him. We have been praying for his salvation for many years and I know many of you are praying too. Please pray that even in his unconscious state, God's Word that he heard down through the years would come back to him."

I don't know how one can feel such love for someone one has never met, but the sorrow that descended at this devastating news, no words can convey. It was worse than if we had been preparing for a funeral. We were crying. How could God, after all He's done to show Himself in such a powerful way, allow Jemoshawä to die without Him? My little Warrior and I knelt but neither one could pray. I looked at him and said the Spirit will have to take the prayers of our broken hearts and perfect them before God. Our cry was that the mercy of God would prevail and He would send all heaven to rescue the soul of this man. The verse in Romans 8 was a great comfort: *In the same way, the Spirit helps us in our weakness. For we do not know how we ought to pray, but the Spirit Himself intercedes for us with groans too deep for words.* We knelt while each one quietly cried out to God for mercy.

Friday was a very long day. Jemoshawä was never far from our minds as we prayed all day that God would speak to him, even in his unconscious state. We knew that would be a very small thing for our heavenly Father to do.

Saturday morning as I struggled with this great heaviness, I opened my devotional for the day's reading and as is characteristic of a loving Shepherd, God wanted to lead me out of the despair and heaviness I felt. He reminded me He is completely trustworthy and that my love for Him should be the motivation of our prayers for Jemoshawä, not for any desired outcome. I immediately embraced that truth and whew, the deep sorrow I felt just vanished. Realizing anew that God is just, holy, and righteous and that I can trust Him in all things in regards to an unconscious, dying witchdoctor, gave me incredible peace. We were unsure how to pray for him the rest of the day, so I would just tell God, "You know everything that is transpiring thousands of miles away in a remote village; I commit him to You." The rest of the day was very peaceful as we placed our trust in Him.

Sunday evening as my husband, Daryl, and I were preparing to retire for the night, my thoughts briefly went to Jemoshawä again, wondering if he was still living or had died, and in an instant, just like I had read it, two verses came to mind from I John: *Now this is the confidence that we have in Him, that if we ask anything according to His will, He hears us. And if we know that He hears us, whatever we ask, we know that we have the petitions that we have asked of Him.* And in an instant another scripture: *and we know it is not His will that any perish but that all men come to repentance.* There was no doubt that God had just spoken.

I was awestruck! In that moment I knew God had conveyed through His Spirit the good news that He had either already saved Jemoshawä, or that He was going to. So sure was I of this, I ran over to Devon's bedroom and shared with him this marvelous revelation! I told him we are no longer going to ask God to save Jemoshawä but are going to begin thanking

Him for hearing our prayers and saving him. Immediately we prayed and gave thanks to God!

What a good, good Father we have!! He did not have to reveal this but His goodness and mercy continually pursues us beyond anything we deserve or imagine. "Oh that men would praise the Lord for His mercy and His wonderful works to the children of men!" Monday, all day, our prayers were filled with thanksgiving as we waited to hear further news from Michael.

Tuesday evening the long-awaited update finally came. Here it is, in part, as Michael wrote it:

"Daryl and RuthAnn, I wanted to message you all first and let you know we got word yesterday that Jemoshawä died on Saturday. His brother-in-law told me that right up to the end before he went unconscious that he kept Devon's card with him and told everyone a friend had sent it to him all the way from the North country and it told him he was being prayed for and that this card was telling him how to get to *Yai Bada* (God). His brother-in-law also said right before he died, he did regain consciousness, and even though he could not talk, he pointed up and nodded his head, then died."

God's incredible love and mercy pursues and saves another soul from the fires of hell in the eleventh hour.

8

YANOMAMÖ HUMOR

Our daughter Mia loves all things natural and of nature. We were over at my mom's house visiting and Mia came out of a room where she had gone to put something saying, "Grandma, when did you get your pet tarantula?" Mom's shocked expression said it all, so the "pet" was taken care of.

❖ 回 ❖ 回 ❖

I have always been fascinated by the Yanomamö legends that seem to have a biblical connection. A really interesting one is how Sujilinawä, the best archer in the world, shot the sun and his blood came pouring out, and from that blood came the fierce Yanomamö. Then the sun gathered all his followers and while they watched, he started spinning and rose up out of their sight, and now lives in the heavens. Do any of you see a link here between Jesus giving his blood for our new life and then being taken back up to heaven? I find this fascinating!

Here is a legend that is interesting for a couple of different reasons. It goes like this: One day, the rains started and would not quit. The Yanomamö kept fleeing to higher and higher ground. Finally, they arrived at the peak of the highest mountain with nowhere else to run or climb. One of the shamans decided that in order to appease the deity of the water, they would have to throw a young lady into the water. If the *lajala* [water deity] would accept their sacrifice, the waters would go down.

Now, young ladies are in short supply for the Yanomamö and not to be given up on impulse, so someone came up with the idea that the deity might not be so discriminating. Why could they not take an old lady, paint her up as a young woman just finishing up her first rites, and throw her in? Perhaps the *lajala* would be happy with her. So they did that. The *lajala* accepted the gift and the stormy waters receded. This legend is interesting for two reasons. The first reason is because this is the only Yanomamö story that I know of that mentions a sacrifice taking place. The second reason is that it almost seems that in this one legend are mixed up two great stories from the Bible: the story of the Flood and the story of Jonah.

◈ ▣ ◈ ▣ ◈

Two visitor ladies ran up from the port. "We want to get three light bulbs for hunting," they panted. I purchase them in the USA for $1.10 a bulb, so I quickly did the conversion into the Venezuelan currency. Then, giving a nice discount, I told them the price.

"OK, give us the bulbs, and we will drop the money off on our way back upriver," said one of the ladies.

Having heard this version of that particular song more times than I care to remember, I told her, "Well, I will save your bulbs here; when you drop the money off, I will give you your bulbs."

"No, my husband said he won't stop again, so give me the bulbs now."

I smiled at her. "If you won't stop again, how am I going to get my money?" I asked, trying to keep a straight face. The other lady, who up until then had not said a word, spoke up.

"I told you he wouldn't go for it," she chided her friend.

While swapping yarns with a group of Yanomamö men out in our cookhouse, our tales became a contest of sorts to see who could tell of the greatest calamity that had occurred on our trips into the wilds. I felt good about my entry in that contest: a story of our motor being broken down on the island of Chiwidi one dark stormy night, during one of the local monsoon-type rainstorms, when, while trying to start a fire using a hose full of gasoline, I ran off a thirty-foot bank and splashed into the cold, dark, deep Orinoco river.

Feeling around me, I found out I had somehow slipped between two huge fallen trees without hitting them on the way down, so I slowly felt my way around, crawled up on one of the logs, and waited to be found. For some reason (perhaps due to the shape of the high bank), even though I could hear every word the guys were saying as they looked for me, they could not hear my frantic calls for help.

My story was good and I was grateful for the laughs until Nando started his story. My story paled in comparison and, to be honest, after hearing what he had had to live through to get his story, he deserved all the laughs he could get. I have faithfully related his story, only translating it into English:

My day was not bad. We had found a swamp full of fish early and had already killed many of them. Suddenly, the young man next to me grabbed his stomach in pain and rushed to get out of the water. I was shocked to see a large piranha still hanging onto his flesh. I, too, moved to get out of the water when suddenly, down near a small root, I saw a flash of a fish, so I decided I would get one more before leaving the swamp and piranhas. I slowly moved my hands around the stump when all of a sudden, something grabbed my finger and tore a big chunk off of it, on the inside of my hand right about the first knuckle. Wow! That hurt! I should have turned around and headed straight on back to the village, but decided to keep hunting.

I wrapped a piece of rag I tore off my shorts as a bandage around my bleeding finger. I left the swamp and, while still walking on the small stream feeding the swamp, I found a large anaconda snake. I was happy to get it. After killing it with a sharpened pole, I decided to leave the head on the pole I had killed it with, sticking in the middle of the trail so any one coming behind could see the large snake I had killed. I cut the head off and forced it down mouth first over the sharpened end and jammed the other end into the ground. Somehow, when I jammed the end into the ground to stick the pole up, it dislodged the snake's head and flipped it right over to my other hand, the one not bitten by the piranha. It landed on the top of my hand with its mouth wide open, sinking its fangs up to their bases in my hand. It was a terrible thing to be bitten by a snake's head. I finally forced each fang out and looked down in sadness at my hand. Each tooth mark was bleeding profusely. Now, both of my hands were hurting. Truly, I should have retraced my steps back to the village, but I continued hunting.

By this time, it was after noon. I saw some palm fruit up in a palm tree and decided to get them to take home. I needed a vine for my feet for climbing. Finding one, I grabbed it and started pulling it down. I did not realize it was wrapped around a dead limb up in a tree. It gave with a crash! I ducked, trying to make a smaller target, when all of a sudden, this branch crashed into the side of my head, almost knocking me out. Thankfully, it was not falling down point first or it would have killed me, but even still the glancing blow to the side of my head had me dizzy and bloody. Now I am wounded in both hands and my head. I know … I should have just returned to the village. But I kept going.

After hunting for a few hours longer with no luck, I decided I needed to hurry home or I was not going to make it back before dark and I did not have a light. Sure enough, it got dark before I got home. I was hurrying down the darkening trail when I sensed something in the trail. Feeling with my foot, I could tell it was a branch across the trail. I tried to catch my step and jump over it but misjudged it in the darkness and came right down on it. It was a huge thorn tree! The thorns were so big that even in the darkness I got some of them out and then continued on.

The trail cuts close to the river bank at the Wadawada Creek and I was almost passing that when all of a sudden, I blundered into a huge ant nest. I was being bitten unmercifully so I took off running in the night. The trail makes a sharp curve there and I failed to see the curve and the next thing I knew, my feet were running on air and I was plummeting down, down and into the dark river. Remembering the snake and piranha I had already fought with, I made haste to get out of the river.

By the time I got home I looked like a warrior who had gotten the worst of the fight. The sad thing was, everything was self-inflicted, so I could not even expect any sympathy from my wife. Thankfully, I did have the palm fruit and the snake to make it easier for her, but I was very relieved to finally get home.

Well, none of us even tried to top that! Especially since he had the half-healed scars to prove his story.

Have you ever had one of those "good news, bad news" days? I had to take my brother, Jerald, down to La Esmeralda to catch a plane we hired to come up and fly him back out to town to catch a flight to Caracas and then on to the USA. Gary notified me that he had found a barrel of gasoline down there that we could buy, so we should take an empty barrel, which I did. So far, good news.

The bad news: With that much of a load for the return trip (one barrel of fuel we were purchasing down there, plus 450 kilos cargo on the plane), my speedboat would be too overloaded, so we had to take a large dugout to La Esmeralda.

Not the end of the world, but instead of an hour-and-a-half travel time, we would now be looking at four hours. We asked Gary to explain that we might be a little late, so the pilot should please wait for us. We took off for La Esmeralda with our empty barrel and large boat.

More bad news: The engine started running badly, so it took us four and a half hours to get down there, and the plane had already left. Very bad news, as Jerald had a flight to catch to Caracas, and then on Saturday another on to the USA. He was starting to get nervous.

Good news: We called the owner of the air taxi company and he had another airplane in the area and could swing by and still get Jerald out to town.

Bad news: They could not swing by until 3:00 p.m. For you all, our dear prayer partners, La Esmeralda is about the most awful place on earth to have to kill time, as you spend so much of your time killing gnats that time literally gets down and crawls — nay, reverses itself! — several times during your wait.

Good news: While walking back from where the planes park to the little store area, a guard asked me if we wanted to purchase seven barrels of diesel. Extremely good news! We said yes, absolutely, and after Jerald's plane landed about three lifetimes later (at 3:30 p.m., to be exact) and took off with him aboard, we picked up our barrels of fuel and started home at 4:46.

Bad news: The river was at almost record low. I have seen it a bit lower only one time before this, and my memory about this river goes back longer than I care to even think about, let alone confess to. Then, to further compound our troubles, our engine started running rough again, due to a clogged fuel filter. We were running a Honda four-stroke on this boat and it is a really good engine, but the guy who designed the fuel filter assembly probably has laughed himself to death by this time, or someone might even have bumped him off, as it is the most awfully designed piece of filtering equipment it has ever been my misfortune to have to work on.

Good news: It was 8:30 p.m., no gnats, no sun. I had a good light, so we started working to disassemble the filtering assembly.

Bad news: A small type of kamikaze moth rose up and smote us! Well, they began swirling around us, into our eyes, ears, noses, and mouths, into the filter assembly, and anywhere else they could be. Felt as bad as a smiting, I can assure you.

Of course, you realize I did not count them, but I don't think I am being untruthful to say those moths were swirling around by the millions, perhaps billions. Trust me, I was feeling overwhelmed at this point. It was totally impossible to work. Trying to work under these conditions despite it all, I dropped a tiny but indispensable O-ring. After spending half an eternity trying to find it, I remembered that the O-ring on my little mag light looked to be about the same size. We tried to put it on, and promptly dropped it down into the same recesses of the motor where the original O-ring had escaped to. Actually, maybe a moth either ate it, or took it away as a toy... but what to do now? It looked like we would have to spend the night with the moths, which would have been very, very bad news. As a last move, more in desperation than with any real expectation of good results, I took the fuel line and cut a tiny O-ring off the end of it. My nephew, Andrew, further carved it down to fit into the tiny groove it had to sit in and we screwed it back down. Praise the Lord, the motor started on the first try and we made it home this morning at 7:30. This was very good news — even better because we were able to get home with one barrel of gasoline and seven barrels of diesel fuel for our generators. Praise the Lord with us!

Out in town, Gary had purchased six large calves for his cattle project, and they arrived by boat shortly after we got home ourselves, tired from our all-nighter on the river. Did I ever tell you I hate cows? While we were taking them off the boat, we carefully opened the corral and got one cow out — so much easier to say than to actually accomplish, trust me. My nephew, Jody, and I led it up to a tree and were tying it when Tomas, the boat owner, possibly figuring they had done enough damage to his boat (cows being what they are when it comes to good hygiene or lack thereof), opened the makeshift corral bars and just let the other five jump off.

Since then we have been trying to catch them and get the ropes off of them ... with no luck, I might add. Also, one calf refused to go into the project area and we could not find it. So, that evening, I offered 2,000 bolivares to anyone who could find it and bring it in. Four guys left and about 8:00 p.m. came in yelling that they had it. We ran out to take care of it and noticed the rope was too tight around its neck, but as I was trying to get the rope loosened without letting the calf get away again, it bolted. I had the rope and tried to hold onto it, but it ripped through my hands. As the calf raced around the tree, the rope caught me below the knees and cut me right off, banging my tailbone on the hard ground. By that time, I was so close to the tree that the frantic calf not only cut me off at the knees, but quickly tied me to the tree. Our two dogs got into the act, further aggravating both the calf and me, as I was still tied to the tree. Anyway, now I know why cowboys wear guns. I would gladly have shot the calf and both dogs, but since I had no gun, I had to get some slack in the rope to untie myself. Keila was still laughing even as she doctored my rope burns. Some cowboy I turned out to be! As I said, I really dislike cows!

◈ ▣ ◈ ▣ ◈

Speaking of Yanomamö humor, I still have a lot of memories with and of Bautista. One in particular that makes me chuckle is from about two years after Reneé had passed away. Bautista came to my house and sat with me, quietly talking for a while. Finally, he got around to what he had really come over for. "Maikiwä, what are you doing? You need to find yourself a good wife. You have been alone now for long enough. When God created man, He Himself looked at man and said it was not good that he was alone. You are alone and it is not good."

"I know," I told him, "but I live way up here in the jungle with all the gnats and bugs and you Yanomamö. Girls are not exactly standing in line waiting for me to ask them to join me. God gave me one who loved the work, but it would be too hard to expect another one like her."

He nodded. "I know," he said. "But it was God who said you did not need to be alone, so I am going to pray that He sends someone for you that is right for you and she will even like us and put up with the gnats and the bugs." He smiled. His optimism was contagious and I found myself smiling in spite of myself.

"Well, thanks!" I said. "I will let you know when I find her." We went on speaking of this and that, and one conversation led to another until finally we got to talking about his garden and how difficult it was for him to get up to where his garden was on the Metaconi. "OK," I told him. "You said you were going to pray and ask God to send me a wife. So, since you are going to be asking God for me, I will ask God to help me get you a motor so you can get up to your garden."

He smiled. "Maikiwä, don't doubt God. He can bring you a wife even up here to the jungle. Don't laugh. You are going to look back on this time and remember this conversation with a smile as you look at the beautiful girl God has sent you."

I looked at him and swallowed the words that had quickly come to my lips. "OK, my friend. I do not doubt you nor do I doubt God's power. So, I will just wait on Him, but I am not joking about your need of a motor, and will ask God for you."

A few months later, Keila flew up to visit the boys. Bautista looked at her with a knowing smile. He silently nodded at me and his smile widened, letting me know this girl met with his approval.

I frowned and shook my head in the negative at him. I was not ready to let anyone know I was starting to think seriously about this dark-haired beauty. She didn't even know yet, as I had not said a word to her. Fast-forward roughly six months: We were on our honeymoon! And yes, it was with my beautiful Keila! I had finally gotten enough nerve to tell her what I felt and was pleasantly surprised to find out she felt the same way. At this time, we were driving from northern Wisconsin, where we had spent our honeymoon, to Dulles Airport in Virginia to pick up Dad, Mom, and Bautista, who were coming back to the USA to visit churches. Keila and I were going to provide them logistical services.

Bautista was so tickled to see Keila again, this time as my wife.

As I said, months earlier, when Keila had come to visit, he had quietly given me his approval. "This is who I have been praying for!" he had assured me then. So this time, when he saw her as my wife, he was beside himself with pleasure and thankful to the Lord that it had all worked out so well.

"Wait a moment!" I told him. "I am feeling just a bit cheated." He raised his eyebrows in the universal Yanomamö questioning look and I was quick to explain. "You prayed for me a wife. I got a wife. I am happy. But I can't help but feel a bit cheated because I prayed for you to get a motor, and not only did you get a motor, you got TWO motors! This is why I am feeling cheated."

He grinned really big. "Maikiwä, I come from people who can have as many wives as he wants. Trust me. One is enough. Be happy!" We both laughed and I had to fill Keila in on the joke.

◈ ▣ ◈ ▣ ◈

In my book *Growing Up Yanomamö*, I told a story that had been told to me by Bautista and other men in the village when I was growing up. The story always fascinated me and the mystery of who the people possibly could have been has always intrigued me. So, when I was writing the story, I wanted to flesh out the people who had been killed so long ago in the cave.

I went back to Bautista and asked him to give me some details about the people. What did they look like? What about their hair: How was it cut, did they wear headbands of any kind? What about jewelry and clothing? So many details I did not know that would have made the story so much more interesting. Imagine my disappointment when Bautista looked at me blankly and asked, "What people? What cave? What are you talking about?"

"Don't you remember?" I begged him. "You told us a story about stealing some pots and then when it was found that the pots were poisoned, you all wanted revenge and tracked the people to a cave and killed them all."

His blank looked continued. "No, the only pots I know about are the ones where Cläämö (Job) got boils from head to foot and set out on a trash heap and scraped himself with pieces of pottery. People in a cave? I have no idea what you are talking about."

I had to drop it for a time and almost cut the story from my book, but like I said, I have always been fascinated by it and hated to get rid of it. I decided to check around. I guess I was worried that I had just dreamed the story, but after asking all of my childhood friends, and them remembering it just like I had, I decided that Bautista had somehow just forgotten it. Thus, I went back to the story, cut Bautista's name out of it, and just called the man telling us the story "Yacuwä's uncle"—which Bautista is, but this way I would not have to worry about someone asking Bautista about it and him not remembering it.

Fast-forward a few years to 2007: Bautista, Keila, and I were in Belize for the filming of the movie *The Enemy God*. The shoot ended and we had a few days to kill before our departure date. We decided to go to a Mayan ruin and look around. There was also a Mayan museum. We walked through it, slowly taking in the culture of this long-ago people.

Bautista was excited and interested in every artifact I showed him. At one point, he walked ahead of me while I was still reading a long inscription about something. I finally finished and looked up. Bautista was standing staring intently at a large pot standing on top of a glass case. I walked up beside him, but, not wanting to interrupt his thoughts, just stood there quietly because he was obviously deep in thought. He walked around the glass case still staring. He finally came to a stop beside me and continued staring.

Finally, without taking his eyes off the pot, he asked me in a low voice. "Did I ever tell you about some pots I found in the jungle?"

In the same quiet voice, I answered, "Yes."

He continued staring at the pot, "Did I tell you that we killed everyone in the cave that had made the pots?" The sadness and anguish were obvious in his voice. Again, I answered in the affirmative. What could I say? Somehow, seeing that pot standing there brought back memories that he had blocked out for a long time.

We had planned to take a trek to try and find this cave and look around. Bautista believed that the people in that cave had somehow had a connection to the old Mayans and he wanted to look around. I couldn't wait! Trust me, I would have my video camera ready!

But we were never able to do our trek with Bautista. He got sick, so we postponed our trip; then rainy season started, so we decided to wait until the following dry season. By that time Bautista was really showing his age: every time we talked about it, his eyes would light up, but his body was just too weak for us to make the trip. Still, we had many good hours talking about it and I think he enjoyed planning and thinking about it.

9

"VACATION" IN THE JUNGLE

One night I hung my hammock out in the jungle alongside the mighty Orinoco River. We had decided we did not need a roof over our heads. The Yanomamö are an exceedingly optimistic people, and I guess I have gotten that way from being with them. Just a few nights earlier, we were almost drowned by an awful rainstorm, but it was such a beautiful night, and because we had worked late and did not have time to build a lean-to anyway, we didn't bother with one, but rather just figured it wouldn't rain. This time our optimism was rewarded with the almost full moon sending its beams like faded shafts of sunlight slicing through the green canopy above us. You would honestly have to experience a tropical jungle night alongside the river to appreciate how beautifully light it is. The tropical moon is huge and created a beautiful ambiance to think on the awesomeness of our God.

◈ ▣ ◈ ▣ ◈

I received an email with a headline that read: "Michael, you need a break! Here's the bad news: you look tired. But here's the good news: we can fix that! You might not know it, but you've still got time to book a vacation with Travelocity before the end of the year…"

Well, I did not realize Travelocity knew me so well as to know I looked tired, but I decided that since they had taken the time to personally send me an email, they must know what they were talking about. Because my wife was also wanting me out of the house for a while, I made plans to head up the Metaconi River to participate in a five-day hunt to get enough meat for a big village-wide Christmas feast.

It's not much of a "break" to get into a dugout canoe and head hours and hours upriver, then spend four days in a sopping-wet rainforest. Now that I'm fifty-something, it's harder to pull said dugout canoe over the rapids than it was in my twenties, thirties, and even forties. I had begun to arrive at that conclusion even before this trip, as a matter of fact. I guess Travelocity had a different type of break in mind for me. Oh well, maybe next time, because now I need a break from my break. If Travelocity thought I looked tired before, they should see me now!

I learned something on this trip. Although fire ants do give a good aerobic workout, I can't in good conscience recommend them, as I have found something even better. Fire ants are good, but they pale in comparison to the sheer exhilaration and extra cardiovascular workout I achieved by having two large, angry, red wasps trapped in my mosquito net with me. Before attempting this radical form of exercise, you should consult your doctor and possibly have him standing by.

I thought I had achieved the ultimate in fancy exercise moves until the next day, when one of the same kind of large red wasps, possibly even angrier than the two that had had the privilege of spending some quality bonding time with me, found its way into Timoteo's shirt. Timoteo was occupying his shirt at the same time, but not for long after the wasp moved in. His moves made me look weak and lethargic in comparison. Why, if I had had a camera and filmed him, I am sure there would be a market for the new exercise video I could put out. The only difficulty would be finding a music track that could keep up with him.

I did finally get home after being half-drowned by the rain, and I got an email asking "Isn't it dangerous to be out on the river at night?" So, I thought I would address this issue. I will make every attempt to be factual and keep exaggerations and embellishments to a minimum.

I am sure the fine person asking this question is aware that in our jungle there are jaguars and anacondas, not to mention enough poisonous snakes (or, as Mia would say, venomous snakes), to keep someone cataloging for as long as they cared to do the job. However, as far as I am concerned, the four most dangerous things found along the river at night are a type of tiny gnat-like bug, moths, wasps, and bats, in that order.

We hunt at night, not because we want an unfair advantage over the animals, but because most jungle dwellers are nocturnal. So, if you want to see them, you need to be out at night, when (believe me!) most of the advantage remains with the animals.

When you float down a river, your light beam attracts these small sand bugs and whatnot, and before you know it, you are paddling down the river with a cloud of these tiny insects swirling around you. For some reason, these bugs think it is just the height of excitement to dare each other to fly into your eyes, ears, mouth, and nose, and there are millions to take the dare. Before you know it, you are gagging and sneezing, and your eyes are running and red from all the kamikaze bugs.

Your light also attracts various kinds of jungle moths, who also have nothing better to do than run over and join the fun, trying to clog every pore and orifice of the person who holds the light. In all your wild gyrations trying to defend yourself from the bugs, you work yourself into a sweat, and your body makes like a salt factory. It doesn't take the moths long to catch the scent of this salt, and they began to lick you; fluttering their wings in excitement, they end up depositing a fine dusting over you which causes you to sneeze even more.

Not wanting to miss the fun, the *jisiomö* wasp flies over to offer advice. If they would just stay on the outside and shout orders, I could handle the wasps, but not to be outdone, they join in the ruckus. Flying around like crazy, they dive-bomb you, with their greatest wish being to lodge themselves between you and a piece of your clothing where they can begin to sting you, all the while maintaining that it is your fault for trapping them and that they are just trying to defend themselves. It even appears that they have holding patterns established to give everyone a fair chance, but because the moths are larger than the gnats and don't respect them, and the wasp can sting like you wouldn't believe and respect no one, they begin to cut the line and fights break out.

You are now one huge ball of swirling, sweating (and almost swearing) bugs and human paddling downriver, and sometimes you get so caught up in the excitement of protecting yourself from these insects that you forget you are hunting.

Oh, but the best is still to come! All it takes is for one random bat to fly over and observe the show and before you know it, that bat has called in all his relatives and then it really does become a free-for-all. In and out of this huge swirling, swatting, gasping (almost swearing) mess flailing down the river, you now have bats whirling and diving, squeaking and fluttering above your head. It is enough to drive someone absolutely, totally bonkers!

After half a night of fighting those bugs and bats, a jaguar would be foolish to show himself, because by this time the poor hunter is so frustrated—with all the sand gnats in his mouth, eyes, nose, and ears; river moths landing and licking him, leaving a powdery film that further makes him sneeze; wasp stings; and bats scaring him to death—that he would jump out of his boat and attack *anything*, including a jaguar, just to relive some frustration! as anyone knows, there just is no getting away from bugs, moths, wasps, and bats on the river at night.

After reading about someone's extreme adventure trip, I figured even my outreach trips qualified for the "extreme" label, though a few friends have expressed doubts about this. Personally, I figure just trying to scale the steep, muddy, slippery, high bank that is a given at every Yanomamö village qualifies the entire trip as extreme, but allow me to give you just one other example of an incident that happened and that allows me to affirm, with not one shred of hesitation, that my trips *do* qualify for the "extreme" classification. I will give you the example, and you can decide for yourselves if I am abusing the term.

Remember, our outreach trips are to take the Gospel to the Yanomamö, but we still have to eat on these trips. This means, after our meetings at night, we will head out and try to bring in some meat for ourselves and our host village.

It was a very, very dark 9:00 p.m. I whistled and a tapir answered about 200 yards upriver from our position. We quietly paddled to shore. Ruben quickly climbed the sheer bank and disappeared soundlessly into the thick tropical vegetation. I, a bit more slowly, carrying my gun and light, climbed behind him, albeit with a tad bit more noise. If a semitruck had been passing in low gear, honking its horn, you might not have heard me over the sound the truck was making.

We stood together in the dark. I whistled again, and again the tapir answered. Getting a bearing on the sound, we started in its direction. It quickly became obvious, to me at least, that the jungle in this area was impassable. Ruben did not agree and was already slithering through the vines and underbrush with the speed and grace the Yanomamö are known for. Again, I, with a bit less grace, got down on my belly and slithered behind him. We paused to whistle again. The tapir refused to come to us, but continued to whistle its interest.

If anything, the underbrush had only gotten thicker, and it was also oozing, due to the close proximity of a swamp. In addition, the mosquitoes were in holding patterns above us, waiting their turn for our sweat-streaming bodies. Ruben was still in the lead, and was using his light just enough to keep us out of the worst of the muck. (Remember, part of this time we are on our bellies in said muck.) Earlier in the day, a large anaconda had been killed in the area: large enough that wallowing in muck, a prime habitat of anaconda snakes, was not my idea of a walk in the park. I whistled again. The tapir answered. It was moving. We changed our direction slightly to keep angling toward the reluctant animal.

By this time, my breath was coming in gasps only slightly less than hurricane strength, but still with enough force to dislodge night-crawlers and the occasional unfortunate grub-worm from under the sludgy humus. We were finally able to crawl to our feet. The prey animal was now off to our right. Although it continued to answer our whistles, it was obvious that we were going to get this one the hard way, if at all. Did I mention it was dark? I mean inside-of-a-cave dark. Though we were now on our feet, the vines and underbrush were still so thick that making any headway at all was possible only with the greatest effort and maybe even divine intervention. The tapir finally wandered off, giving us our first reprieve of the night. To be honest, by that time, I was happy to hear him go.

We made our slow, painful way back to the boat. Personally, I think any time you have to crawl though tropical jungle muck in the dark qualifies all following portions of your trip as extreme. To make matters worse (though I'm not sure if there was any connection to the jungle muck), I had an extremely painful zit on the end of my nose: a zit big and glorious enough that it should have been gracing the nose of some fortunate teenager, rather than me, a slightly over-the-hill missionary who doesn't know enough not to slither through the muck on a dark, hot, tropical night.

I will end with this: When you go out on one of these four-day extreme outreach trips and the highlight of your trip is finding some chocolate-chip cookies your wife hid for you, it might be time to admit that age is starting to creep up on you! Just sayin'.

◈ ▣ ◈ ▣ ◈

On a trip to La Esmeralda for fuel, I was filling my boat tank while Keila was shining the light and Mia was asking a thousand questions a minute. Getting distracted, I accidentally spilled a bit of gas. When I bent down to scoop up some water to wash the spilled gas away, I heard a small splash in the darkness, and only then remembered my glasses in my shirt pocket. I was not a happy camper! Getting the light from Keila, I shined it into the murky water of the Orinoco River in vain. I hoped I could find a spare pair that I thought I had somewhere back at the house, because I just was not going to be getting into that river. It was night, and the water looked cold and dark and deep. Muttering to myself about my stupidity, I finished filling the fuel tank and continued preparing the boat for our trip back to Cosh. We were waiting for the moon to come up, which on this night was going to be about 8:30 p.m.

"What are you doing here?" said a familiar voice? I turned to see Vicente, and he was happy to see me. He and his wife had been out in Puerto Ayacucho and they had gotten back to La Esmeralda the day before. In these days with very little fuel, he had no idea of when another opportunity might present itself for him to get home.

"Yes, I am heading home, but I am really loaded," I told him.

"Oh, you have got to let my wife and I go with you. We will squeeze in like a couple of bats, and you won't even know we are in the boat," he pleaded.

"I dropped my glasses in the river." Pointing down to the dark murky water, I told him, "Find them and I will take you home." I figured if he at least tried, I would go ahead and make room for him. He quickly stripped and jumped into the inky black water. *Boy, he really must want to get home*, I thought, beginning to feel guilty that I had made him get in the black water and look for my glasses. Besides, what would be the chance of finding them? I decided I would tell him to quit the search the next time he came up. Well, surprise! The next time he came up he had my glasses in hand! Praise the Lord! Though not totally blind, I sure can't do any reading or computer work without them. By the way, I did give Vicente and his wife a ride home. We made it home around midnight, and I still have my glasses.

Now, about that trip home: I know it is always easy to get carried away and start exaggerating about the weather and how bad it was. I can't stand that kind of report! I won't go on and on about the never-ending rain, with drops so big I felt I was being blasted in the face by a sandblaster using buckshot; nor will I go on and on about the lack of visibility, which was so bad I could hardly see my hand in front of my face; but let me just say the following and I will leave it there.

My boat is equipped with a GPS, so even though I had my head down and could not see anything, I could still make my way downriver safely even though visibility was almost zero. Thankfully, the GPS is also a depth sounder. We were driving downriver, being careful to follow my route, when all of a sudden I had to take a second look at my GPS: The depth sounder said we were running ten feet below the surface of the river! It was raining so hard we couldn't even tell that we were ten feet underwater! Can you believe that? Well, I thought, they don't call it the rainforest for nothing! Anyway, like I said, just the bare facts.

◈▣◈▣◈

How do I tell this and not do too much damage to myself? Having to do damage to Keila is a given. Here is the unvarnished truth.

Around midnight, I was woken up from a sound sleep, a sleep that I had just fallen into in spite of my ongoing fight with a tenacious flu. I was woken up by the shrill scream of my lovely wife. She had seen a rat!

I bravely stumbled up to do battle with said rat, which had taken shelter behind a cabinet. I got an arrow and then found another suitable weapon for Keila. Placing her at the end of the cabinet from which I did not think the rat would exit, I asked her to poke her weapon into the space behind the cabinet and drive it toward me, where I was ready with my arrow. She poked, but instead of running out toward me, it turned around and rushed past Keila—and from Keila's shriek, I thought it had taken a bite out of her. But no, she was only frightened by it.

I gently massaged my heart to get it pumping rhythmically again. Calmly walking up to her, I cautioned her about screaming so loudly in the night. "The neighbors are going to think I am beating you up. Someone might come over to help you. Please stop," I pleaded. She nodded.

I made a good effort to find where the rat had gone, but by that time it was really gone, so I went on back to bed, shaking my head at my night.

About two hours later, I was once again rudely awakened by another shriek. "The rat is back, come help!" Well, what could

I do? I jumped out of bed and ran over to do battle once again with this tenacious rat.

"Where is it?" I asked.

Keila pointed at the same cabinet. "I-It went back behind there again," she stuttered.

"OK, let's get it this time!" I encouraged her. She nodded. I placed her where I had been standing before and I took my position where she had been. Holding my arrow ready, I noticed that I could not get a straight shot at the point of exit where I figured the rat would appear. I got down on my knees to give myself a better line of attack. "OK," I told Keila. Keila poked her broomstick into the space and I got ready, but I was too slow. I am sure it was because of how weak I was due to my sickness. Anyway, the rat bombed out of there so fast all I could do was stare as the crazy rat ran up and over my bare legs. I shuddered. Now, Keila says I shrieked like a girl, but I don't recall a shriek. I did try and yell a warning to Keila—and that was the thanks I got!

We still have yet to rid ourselves of this nuisance rat, but the battle will go on. The worst thing about the entire incident was this morning, at our early morning Bible class, when one of the church elders asked me what was going on in our house last night. "Why do you ask?" I replied.

"Well, I heard your wife scream and other noises and then, I am not sure, but someone else screamed." He looked at me as if I was supposed to tell him that it was I myself who had broken down, but I distracted him by giving a blow-by-blow description of our fight with the rat. And the fight continues.

Well, now it is Vermin 2 Dawson 0. Last night, to show his utter disrespect and disregard for us and our feelings, he broke into the pantry and chewed holes in some of Keila's hoarded apple juice, spilling the juice all over the place. Progress is being made on the rat trap, but we are running short on some of the necessary materials. But it is coming.

Last night was an up-and-down time again with the rat — or rats; at this point I am not sure if there is just one or more. There might be as many as three. I think it is probably partly due to the huge amount of rainfall we have had for the past three weeks. Anyway, I entered into hand-to-hand combat; actually, I had a pole, and the rat only had his "hands," but sad to say he eluded me again. Then, almost as soon as I got back in bed, there he was again, all the way over on the other side of the house. Again, he was too fast for me. He got away! After I got back in bed I wondered if I might not be fighting at least two rats. I finally fell into a deep sleep ... Keila swears it was really deep, as she could not wake me for the rat's third appearance.

Our trap is finally built and ready for testing. It is a rolling log trap. It was fairly easy to build. Talking Keila out of her large, round trash can for the base? Now that was hard! Talking her out of some peanut butter for bait has so far proved to be impossible. She offered to let me use some of my last bar of chocolate for bait, but everyone knows a rat hates chocolate! Still, I mean, the nerve!

Well, the trap spun and the rat is ... suffice to say that he is not going to bother us any longer. I just hoped he was a lone fast rat.

But alas, it was not to be. So true what the old timers used to say: "No rest for the weary." As I surely have not had any rest from these rats, scarcely a few days after we dispensed with the afore-mentioned first rat, then this. "You were not the hero this time!" My wife's lovely eyes were hostile as she glared at me.

What happened? I can hear you asking. Good question. What

happened is that there was more than one rat, and the next one made his appearance while Keila was alone. She sometimes wakes up in the early morning and can't go back to sleep, so she gets up and does her devotions. Well, it seems she was interrupted this time by a rat that was not afraid of her at all and, as a matter of fact, according to Keila, tried to get way too close to her for her comfort.

I finally heard her calling and jumped up to rescue her, only to find her standing on her tippy toes on our couch. I coaxed her off her perch on the couch long enough to show me where the rat had gone. "Let's not scare it any more than you have," I told Keila. "Let me set up the trap again." She nodded and watched me set up the trap from the safety of her perch.

I finished setting up the trap and told her to come down. "No! You are no hero to me!" she said again.

Shocked at her angry words, I said, "What do you mean? I set up the trap. I can't fit under the couch to dig it out, the trap is the best bet..." My voice trailed off.

She continued glaring. "You did not answer any of my texts!" she finally said, still pouting.

"What texts?" I asked.

"The text I sent you after the rat treed me on the couch," she answered.

"Honey, it is almost 4:00 a.m., my best sleeping time. I never heard my phone ding for a text message. Why did you not call me? I would have heard that. I never even heard your texts come in."

Just to verify that she had in fact sent me some texts, I went to my phone and saw her supposedly frenzied "calls" for help. I was so sorry I had not heard her text come in. Here is what she sent:

[3:36 AM, 9/17/2018] Keila: Mike
[3:37 AM, 9/17/2018] Keila: Love
[3:38 AM, 9/17/2018] Keila: Your mouse wants my couch

Can anyone blame me for not having heard that?

◈ ▣ ◈ ▣ ◈

This morning, after our men's prayer and Bible study, I mentioned my sleepless night due to the rat scaring Keila again. My friends all got a chuckle out of trying to picture Keila up on a couch and they laughed at me when I told them, "Yes, but the real problem is now she is angry at me because the rat scared her." They reminded me of what happened to a friend up in Cavanabe a few years ago. Here is his story:

Pedro and his wife had a nice little flock of chickens which they made sure were in their shed every night. One morning, they were saddened to find out that something had gotten into the shed and killed a half dozen of their hens. This was a terrible loss! Quickly reading the signs, Pedro knew that an ocelot had gotten in and killed his chickens. He was furious and swore he would tear the cat apart with his bare hands.

The cat, possibly because it spoke no Yanomamö, did not realize what dangerous ground he was on, so the following night he broke back into the chicken coop and killed more chickens. Because the Yanomamö counting system only consists of one, two, and many, it's hard to know exactly how many chickens had been killed, but both husband and wife were furious. As is the case too many times, they began to take their hostility out on each other. "You talked so big yesterday about tearing the ocelot apart with your bare hands, let's see you do something. I am tired of hearing your talk!" By this time the wife's chiding was shrill enough to be heard by the entire village.

"OK, you want to see me do something, just watch me tonight!" Pedro shouted back. That evening, right before dark, he crawled through the low doorway into his chicken shed and took up a position next to where the cat's tracks showed him coming and going. Because of his bragging, he was barehanded, taking not even a knife in with him. What he did not know was that his wife, waiting until he was inside, quickly and quietly locked the door from the outside.

Right before dawn, he heard the cat enter the shed. In the predawn light, he could barely make out the jungle cat. Pumped up by his own talk, he reached down and grabbed the cat around the middle in a bear hug, jerking it off the ground. He hung on for dear life. The cat went crazy! In a fighting frenzy, the cat began to rake Pedro's arms and head with furious clawing. Pedro's arms and head were soon covered in blood. Head wounds bleed worse than most other places and it wasn't long before Pedro had so much blood pouring down his face that he could not even open his eyes. The cat was snarling and Pedro was yelling for help. By this time, he had made his way over to the door and tried to back out of it, but he was shocked to find it locked. He began yelling in earnest for his wife.

Hearing her husband's frantic yells, she ran up to the shed, but had to get in one more dig before opening the door. "Have you ripped him apart limb from limb yet?" she yelled.

"Just open the door! This *yaocole* is killing me!" Pedro shouted. By this time most of the village was standing outside the chicken hut, some of them yelling encouragement to Pedro, others egging on his wife. Finally, she took pity on him and opened the door. Poor

Pedro had just about lost the battle with the furious cat. To add insult to injury, the little lady picked up a stick of firewood and dispatched the cat with a well-placed swing to its head.

Pedro sagged to the floor, still holding the dead cat hugged to his chest. Blood dripped in big drops from his head and arms. He finally opened his arms and let the cat drop to the floor. Taking pity on her bleeding husband, his wife took him by the arm and led him home. Poor Pedro was laid up for weeks fighting infection from the claw wounds inflicted by the furious cat. His wife could never say enough about how brave her husband was to fight a full-grown ocelot hand-to-hand in the predawn darkness of their chicken shed. I don't think either of them ever brought up the locked door again … at least not while the other could hear it.

After all the laughs, I realized that Keila and I are still doing pretty well. She has not locked me in anywhere with the rat yet, although, after telling her this story, I sure am hoping I haven't given her any ideas!

10

LETTERS HOME

Because so much of a missionary's life is spent writing letters to his support team back home, I thought I would include some of our letters from the past few years to give you a better grasp of exactly what happens to us, and our thought process after it happens. When writing a book, many times we can look at things through the corrective lens of time, which everyone knows is 20/20 and present them in a mostly positive way; when you read the actual letters that were written soon after the occurrence, it shows a more realistic picture of the event.

July 28, 2008

Just a note to bring you up to date on different issues facing us here in the jungle. First of all, we do covet your prayers as we know we are going to face some tough days, but at the same time, we know God is in control, so we remain optimistic that He is going to keep the door to the Gospel open here in our little area of Venezuela. We are not sure why this area has been so singled out for treatment, but some days it seems all we can do is hang on.

Up in our area, everything is getting harder and harder to find. It has been months since we have been able to get any bottled gas. I was finally able to find two bottles in Puerto Ayacucho a couple of months ago, but while they were being shipped upriver, one was taken by a guard because they did not have any for their stove. We did get one up here, so Dad and Mom still have bottled gas to cook with. This last month, I have been working on an outside cookhouse and we will be cooking on wood. Faith and Sharon, my sisters, have already been cooking over a wood fire for months now. It is an inconvenience but basically not much else. I almost said "not even worth writing about" until I realized I was in fact writing about it, so either there just is not that much to write about, or it is a bit larger area for concern than I am letting on.

Another area that we are a bit more concerned about is the difficulty of getting food supplies up here. While cooking over a fire is time-consuming and all, having no food to cook gets old much quicker. Now, let me say, no one is starving, but it was a sad day a couple of weeks ago when we ate the last of our potatoes, I can tell you that. I did not know whether to eat mine or frame it and display it. I ate it! Other fresh stuff has been gone too long ago to mention.

Gary and Marie ordered food from town, but the military authorities turned down the request to allow a flight to bring their supplies. We are not sure how long this impasse is going to hold, but we are concerned about this new twist. Seems like they have orders to make it difficult for us.

Another impossible-to-find item — well, almost impossible — and it seems unbelievable, is fuel. Remember, Venezuela is one of the largest oil-producing countries in the world, and actually sits on the largest known oil reserves in the world! We can barely keep our generator running even reduced hours. Gasoline for outboards is a fading memory. As many of you know, we have always depended on local fishing and hunting for fresh meat and fish. With no fuel, it makes it almost impossible to go where you have any hope of finding an animal; so one good thing, with the generator running the reduced hours, if we had much fresh stuff, it would only spoil anyway, so it is kind of balancing out.

I honestly don't want to bore you with a bunch of discouraging information, but we so depend on your prayers, and in order for you all to be effective prayer warriors before God's throne, you have to know what we are facing. I really don't want to sound like we have it so bad. That is not how we feel at all: most days, life is pretty good here. We have much to be thankful for. We are all in good health, for which we are grateful. We rejoice to be granted an open door for the Gospel of Jesus Christ here. Thanks for your prayers!

Honored to be partnering with you in the Gospel of Jesus Christ!

Friday, September 5, 2008

Just a note to say hi and thank you for your continued prayers and support of us here. The Lord continues to teach us that His time is not our time. I have been reading the book of Esther and am encouraged how the Lord worked out the changes in government to accomplish His purpose in His time. Sometimes I find myself worrying over the fact that it seems there is no stopping our king. But I am reminded from this verse in Proverbs that *The king's heart is in the hand of the Lord, as the rivers of water: He turneth it whithersoever He will.* Proverbs 21:1.

Now, on a practical level, sometimes my actions don't follow what I know in my head and heart. While we were able to get some food from Las Esmeralda last month, our pantries are once again starting to go bare, causing us to start worrying just a bit. Let me be quick to make it clear that we are not even close to even losing the weight that would be healthy to lose, let alone in any immediate danger of starving. But sometimes one gets to remembering the "leeks and garlics of Egypt," in this case, more remembering the meals at the Golden Corral and like restaurants.

Our greatest problem is fresh food and fresh meat, the lack of which has made me start eyeing our pet macaw parrots. We have two of them, and they, perhaps not realizing how meat-hungry we are getting, sit out on their perch outside our kitchen window and make obscene comments at us when we are a bit slow with bringing them their food. When our blue-and-gold macaw catches me looking out the window at him, he throws his head straight up and makes a motion with his beak as if he is being fed (looks a lot funnier than I make it sound), as if I need a hint. He's not realizing that I am eyeing him more with wondering how much meat his short little drumsticks might have than thinking about what I am going to take him to eat. But he is still safe. Parrot meat is blacker than boot leather and even tougher. So, I just shake my head and mutter about my beans and rice. But God is faithful and through all this, we are learning to trust Him.

PS: Keila says I need to make sure you know I was joking about eating our parrots. Regardless of how meat-hungry we get, she says we are *not* eating them. So that is official.

December 8, 2008

At the risk of sounding like a whiner, I would like to share my latest grievance. As you know, in the past, I have asked for prayer for all the government harassment, lack of air support, lack of fuel, lack of fresh foods, etc. These are large areas and needful of prayer, but I hesitate to bother you with something as small as what is eating me. Literally! Now, I know we are to bear our burdens with not only a stout heart, but also a stoic demeanor befitting a humble servant; however, this burden I am being called to bear is keeping me awake at night. I thrash and turn all night long and wake up not only exhausted, but bruised, scratched, and bitten.

What is this added burden I have been called to bear? Well, it seems I have become the latest gourmet food for a vicious horde of tiny fire ants. They are into everything, sad to say, even my bed. I am not sure where they came from, or how long they plan to stay around, but during the night, I move from our bed to my hammock and, you guessed it, they beat me to the hammock and they drive me from there to the couch, where, yes, an even larger convocation somehow get there ahead of me and are waiting, as if I were the main course, which in reality, I have been.

What really bothers me is the ants don't touch Keila! It's as if they know if they taste her, they are history, but I am fair game! Sure, she makes a rudimentary, cursory attempt to make sure the ants are gone, but I think they have made some kind of a treaty with each other. They hide, she does not look very hard, they leave her alone, they eat on me all night.

After about a week of this, I trudged my way over to my parents' house this morning after my early morning Bible class. While nursing my second cup of coffee, we got to talking about the day's activities and I said I was not sure I could do much, as I fought ants so much during the night that I woke up more tired than I had gone to bed. Mom, ever quick to see a silver lining in my dark cloud, told me, "Well, look at it this way, you are getting your exercise and your sleep at the same time."

Well, I had better quit, as I can hear many of you-all getting ready to start typing your replies back to me asking if I would like some "cheese with my whine?"

January 8, 2009

About the ants in my bed, thanks again for all who gave information on how to remove same; I hate to tell you, but not much of it worked. But I am glad to report the last week has been ant-free! I am not sure where they went, but before they left there was a great whining and moaning sound all through our house. My wife finally told me if I would stop whining and moaning, she would take care of them. I did and she did, so the rest is history.

Speaking of history, back in 1990 I had some bridgework done. I am not sure why, but about three days ago, for some reason, while lying in bed, I thought of this bridgework and what a fine job the dentist had done to last me so long with no problems. Well, tonight I was over with some Yanomamö friends eating some wild pig and *casava* bread when all of a sudden, I felt that same bridge break loose and began to move about my mouth. My tongue sprang into action and the wayward bridge was coaxed back into place. It is there now, but my tongue has about worried it and myself to death continually checking to verify that it is, in fact, still in place.

My big question now is, what is going to happen if it comes loose while I am asleep? I don't think I snore, but Keila swears I do. What if Keila is correct and sometime during the night while deeply breathing in, I should accidentally inhale my gold bridge? Not only would this be a monetary loss (it is gold, after all), but I am a good long way away from a dentist of any kind and I really don't like pain all that well. Again, a small matter, hardly worth mentioning.

Now, I am not in any pain yet, but tomorrow, I am going to have Keila try and superglue it back in place. Hopefully, she can get the wayward bridgework glued down. More importantly, can she get it glue it down without supergluing my tongue to the side of my mouth? I guess a better question might be, would she ...? Nah, surely better not go there.

❖▣❖▣❖

January 10, 2009

About my bridgework, Keila superglued it and so far it is holding. I might never get my mouth closed again. Keila made up for her lack of experience with enthusiasm and I think at one time she had both hands and a foot in my mouth, but she got it glued down.

Months later, while on furlough at the dentist's office:

Regarding my bridgework, I guess Keila missed a calling. The dentist x-rayed my tooth and bridgework area and he said Keila had done a superb job of supergluing the piece back in place. He said it was seated perfectly and I should just wait a bit to let the superglue begin to unbond, as it was down so tight that he was afraid he might break something getting it loose. Made Keila's day, I'll tell you that.

I have not been able to get it out of my head for about a week now.

> Got any rivers you think are uncrossable?
> Got any mountains you can't tunnel through?
> God specializes in things thought impossible,
> And He can do what no other power can do!
> Faith, mighty faith the Promise sees and looks to God alone
> Laughs at impossibilities and shouts it shall be done!
> "Got Any Rivers / Carry You", Selah

❖▣❖▣❖

Then this note: This was in regard to our fuel barge sinking on its way upriver. When it sank, it flipped over, dumping its entire load of building materials and fuel. This was a huge loss for us. For about a week, as we worked with only people power to get it flipped back over, we despaired of ever getting it back.

❖ ▣ ❖ ▣ ❖

October 18, 2010

And we know that all things work together for good… Romans 8:28

We take this by faith, not seeing yet the fulfillment of this verse in the sinking of the fuel barge, the rain that beat us silly one night, and the fact that we could not get the barge tipped back over, but we are excited to watch it play out. We came home to catch our breath, get some eats, and try and come up with some better ideas. Ain't life exciting!

Years ago, a good friend gave me a giant-size Stanley stainless steel coffee thermos. Well, I loaned it to Nando who was going to be driving the barge. I, of course, read him a riot act about guarding it with his life before I loaned it (partly in jest), but I really very rarely loan it. Well, I think Nando felt worse about the thermos than he did about the barge. To be honest, I partly did, too. Anyway, yesterday late, on one of the last dives back down to the barge for the day, one of my friends came up to the top holding that crazy thermos.

This thermos is either the luckiest thermos made or it is a Jonah thermos. This is the third time I have loaned it and it was sunk all three times, and yet we got it back. I am extremely happy to get my thermos back, and yet, to make it less traumatic on my friends, have decided I am not going to loan it to anyone again, at least not if they are heading off in a boat.

We appreciate your prayers that we might be able to figure out a way to get our barge tipped back over right side up. It is a huge undertaking with just people power, but Lord willing someone will come up with a good idea. We have tried a number of ideas already: some seemed good, others seemed stupid, and so far, none of them have worked.

October 28, 2010

Praise the Lord with us! We finally got the barge flipped back over! We honestly despaired of ever getting it right side up again and had all but given up when some Piaroa friends from TamaTama, hearing about our troubles, came up by dugout canoe to see if they could offer us some help. When New Tribes missionaries left TamaTama, they gave a lot of the tools that had accumulated over the years to the native population. One of the tools Fran Cochran had given was a large come-along. Just what we needed! This tool made all the difference in the world. We quickly took heart and jumped back into the task.

We attached the come-along to a large tree with a long piece of chain. Then, looping the cable of the come-along over the far side of the upside-down barge, taking the cable under the barge, we attached it to the near side. As soon as we had everything tightened down, one of the guys who had brought the come-along took the place of honor at the handle and began to work the handle back and forth, slowly taking up the slack in the cable. We watched in silence, hardly daring to breathe, as the cable tightened and slowly started pulling the upside-down barge right side up. It was actually amazing to watch this tiny tool move the huge fuel barge. At one point, the barge hung in the balance, then splashed down right side up. All that was left to do was bail it out. Setting up our large diesel pump, we watched our fuel barge come out of the water as the water was pumped out. Within a few hours the barge was floating empty. What a beautiful sight!

September 7, 2014

After 60+ years of there being a ministry to the Yanomamö, one should be able to think news of raiders, grisly murders, spirit killings, and shamanism would be things of the past, but unfortunately, that is not the case. Erico, from Cuwa (he was the son of a really good friend who died a few years ago), was captured in an ambush and killed a few days ago. He was from the village of Cuwa and was related to many people here in our village. The young man had been here in our village until about a month ago and had gone back home after staying here for about six months. He and a cousin had gone visiting to Wachaquito, a village just a short half-hour boat ride below their village, and after a one-day stay, Erico decided he wanted to go home. They had gotten a ride down with someone else, so now, unless they waited for someone heading back upriver, they would have to walk. Wilson, the other boy with Erico, decided he did not want to walk home, as by trail it was a lot longer trip, but Erico insisted and decided to leave by himself. Since his village had no communication with the other village, no one was aware he was even heading home, let alone that he had not arrived.

Three days later, Wilson did catch a ride and was shocked that his friend Erico had never gotten home. Search parties went out, but his tracks were difficult to follow, as we have had so much rain. But persistence paid off, and they found where Erico had slept and were concerned to find his clothes and other personal belongings still in the little lean-to he had built. They continued looking, and the stench of death permeating the area made the search easy.

They found the boy impaled on a pole, his body broken from the many times he had been clubbed. The short hand-carved club lay beside him as a further insult. He was lifted down and taken back to the village of Cuwa. Word went out and surrounding villages gathered for the cremation and also to try and figure out who had done this deed and what was going to be the response. As

I said, many people from Cosh went, as he was related to many people here.

[In situations like this, it] is extremely difficult to even know how to counsel the people. We know God's Word says we are to love our enemies, yet, in our cultures, we have police and armies to defend ourselves when trouble occurs. These people have nothing except themselves. To the best of our knowledge there was no reason for this brutal killing. Erico was a good boy. He had accepted the Lord and, as far as we have ever heard, lived for Him. It seems these were raiders from some far-away village who were lying in wait for anyone they could find and Erico stumbled on them and died. When the village really confirms who the guilty village is, many people feel they have to take action, as this kind of brutal killing cannot just be ignored, as doing nothing only increases the very real possibility that the guilty village will try again. Possibly, even against our village.

◈▣◈▣◈

Just days before the 2016 presidential elections, I posted a letter to both Facebook and my update list. The crazy thing was, I use Mail Chimp for my update list and evidently, I must have made someone at Mail Chimp angry because they froze my account. They made me delete all my addresses, and those who wanted to be on my list again had to sign themselves up. I could not sign anyone onto my list for many months. Anyway, here is the letter that got my account frozen.

November 2016

I normally try and keep my prayer and praise updates [about] personal and cultural adventures with the Yanomamö. However, I feel so passionate about the slaughter of the unborn going on in this country, I am going to send this out to you all.

The other day, while listening to the presidential debate, I listened in disbelief to one of the candidates for our highest office, not only defend late-term abortions, but PROUDLY defend late-term abortions. Thinking of the horror of murdering all those innocent babies caused me to remember something I had seen many years ago in our small Yanomamö village of Coshilowäteli. Some visitors had come over from the village of Jalalusiteli and the women were visiting Mom in our house. One of the ladies, obviously big in pregnancy, told Mom in hurried whispers that if her baby was a girl, her husband was going to make her kill it. She already had four girls and her husband wanted a boy.

While shocked, Mom was not quite sure the lady was serious. A short few days later, early in the morning, some women stopped at the house and told Mom that Oracio's wife had in fact given birth to a baby girl early that morning and had thrown it away. "Why didn't you all take the baby?" my mom demanded, almost in tears.

"We can't take care of another baby, we all have babies," they explained. My poor mom felt so badly and wished she would have tried harder to talk the lady out of killing her baby.

Around 2:00 p.m. that same day, Dimiyoma came in agitated. "Milimi," she called my mom, "the baby is alive. I heard it crying."

"Why didn't you take it up?" Mom demanded. "How could you leave that little baby out in the jungle all alone?"

"Milimi, I can't take care of another baby, I have my own," Dimiyoma explained again.

"Well, will you take me out there and let me see it?" Mom asked. With a few other women, they made their way out to where the little newborn girl was lying in an ant hill. Though still alive, her little cries were weak. Her little body was covered by large ants and by large bleeding ant bites, especially around her little nose, ears, and uncut umbilical cord. Mom picked her up, unmindful of the ants that were now biting her.

She gently started removing ants and was horrified to see that around the little girl's neck was a vine that the mother had hurriedly tied and pulled tight: so tightly it had cut the soft baby skin on the child's neck, now further aggravated by the hungry ants attacking the baby around the cuts. Evidently after being thrown, the baby had hit with enough force to cause the tied vine to slip loose.

I will never forget Mom carrying this bleeding newborn into the house and gently washing the blood and dried afterbirth off, then doctoring the bites. By this time, the little girl was barely alive. But after much gentle love, she did get better. This left a lasting impression on me. While on furlough a few years later, I listened as Mom told about this little girl, who now had a new family and a new chance at life. I will never forget the response from the listening women.

"What savages!" they exclaimed. "How can any woman do that to her own baby? What barbarians!" The horror was real in their faces as they thought of this violent mother, having her baby, taking a vine and wrapping it around her infant's little neck and pulling it tight and then callously throwing the baby down and turning her back and walking away. As a kid who had seen the little, bloody infant, I found myself agreeing with these women's assessment of this primitive culture — a culture I was more comfortable in than my own. My views on abortion have only grown stronger as our American culture debates how to sugar-coat the murder of an unborn child.

I read an article on what really happens during a late-term partial birth abortion and I realized the Yanomamö know nothing about being barbaric. Here is what happens in our "civilized" culture. This is a quote from a townhall.com article by Rebecca Hagelin (Oct. 16, 2016):

> Let's be clear about what partial birth abortion is: a full-term baby is partially delivered up-side-down, feet first. The squirming baby's head is left just inside the mother, with only the base of the neck showing. The abortionist then takes a pair of scissors, inserts it into the soft tissue at the back of the neck and slices through the spinal column severing it from the brain. All the while the "doctor" struggles to hold the now violently moving baby, trying not to drop the child lest the delivery be complete and a bloody, wounded baby fall to the floor. Finally, if the baby isn't dead yet, a suction tube is inserted into the incision and pushed into the skull cavity—literally sucking out the baby's brains.

In the jungle, I have watched animals with young defend their babies with a ferocity that is far beyond their size or abilities, and it is obvious they are acting in this way due to the instinct God has programmed into them. It is a known fact that this instinct to protect their young is strongest in the human female. Women all over the world have done courageous acts that stagger the imagination in defense of their unborn young. But now, due to an evil that is sweeping our country, not only do women murder their unborn young, they fight for the right to do so. And not only do they do so, but we have a woman running for president of this great country who not only says she supports this practice, but she is proud to defend this. America is on a precipice. There is no blood more innocent than that of the unborn. God is not going to hold us without blame for standing by and watching the slaughter of these most innocent Americans. Proverbs 24:11–12 say, *Rescue those being led away to death; hold back those staggering toward slaughter. If you say, 'But we knew nothing about this,' does not He who weights the heart perceive it? Does not He who guards your life know it? Will He not repay everyone according to what they have done?*

Tuesday, October 17, 2017

I just got our big boat off heading downriver to pick up our new bush hog. I decided to forgo the six-hour trip down and the ten-hour trip back up, so will leave here tomorrow at 5:00 a.m. with a speedboat. If I leave tomorrow at 5, I will get down there about the same time our big boat does. Pray all goes smoothly. There is a guy in green down there who strongly does not like us and he is in a position of authority. But God promises that He can make even our enemies be at peace with us.

October 18, 2017

We are back with the bush hog. You know what was funny, last week, we had the CNE, (National Electoral Council) and the National Guard up here for the regional elections. Keila normally cooks for them and just befriends them, etc., but she had been stuck out in Puerto Ayacucho and had been trying to get home for the last almost two weeks with no success.

As soon as the helicopter landed bringing the polling station authorities, they made a beeline to our house as they always do. I felt like telling them, since they had not given my wife a ride up with them, "too bad, kitchen was closed," but I felt like that would be a poor testimony. So I told them that although I would not cook for them, they could use the kitchen, which they did. Everyone was really friendly and they left almost a week later.

Well, we headed down to get the bush hog and guess who was the new commandant down there? The guy that just spent a week up here in charge of the polling station, practically living in our house! Wow! We were treated like royalty. They brought their big forklift down and loaded the bush hog on the boat for us and what a blessing! I had figured we were going to have to do it by hand and have to put up with all kinds of grief from the guys in green. How we praise the Lord for the way He always goes before us, making our paths straight. Thanks for the prayers!

November 7, 2018

This morning, after the Republican defeat in the House and all the ramifications that could spell, I was feeling pretty dejected walking out to my Bible class this morning. After the class, a young man who used to be from this village stood up and asked us if he could say something. We gave him the floor.

"I did not come down here to come to your class," Isaac started. "As you know, I have not wanted anything to do with the Gospel since I left here many years ago. I actually came down here to see if I could steal some needed items like fishline, fishhooks, machetes, and whatever else I could steal or have someone steal for me. I even brought tobacco down because I know some of the thieves in the village will steal anything to get tobacco. But it seems God has different plans for me. I got down here and something will not let me alone. Everywhere I turn something is reminding me of my need for a Savior. I do know I am going to hell and I know I am close, so I am finally giving up and have come here to ask you all what I need to do to get saved. I am so in bondage. I really need to be released from Satan's grasp."

Nando told a story of a hunting trip he had been on with some

Yecuana Indians. They are much bigger in stature than the Yano-mamö and Nando is small even for a Yanomamö. Anyway, they were following a pig herd and Nando was quite a ways ahead of the other guys in his party. Coming to a stream, he saw where on the other side the pigs had clawed their way up the bank, so he started in after them. Getting to about midway across, all of a sudden he started feeling funny, so he turned around and started back down the trail, looking for the other guys he was hunting with. Meeting them about 100 yards down the trail, he told them the pigs had crossed the stream and they were really running, so it was probably a waste of time to keep after them. One of the guys, Mario, ran ahead to look for himself. Nando and others stood there waiting for him. Suddenly, they heard Mario yell in pain and panic.

Jumping to their feet, they ran toward where they had heard him. Getting to the stream, they were shocked to see Mario totally in the coils of a giant anaconda: he was already gasping for breath and weakening fast. The two other Yecuana guys, having razor-sharp machetes, jumped into the stream and started hacking the anaconda. Severing the giant snake's backbone, they were relieved to see the coils loosen. They quickly helped Mario out of the coils and dragged him to shore. It took him hours before he felt strong enough to finally make it to his feet and they slowly made for their home, forgetting the pigs. Nando told me he could not help but look at Mario's big muscular body and compare it to his small tiny frame. He thanked God that God had stopped him from continuing across the stream, because if the snake had gotten him, he would have been gone.

After telling Isaac this story, he asked him, "Isaac, do you think Mario has ever wanted to get back into the coils of that huge snake? Do you think maybe anytime he comes to a stream that he maybe hesitates and nervously looks around trying to make sure there are no snakes in there waiting for him? He has no desire to get back into anything that had such a stranglehold on him. Well, this is how you need to look at your old way of life. Don't get back into it. By your own admission you know you were in bondage. God's Word tells us that now you are a new creature, old things are passed away, all things have become new. So, my friend, allow God's Spirit to draw you closer to him and to help you stay out of Satan's coils."

We spent the next two hours going over Scripture with him and then finished up by leading him through the sinner's prayer. Because he is from a different village and is planning on heading home this afternoon or tomorrow morning, we took extra time to give him verses and encourage him to really stand for the Lord.

Suddenly I was not so discouraged over the elections yesterday. God is firmly in control and I can rest in that. What a privilege to have a small part in helping to reach the Yanomamö with the glorious gospel of Jesus Christ!

11

OUR GOD IS AN AWESOME GOD!

Now, I am not sure what a group of termites is called, but somehow a bunch of them got through the wall behind one of our bookshelves and got into the books. It was a long job to go through all the books to find the ones that had been damaged. Some were so heavily eaten out that the books were only a shell; other books, right next to them, were not touched at all. If any of you are interested in the taste preferences of termites regarding books, let me tell you: they love Jerry Jenkins, Dave Hunt, Frank Peritti, and Louis L'Amour better than any of our other books' authors. Most of the books by these authors were reduced to only a very thin shell (I'm not even sure how they managed to keep the shape of a book)—but not a bite out of any of the volumes I had to wade through during my Bible school days. Remembering how dry those were, I had to admit our termites seemed to be creatures of discernment and good taste.

◆◻◆◻◆

In missionary work, so many times, after going through something that at the time felt like a tragedy, when it is finally all played out, we see that really God had been orchestrating the entire script; as we look back at the story, we see how our God was in control the entire time. Actually, we see where He had started putting in place things long ago, we just did not know what it was for. Now, I am not saying that the people who broke into my sister's apartment were right, but Romans tells us that *all things work together for good*, and once again we were able to live that reality. Here is the story.

Keila and I had gone over to the apartment building that our mission rents in Puerto Ayacucho and we were disappointed to see that someone had broken into the apartment. The room where Jerry and Susan Lee (my sister and her husband) have their stuff stored had been ransacked. Keila noticed a box tossed on the trash and picked it up. She saw some important-looking papers in the box. Not knowing what else to do with it, she brought it over to where we were staying.

A few weeks later, we received word that Susan's and Jerry's son, Andrew Lee, had gone down to Las Esmeralda to help try and get a bit of fuel. While he was there, the guards told him he did not have the correct permit to be up in this area. They went back and forth, but because the guard had the gun, it was pretty one-sided. Finally, Andrew called me and told me he had been arrested and was being brought out. To make matters worse, he realized that his identity paper was expired, so he was really nervous. I told him to calm down, although I was not feeling too calm myself. Just a few months earlier, a missionary family had been picked up and deported. They were not allowed to let anyone know, nor take any of their belongings. They were just deported. So, I was nervous.

I got off the phone and told Keila what had happened. She remembered the box of papers she had picked up over at the apartment and went and got it. Inside the box were my sister Susan's Venezuelan birth certificate, her marriage certificate, copies of her passport, and identification papers, among other papers.

We made copies and, after getting our lawyer, went down to the civil authorities to give them a heads-up on what was happening. I was so pleased to see that the lady in the director's office was a lady who had been part of a commission that had come to Cosh months earlier. I hoped she remembered our pet macaw parrot that she had fallen in love with and that we had given her. Thankfully, she not only remembered us, but gushed about how much she loved her macaw.

We explained that Andrew had gone up to Cosh before the new permits were even required. She told us the military had already called her and told her to pull his file and have it ready, as they were going to deport him. She had all his paperwork there on the desk in front of her.

Our hearts sank when we heard "deportation." We knew the military had already gotten away with quickly whisking another missionary family out and deporting them, so we thought they were going to get away with it again. In our jungle area, it seems legality is not that much of an issue. The official we talked to was very attentive and said she would do all she could to help.

Our lawyer pulled Susan's birth certificate out and showed it to her, asking, "Is it legal to deport someone who has every right to be a Venezuelan citizen? His mother was born right here in this town."

The lady took the paper and said, "Absolutely not! What is this?" She then got very excited and said the military needed to be reined in. She called the military and told them that under no circumstances were they to deport anyone, and that they had no right to, first of all, arrest him and, second of all, to bring him out. But since they were already bringing him out, she was ordering them to bring him straight to the office. It was once again a time to just sit back and see the provision of the Lord!

We met Andrew at the airport with our lawyer, and in spite of the guards' reluctance, the lawyer and Keila boarded the jeep with them to the military base and refused to leave his side. Our lawyer kept telling anyone who would listen that there were not going to be any further illegal deportations. As you can imagine, this did not go over very well. Finally, it seemed they accepted the fact that she was there to stay, so they took off to the immigration office: the lawyer inside the guard jeep with Andrew, with Keila and me in hot pursuit.

I might add that they had waited until ten minutes before closing: I am sure they were thinking the office was going to tell them to hold him over the weekend as it was too close to closing time. The director must have really loved her parrot, because even I was surprised at how fast her office handled it. Ten minutes after our arrival at the office, we walked out with Andrew, with his new identification papers clutched in his sweaty palm. Praise the Lord! We don't profess to know what God has in plan for this country, but we feel it is going to be something great.

This "something great" might just be that God continues to build His church here! I sat and listened in awe as Vicinte and his wife Teresa shared what the Lord was doing on the upper Padamo River. They are possibly the first "real" Yanomamö missionaries as we understand the term. They left their village of Cosh and moved to a Yanomamö village upriver where some of Teresa's people are from. Their only reason for going was to share their faith and to help the fledgling church up there. They came back downriver to our village for a visit and to share what the Lord was doing up there. They had recently returned from a trip further upriver where they had gone to share their faith and were excited to share all they had experienced.

We listened in rapt attention as they told of their reception in the many different villages upriver. Honestly, I could not help but think this might have been how the church in Antioch sat and listened to the Apostle Paul and friends as they related all God had done through them. In Acts 14:27 it says, *And when they arrived and gathered the church together, they declared all that God had done with them and how He had opened a door of faith to the Gentiles.* They surely declared all God had done, and it certainly sounded like miracles done through the early church. How we praised the Lord for the profitable trip that Vicente, Teresa, and their friends had!

This is one of their stories: In the village of Wasareco, there was a boy about fifteen years old who had never walked since birth. His legs never developed enough to support his weight, so at best he could only shuffle along on his hands and knees. The small group of believers had decided to meet together and pray for this boy before Vicente and his group had even gotten there, so as soon as Vicente's group were told about this, they joined the believing villagers wholeheartedly. They prayed for the boy way into the night, reminding God of all the recorded incidents in His Word where He had healed lame people.

During one of these prayers, the boy sat up in his hammock and told his mother, "I am going to go to the river. I am really hot and need to take a bath." While his mother was still getting up to help him, the boy stood up and walked out of the house and on down to the river, with the entire household looking on with mouths hanging open. I had to smile at this picture, because I too have been surprised by answered prayer even while assuring myself my faith is strong. Well, we were all ears! Vicente went on to tell what a follow-up praise time they had. "But after the meeting, I just had to be sure of what we had seen, so I went to people who were not believers and were not at the meeting and secretly asked them if the boy had ever walked before. I was assured he had never walked since he was born! And he was still walking around when we left!" Vicente assured us.

This was only one of the stories told. However, the news that excited us the most was that there were forty-three people from seven different villages who had made clear professions of faith and been baptized during this trip! We are incredibly encouraged by these reports and praised the Lord with them.

◈ ▣ ◈ ▣ ◈

I hesitate even to tell this next story, as I am afraid some of you, maybe with reason, will say: "Mercy, you just need to hang it up already!" But the praise part is so great I did not want to cheat you out of being able to say with us, "Praise the Lord!" This was such a miracle that I would say, in light of the fact that this involved humans, it is an even greater miracle than the parting of the Red Sea and feeding the Israelites for forty years combined. Here is what happened.

I left my briefcase with my computer, pilot's license, airplane and pilot log books, and other valuable papers at the Simón Bolívar International Airport outside Caracas. I have no excuse: I just walked off and left it! We did not even notice it was missing until about three hours after we had arrived where we were overnighting before catching the national flight to Puerto Ayacucho the following day.

Keila said, "Let's go and see if we can find it." *That is such a waste of time,* I thought. But as I could not come up with a better idea, I went anyway. Here is the miracle: Someone had found the briefcase, with an almost brand-new MacBook Pro fifteen-inch computer in it, and turned it in—with everything still in the briefcase! Can you believe it? Like I said, this is a miracle on par with parting the Red Sea and feeding the children of Israel for forty years! God is certainly still in the miracle business!

Speaking of miracles, when we purchased a new generator, we were told it was a three-phase generator, which is what we needed. After a long truck ride from Caracas to Puerto Ayacucho, where it sat for months waiting for a barge to bring it the ten days up the Orinoco River to our village on the Padamo River, we could not wait to get it unloaded and hooked up. Our hearts sank when we read on the data plate that it was only a single-phase unit, and worse yet, was single-phase, 220 volts: totally unusable for us. The length of time that had gone by since we purchased the generator made it impossible for us to just return it. Also, we had no way of returning it anyway, as the barge it had come up on had already left to make its slow way back downriver.

We prayed, asking the Lord for wisdom. I sent out word to our prayer partners to be praying for us, as we really needed this generator to allow us to continue using our well for drinking water. The well is deep and water can only be brought up using a submersible pump. Most of the response only echoed what I thought: "It cannot be done. You will have to somehow get a different generator."

Then, a lady at one of our churches wrote back that in her church was a man who worked on generators for a living: would we want her to ask him for advice? I not only said yes, but asked her to give him my email address so he could email me directly. A few days later I was happy to be able to email our prayer partners that the generator was hooked up and running!

Someone wrote, "You have to be experts at everything to live where you do!"

I answered, "No, we just serve an awesome God and He has given us a support team that is second to none." We are not experts, but the gentleman who emailed me asking what we needed done on our generator surely was: expert enough that, in spite of the distance and only going by a few photos, he could figure out something that most people said couldn't be done. The mind-blowing part of it is, not only did he figure it out, but God gave him the wisdom to be able to tell us, way up here on the backside of nowhere, how to rewire it. How we praised the Lord when we flipped the switch and not only the water pump, but our entire house, came on!

This side of eternity, we will never know how many people take our problems to the Lord, asking the Lord to give us wisdom.

◈▣◈▣◈

Sometimes our days are so bizarre it is hard to explain what our thinking was and what made us do or not do certain things. To give you an example of how this affects our lives on a daily basis, here is a typical day (or days) for us.

I made plans to make a quick trip upriver to take some medicine to a young man who had a really bad case of leishmaniasis. It is a terrible disease caused by a living microscopic bug that literally eats the person away. In Javier's case, it was in his nasal cavity: it had already almost eaten his entire nose away and had now started on his upper lip. Javier lives in Arata, a village that is about 250 kilometers up the Ocamo River; depending on the boat used, it can take anywhere from eight hours to two or three days to get up there. Well, using the boat I wanted to go in, the trip would take me eight hours, but the day before I was to take off, four guys came to our village asking if they could catch a ride with me. I frowned. With the fuel I had to take, plus the two guys who were already going with me, I could not carry any more weight in my small boat, and I really did not want to change my plans of a quick trip.

"Who are you all, and how did you get here?" I asked them.

"We are Shitali" (a different branch of Yanomamö) they told me. "Our village is about three days' walk inland from Arata, and we heard you were going up there. We need a ride so we can go home.

About three moons ago, a helicopter landed in our village and we took the opportunity to come out so we could find some much-needed axes and machetes for our village. The helicopter people told us they would give us a ride back on the helicopter, but we have been waiting in La Esmeralda for over two moons now, and they are telling us it will be the moon of October before the helicopter comes back and we are already really tired of waiting." They looked at me expectantly, waiting for my answer.

I did not have the heart to tell them I was in a hurry and only wanted to do a quick trip, as they had already been waiting almost three months and had another two or more months to go if they waited for the helicopter to take them home. So I nodded my assent. "OK, you can come with me, but we are leaving really early," I told them. The joyful expression on their faces was almost worth the fact that I would have to take a larger boat and had just added at least two days and another barrel of gas to my own trip.

I decided to give myself the flexibility to be able to visit in villages along the way without having to stop the large boat by taking my small aluminum speedboat and getting ahead of the other boat and visiting as I wanted to. We quickly outdistanced the larger boat and were a couple hours up the Ocamo River when we passed another large boat making its own slow way upriver. Recognizing people in the boat, we slowed down and pulled alongside at their insistent hand motions.

"Do you have any extra gasoline?" they begged. "We are still a long way from home and are almost out."

"No, you know, these days, no one has any extra gasoline. Why didn't you get enough before starting your trip? I am really sorry, but I only have enough to get up to where we are going," I told them.

"At least let me and my mother get in with you, she is not feeling well," a man named Pelayu pleaded.

"OK," I said. But then, along with his mother were four kids, and there was just no way I could fit Pelayu, his mother, and four kids, two of whom were not so small. So I told Pelayu, "I have a big boat coming behind me. You and your mother can get in that boat. I don't have room or enough power to put everyone in this boat."

"OK!" he said quickly. And we took off back up the river.

We arrived at the first village and visited for hours — enough hours that our big boat should have caught up with us. Remembering the big boat we had passed and Pelayu's quick agreement to stay behind, I got a sinking feeling in the pit of my stomach. Looking at the time, I realized we were not going to get to the village of Yojobä where I had wanted to sleep. Not willing to continue upriver without knowing what had happened to our big boat, I turned back downriver to see what was taking them so long, already figuring I was not going to like what I would find.

Sure enough! Just upriver from where we had left the other large boat, here came our boat, *pushing* the other boat. *Oh no!* I thought. *How could my guys have done this to me?* I pulled alongside.

"What are you doing?" I asked Ramon, the driver of the big boat.

"Pelayu said that you told him to tell me to push them up to Arata since their motor was not working good." I looked at Pelayu and he grinned weakly.

"You did say I could catch a ride with him," he defended himself.

"Yes, but not your boat and everyone else! We don't have enough gas to push both boats up there! Where is your motor anyway?"

"I sent it home, it was only borrowed. But I kept three tanks of gas!" he stammered.

Ramon quickly pointed out that the motor had already been sent back downriver before he had even gotten there, so when he saw them with no motor, he really had thought we had told them to stop him. I bit my tongue on the harsh words that came to mind. What should I do? What could I do? What would you do? Remember, my eight-hour trip had already become a two-day trip. Now, with this other boat tied on, it was going to take us at least another day! But I decided, sitting there in the prow of my boat, with all the people in the other boat looking at me with worried looks, the most important question was: How would Jesus respond to people in this kind of need? *Oh well,* I thought, *what did I expect anyway?* Just another typical day with the Yanomamö! Then, as if that weren't enough, it started to rain and *rain* and RAIN!

An MAF pilot (a great friend) used to respond to people with poor planning by saying, "Your lack of planning does not constitute an emergency on my part." All fine and good, but even as well as I speak Yanomamö, I have never even tried to translate that, as it would probably just give me worse heartburn. I can imagine them looking at me like, "What do you mean lack of planning? I am here, what are you going to do with me?" And you know what? It is with unplanned issues like this that we have the opportunity to really show God's love. Oh, but it is hard some days!

In the end, I am sure this trip turned out just how God wanted it to, because over the next couple of days we not only had opportunities to show the Jesus/Passion movie to different villages, but I was also able to spend time talking to the four Shitali guys. These were people who had never had an opportunity to hear anything about the Lord, and they listened very well. After having watched the movie a few times, they had a lot of questions, and — to make a long story short — they have invited us to come to their village to show the movie up there. It is a long way: two days by boat, then a three-day walk one way to their village, but Lord willing, we are going to try to make a trip in there in November or so. The four guys said they would walk out to get us and carry our stuff. Pray for these guys and their village. May the seed sown find good soil and give good and abundant fruit.

◈◙◈◙◈

There are shortages of everything, including coffee! Yet we love drinking coffee during our early morning prayer and Bible class. So far, God has always faithfully provided enough that we have never not had coffee. Funny thing is, while out in town, we could not even find it in restaurants, as there was just none available. But we still have coffee up here in our men's class of forty-five to fifty men every morning. So, figuring that if the Lord could provide it for us, He could provide enough for us to also share it with the women's class, we had shared with them for the past few months.

Now, though, we were getting desperately low. I announced to the class and also to the women's class that after this coming week, unless something changed, we were all going to be out of coffee. Well, that drove everyone to pray! And we serve an awesome God who even cares if we have coffee, because yesterday, before Lanzo and the others left with the boat heading back up here, I received a message from someone in La Esmeralda telling me he had eight kilos of coffee. So, big smiles with this coffee. Amazing how God continues to provide something as insignificant as coffee for us in His time.

Speaking of providing: Nothing like a socialistic country to keep us on our knees! We headed down to the little town about fifty miles below us by river, as we had heard some food had finally arrived down there. Because the last food was brought up to our village months and months ago, we wanted to make sure we got down there while there was still some food available. Venezuela is facing desperate shortages of everything, especially food items.

We got down there after dark, figuring that we would try and make our food purchases then and load up in the morning to head home. However, the lady owner of the little dirt-floor store told us that although she did not have some of the items on our list, she did have rice, sardines, some pasta, and a few other items — but if we wanted anything, we had to take it *right then*. We purchased all we could afford. After we were finished with our purchases, the owner told us we needed to get the stuff out of her store and down to the boat and get it loaded up as quickly as possible. "Don't even overnight here!" she said.

Wondering why she was telling us that, I asked her what was going on. Her answer floored me. It seems she had been warned that the boys in green (the military) were coming in the morning to confiscate her entire inventory! Boy, that got our attention! I just wish she had told us that before we agreed to buy her stuff. What a time! We loaded as quickly as possible — well, as quickly as you can carry about a thousand kilos about half a mile down to the river by foot! I didn't think we would ever get it all on the boat. We then shoved off immediately and quietly.

The channel we had to use would have us hugging the bank for the full length of the town, right past the guard post. Funny how the stress of sneaking, watching, and lugging in the dark made me feel guilty; I honestly felt like a criminal. The lights along the shore took on an ominous look and I thought I could feel the eyes of countless people looking at us.

My nerve broke. Switching off our lights, we cut out of the channel and slowly, carefully, picked our way across the dark water. It was way too shallow for our heavily loaded boat, but we managed to creep along, almost by feel, all the way across. We felt the boat touch bottom twice, but managed by everyone taking a deep breath and, raising our feet, helped the boat over the sandbar. We then crept along, barely at idle, until we were about a mile above town and out of earshot.

We traveled all the way home in the dark in spite of the very low water and arrived back in our village at 6:30 a.m. Whew! Good trip except for one incident: We were shining lights, mainly to announce our presence to some other boaters on the water who might be running downriver with no lights, and directing our driver where to go to stay in the channel. Suddenly, our driver was no longer following orders. A friend and I started yelling and banging on things to get the driver's attention, to no avail. The bank loomed up close and we yelled and banged louder, then gave up and ducked for protection. The driver finally started turning the boat, but we were too close. We crashed into the trees, but then veered back out into the channel. We harshly bawled out the driver for having fallen asleep. He told us if we didn't like the way he was driving, one of us could drive, so we apologized and started back up the river. Glad to be home.

12

MEDICAL PROBLEMS

Parasite treatments are a nasty part of missionary activity. Now, my intention is not to gross anyone out, but only to share the good and the bad of missionary work. To make matters worse, Keila (bless her heart) is hung up on home remedies, which mostly translates to vile, foul-smelling, terrible-tasting concoctions that we are supposed to drink all in one gulp on an empty stomach. I am not sure why, but almost without fail, the concoctions look, smell, and yes, even taste like (can I say this in public?) cow manure. Whew! It is one of the least pleasant parts of missionary work... almost rates up there on the pleasure scale with support/fundraising.

◈ ▣ ◈ ▣ ◈

It seems that medical problems for the people are only getting harder and harder to deal with. Back when there were many missionaries working up here and there were also many missionaries working out in Puerto Ayacucho, the medical burden, though still difficult, was spread out among enough people that it was at least manageable. Now, with just our family up here, I feel that most times we are being stretched past the breaking point. To be honest, I don't have to deal that closely with the actual medical issues, except when the circumstances call for my help with transportation logistics, but even so I still feel stretched.

A young man from Yajanama, Manuel, spent the past six months in a hospital in Caracas. He first went out to town on a military flight, sick with malaria. He was then diagnosed in Puerto

Ayacucho as having liver and kidney damage and was sent to Caracas. It has been a horrible battle for him and he is losing. The hospital told him his condition is terminal and there is nothing more they can do for him. He was unconscious for about three days. He also had a lot of hemorrhaging. When he regained consciousness, he called his people here in Ayacucho and told them he wanted to go home to die.

Because Gary happened to be out in Puerto Ayacucho, he tried everything he could think of to get Manuel back to Puerto Ayacucho so we could help him get home. He and Andres, the young man's father-in-law, went to every government office they could reach, but to no avail. They filled out more paperwork than you can imagine and it was all for nothing. They were finally told to just let Manuel die in the hospital and then the government would fly his body back. Finally, in desperation, Gary and I hired a taxi to go pick Manuel up and bring him back to Puerto Ayacucho; then Gary spent a full day arranging a flight to get him to La Esmeralda, where I was to pick him up and take him to Cosh and then to his village.

We had not had much contact with the village of Yajanama since we lost air support in 2006, so we don't know the younger generation up there like we know the older ones. As a matter of fact, there is no longer an airstrip in Yajanamateli: the jungle has reclaimed it, as it has reclaimed most of the airstrips in Amazonas State. Thus, we didn't know if the young man was saved or not. Gary did ask the man's father-in-law, and was thankful to hear that Manuel had made a profession of faith while our sister Velma and her husband, Paul Griffis, were working up in the village of Yajanamateli.

Then on the morning of the return, while waiting for the flight to bring the patient home, Gary had an opportunity to talk to the young, dying, Yanomamö man at the airport. Gary wrote:

We sat there and I talked to him about his salvation and about the hope that we have in Christ. He told me that he had given his life to Christ and that he has complete peace. He said to me, "My body is dying but my spirit, my inner being, is strong in the Lord and I am ready for whatever He has. I would like to stay here with my wife, I would like to grow old, but I know that what God wants for me is the best. Thank you for getting me back from Caracas, thank you for sending me on this flight to Esmeralda, and thank you that your brother Mike is going to pick us up. I know that you did this because you all love God, not with just your mouths; because you all did it for me even though you did not know me, knowing that there is no way I could ever pay you back."

I sat there and just quietly cried with him. Thank you all who so faithfully pray for us. I sat there a very humbled servant of God and in my heart just thanking God that we had responded to this need. Please pray for us, as the needs here in the rainforest sometimes are just overwhelming for one small insignificant family.

The airplane delivering Manuel took off heading to La Esmeralda. To try to make it easier on him, we decided to do the trip in small steps. This young man had a rough trip ahead of him: the flight to La Esmeralda, then speedboat to Cosh, then a terrible two days through whitewater that would curl your hair.

When I got him to Cosh, I could tell that after only a few hours in the speedboat, he was exhausted. What breaks your heart is knowing that by air, it is only twenty-three minutes from here with a Cessna 206, but that is no longer an option. We still dream, though.

A couple of days after getting home, Manuel passed away. Though our hearts were saddened by the news, we were happy to know that he is present with the Lord and doubly happy to know that he was able to be with his family before he died.

◈ ▣ ◈ ▣ ◈

Javier, from the village of Alata, had a bad case of leishmaniasis. It advanced to the point that it had eaten away his nose, upper lip, and parts of his face. We had sent him out to town but as no medicine was available out there for his treatment, he was sent home. After speaking with a doctor friend of ours in Michigan, he was able to find the proper treatment, so I started taking him the medicine and keeping up with his progress.

I made another trip up to Arata to check on Javier. We had been treating him and checking on him every thirty days. The treatment was working for him and he looked quite a bit better. I wanted to get back up there, but I had been fighting allergies—well, I thought it was allergies. I kept getting worse and worse; some nights I was up all night long. I could not breathe and there were some days I despaired of ever coming out of this. Well, after spending almost two weeks with me a prisoner in my own home, Keila finally diagnosed my sickness. She says I have cabin fever!

Aside from my breathing problems, my symptoms were looking more and more like malaria. I have been malaria-free since 1998, and have faithfully taken my drink of neem tea every day. But looking back at when these symptoms started, it was too close to matching my Arata trip, when I went to take Javier his medicine: a trip, I finally admitted to Keila, on which I had forgotten to take my little bottle of neem. So now, as if my cabin fever were not enough, I was going to have the added effects of mefloquine, which include dizziness, nightmares, and many other horrible side effects.

For those of you who have not ever had malaria, symptoms include (but are not limited to) the most awful headache you can imagine, nausea, high fevers, chills, spaciness, and (once you start the treatment) insomnia like you would not believe. Actually, it might not be real insomnia: it might just be my body's refusal to fall asleep because once I finally did fall asleep, I would have the most awful nightmares you can imagine. Someone wanting to write or direct horror movies would have their work done for them if they would get a good case of falciprum malaria and then take mefloquine as a treatment. Their success would be assured just by writing down their dreams and hallucinations.

Since 1998, we have been drinking a tea made from the leaves of the neem tree. We planted seeds in 1995 and had a mature plant in two years. It is a bunch of leaves growing in a sprig, with quite a few sprigs making up the entire branch. We dry the leaves in the shade. If the leaves are dried, the tea lasts without going bad. I am sure tea made with undried leaves would be just as effective, but the shelf life of the tea is short. We heat up water until it is boiling, toss the dried leaves (stems and all) into the boiling water, and then let the leaves steep for about an hour (the longer they steep, the more bitter the brew). I will even let them steep longer, as for me, the more bitter the better. We use a ratio of three or four sprigs of leaves to a gallon of water.

My sister Faith started drinking the tea in 1997 and she has been malaria-free since that time. Personally, I did not really believe it: I just did not think it could be that easy to prevent one of the worst all-time killers in the world. But after a really bad outbreak of malaria in 1998, Faith started bringing neem tea down to me and my family, and stood there until we drank it. We drink about three or four good gulps of it: in an eight-ounce glass, it would be about one-fourth to one-third of a glass, I guess, so about two to three ounces. In twenty years, none of us has had any side effects that I am aware of. All of us who have faithfully taken the neem have been malaria-free, both missionaries and Yanomamö. The ones who either don't take it or only take it when they remember it, get malaria quite often, so I am pretty much a believer in the stuff.

It is bitter as all get out! But after being forced to take it for a while, and not getting malaria, I slowly became convinced the benefits were for real. I have been malaria-free since that time!

Everyone here in the village who drinks the tea faithfully has also been malaria-free. It is unreal! It is so easy that it almost reminds me of salvation: so easy, so free, yet so few take advantage of it. Like I said, it has kept us malaria-free for twenty years now! Before that, I had three or four bad cases of malaria a year. It seemed like I was always sick with malaria or relapsing from malaria. Then, between malaria attacks, I was so drugged up on malaria medications that I was a walking hazard.

Groups coming down would bring neem pills and when they departed, they just left whatever pills they had not used. Keila much preferred the pills. I believe she would take one pill a day. She used those for about five years and stayed malaria-free, so the pills seem as effective as the neem tea.

Another reason for my not being able to take Javier his last thirty-day treatment was that fuel has been almost impossible to get up here. They are not stocking enough fuel at the government gas station downriver, so our meager ration has been cut by two-thirds already. It takes a lot of fuel to get to and from these faraway villages, so this lack of fuel really does affect our ability to do our job and to visit the people we need to visit.

When we finally heard that fuel had been brought in, I took off to try and get our ration. They allowed us to buy about one-fourth of our ration at the pump, but then, thankfully, they sold us the rest of our allotment under the table at about a hundred times what it cost at the pump. Still, because buying that amount gave me enough to get up to Alata, I did not complain.

I had just arrived back in port here from going after the fuel. I felt a lot pressure, as I knew Javier was waiting for his last treatment. I was still not feeling well and was really short of breath, but I knew he would be finishing up the treatment I had left there the previous month and that he needed to go right on to this last part.

We hadn't even unloaded yet, and here came KK, a friend from a village upriver. He was panicked like he'd seen a ghost. "My wife is in heavy labor, has been for days, and she is losing it," he panted. "We think the baby is dead!" We jerked my motor off the big boat, put it on my smaller boat, and sent Ramon Gonzales up to Ilomaqu to pick up KK's wife. In the meantime, I got fuel and whatnot ready to head back down to La Esmeralda. Ramon and the lady got back, and the lady did look terrible. We got her moved over to my larger, faster speedboat, trying to make her as comfortable as possible.

Then — can you believe it? — the crazy baby decided to get born right in my speedboat! In "medical" terms, I think the boat ride down from her village must have jiggled something loose! Thankfully, we were still in port — but I was panicked! I sent guys to get Keila and my sisters.

Biggest loser in this whole thing was — follow me here — was me. Here is why. I am afraid Keila was a bit panicked herself, because she grabbed string and cutting implements and ran to the port. When the baby was delivered, she brought him up to the house to clean him up, with me behind her barely able to puff my way up the track. Here is where it gets bad: Keila next took one of my brand-new Mission Padamo Aviation and Support tee shirts, instead of one of her own, and wrapped the baby in it! We then sent Ramon Gonzales to take them back home, up to their village. Mother and baby seemed to be fine ... but that was my last MPAS tee shirt!

Whew! Having a baby born in my boat has always been a personal nightmare, since I have had to take so many emergencies down to the little government clinic, but thankfully, the baby was born right at port, so all I had to do was run around and send others in.

At last I was able to made the trip to Alata. Javier was able to go into the next phase of his treatment, and we had nightly meetings where we showed the Jesus/Passion of the Christ movie and the movie *God's Story*, which takes the viewer from creation to eternity. All of these we have translated into Yanomamö, and they have been effective tools in sharing the Gospel. This is my passion. I know you have to do medical jobs to keep people alive, but the Gospel is where we can share eternal life.

I did finally get back from Alata, but I just can't win medically! As if my lung infection and malaria weren't bad enough, I had an ingrown toenail in my big toe so deep I'd have to take depth soundings to find it and so big it would take a backhoe to dig it out!

You all know that I almost never tell of personal pain and difficulties that I might be going through; when I do mention some major source of discomfort, I do so only to solicit prayers, always minimizing my own personal pain. Now, however, I am going to break my tradition of suffering stoically in silence, because that ingrown toenail, even though it has been removed, is still causing me pain (on a scale of 1–10, about a 19). Even more, I broke a tooth, and though I couldn't see the problem area, my tongue wore itself out assessing and reassessing the damage and reporting to central control. According to my tongue, the damage is extensive. The crater feels (to my probing tongue) to be about the size of Barringer Meteorite Crater outside of Flagstaff, Arizona. So, there I was, three hundred miles from the nearest dentist, with a crater in the side of my tooth that threatened my very existence if not taken care of!

Somewhere Keila had heard that dry coffee is good for "proud flesh." Now, not only do I have pain in my big toe, but it is on a caffeine high that won't quit!

Toe is really starting to hurt again, coffee must be wearing off!

The work has to continue, whatever our problems. We were taking all our barrels down to our big cargo boat to go get our quota of diesel. We had had municipal elections the preceding Sunday and they did not go well. At 8:00 p.m., we also received word that a guy in green who had made many threats against us was down there, so while loading, I kept having a really uneasy feeling about going. My guys were surprised when I called them over and told them we were taking everything home and we would try another day. I explained why and they agreed, so there we stayed. Not sure why, but sometimes it is hard to ignore your gut.

Now I know heeding the gut feeling was a very good thing, for two reasons. First, some men arrived from a different village late in that day. The next morning they came to our early Bible and prayer class and said they had come down wanting to be taught for the next three days. If we had left yesterday, we would have missed them and they probably would have returned to their village with no teaching. From where I sit typing, I could hear Timoteo, as it is his turn to do teaching.

The second reason was that, about noon, a guy came running up in a panic. His wife was in heavy labor and it looked like the baby was breech. My fast speedboat was down with a faulty coil just then, and my little speedboat takes an extra one and a half hours to make the trip. Taking a pregnant woman down to the clinic is one of my least enjoyable jobs, because there are too many things that can go seriously wrong. I have already had one baby born in my boat and, to be honest, that is one too many. Now, to have to think about a ride down that would be twice as long—well, I could foresee many potential calamities happening, so I possibly took the coward's way out. I quickly sent the father to call Ruben, one of the guys who goes with me a lot, and another guy. I got the boat ready, and as soon as they came, they were off. They got back later that same day, having safely gotten the lady in labor to the little government clinic. They were able to confirm that the guy in green who had been muttering threats had left yesterday to go back out to town. So, the next morning we once again headed back to the port with our barrels to get our quota of diesel for our generator and to get an update on the lady in labor.

We were able to get our quota of fuel, and the boat we loaded took off upriver; we knew it would take some extra time because the river was very low. Thank goodness, I had towed my small speedboat in case of trouble. I was not going to use it unless we had trouble, but the pregnant lady whom we had sent down on Monday in hard labor had finally had her baby, so she was ready to come home. I brought her, the baby, and her sister-in-law home, so that saved Timoteo and me from having to spend another night on the river. No complaints from us, I can assure you!

13

TRYING TO REESTABLISH AIR SUPPORT

By the way, none of you should think that we get to run down to this quaint little Venezuelan town and we can relax in town for a few days: I am sad to say that is not the case. La Esmeralda is not quite big enough to be called even a one-horse town, but we are grateful for it. It does boast a number of small, open-air stores with dirt floors, a few disjointed sidewalks, a government clinic, a huge military airstrip and, most importantly, a cell phone tower! Depending on the boat used to go down, it takes anywhere from two to eight hours to get there by outboard motor, and a bit more to get home. It is less than twenty miles away as the crow flies and is less than twelve minutes of flight time away. Actually, it used to be a one-horse town, but the horse died a number of years ago.

❖ ▣ ❖ ▣ ❖

God continues to do a work in the country of Venezuela in spite of all the opposition Satan has hurled against us. We don't know how much longer the Lord will allow the door to the Gospel of Jesus Christ to be kept open, but we do know we want to be found working until either Christ returns for us in person or shows us that it is He who is closing the door. We also know that none of the trials we have gone through have taken God by surprise.

Missionary aviation came to Venezuela more than fifty years ago, while I was still just a young boy, and for all that time, although we appreciated it, we never really thought much about how life would be without it. It was just something that became so normal, so necessary, that I don't believe any of us ever thought much about how life in the jungle would be without it. Missionary aviation was just there: something to count on, dependable. Not that our pilots and aircraft were perfect, but we did know they were dedicated to making life in the jungle as bearable as possible.

Back in about 1972 or so, my best friend, Fran Cochran, and I were asked to go to the village of Buena Vista to help the people up there build an airstrip. We were both about seventeen years old at the time. After fighting whitewater for more than two days and portaging over waterfalls that would take your breath away, it was pretty easy to figure out why the people wanted an airstrip. We arrived up there, and after much walking around through dense jungle, we finally found a piece of relatively level ground. We marked the trees for one end, then measured off the relatively level ground, and found out we only had about 330 yards. The pilots (a surly lot, for the most part) almost always insisted on 500 yards. But all we could find was this 330 yards of level ground.

Thankfully, we had a radio, and we called out to explain the lay of the proposed airstrip to the aviation program manager. Although there was only one approach, it came in over the Padamo River and a nice uphill slope that gave it the extra margin to be long enough for landing. Thus, we were given the OK to have the people start clearing the ground for the airstrip. For about two weeks we helped the people chop down thousands of trees, as that was the first step to clearing their airstrip. We would notch the smaller trees and leave them standing, and then, after all the smaller trees were notched, we started on the huge trees. Mercy! When those giants fell, they took out all the smaller notched trees with them and wow, the ground literally did tremble!

We basically had the airstrip roughed in when we left to head back downriver. "Call us when you want us to come back," we told the villagers. They assured us they would. Sooner than I expected, we did in fact get word that they wanted us to come up and check it out. Again, we took our fancy two-way radio with us, and Fran and I each took a younger brother. Fran took his brother Matt, and I took my brother Joe, called Pepito by everyone. Again, the whitewater took years off our lives and made my hair prematurely grey, but we arrived.

The airstrip actually looked incredibly good! Those guys had really worked hard. After spending a few days lengthening the approach by chopping down some taller trees at the end, we called for the plane to come in. They gave us a date a few days in the future and we settled down to wait. While we were there, two of our friends from the village of Lapateli asked us to name two little boys who were constantly underfoot. As I said, we also had two little brothers with us underfoot, so we named one of the boys Mateo, after Fran's brother, and one of them Pepito, after my brother.

The day for the plane to arrive finally dawned brightly and the people were worked up to a feverish pitch to think that they were finally going to be able to have an airport of their very own—a landing strip in their very own village! Well, everyone was happy except for the village shaman; I never did figure him out. He was rude and ugly and obnoxious, but we ignored him as best we could. Finally, off in the distance we heard the sound of an airplane engine! I did not think it possible, but the excitement mounted by a huge factor. Cochran and I looked at each other and the weight of responsibility was suddenly real for us. Is this airstrip really long enough? Is the approach right? Our doubts mounted and we wished we had not endorsed it quite so exuberantly. Well, at least I did, and watching Cochran look up and down the strip, swallowing a couple of times, I figured he was as worried as I was. But the MAF pilot lined up on the airstrip and swooped in, doing, in their jargon, "touch and gos," in which the pilot sets up for a landing, touches down, rolls his wheels, and then pulls back up for another go-around. This not only allows the pilot to judge the smoothness and firmness of the ground, but also gives him a very good idea of whether the strip is going to be long enough.

I had thought we had everyone conditioned for the plane's arrival, and most people were beside themselves with excitement—everyone, that is, except the witchdoctor! He jumped out into the middle of the strip and began to dance and chant, waving his arms frantically in a "go away" motion. Either the pilot did not recognize the shaman signal for "go away," or just thought he was one more very exuberant native trying to welcome him down, so he was undeterred as he set up for a real landing. The plane swooped down and touched down so smoothly that you could hardly tell the plane had actually landed. The pilot braked and came to a stop right in front of us. I looked over at the local witchdoctor and only saw his back disappearing into the jungle. He was gone!

Funny how memories come back. The reason for this long story is that Mateo died out in town and Gary had to get the air taxi company out there to fly the body back in here. I went and spent hours with Jaime, encouraging him. Many of you who have read my books know Jaime by his Yanomamö name, Yacuwä; Mateo was married to Jaime's sister and I had to tell him that his brother-in-law had died and his body was being flown here. Some days, it just seems we have to deal with death too often.

Trust me when I tell you that there is nothing like having a young woman in a coma in your boat hurtling down the river in a rainstorm to make me realize yet again how much I miss the pilots and planes who used to provide our air support. With the airplanes, once they took off from Cosh, it was a two-hour plane flight out to town. Now it is a two-hour boat trip, then a wait for an airplane in La Esmeralda (and it is always anyone's guess when that plane will arrive), then it is another one and one-half hours out to town by air.

I had been asked to take a very sick seventeen-year-old girl to La Esmeralda to the little government clinic. She was unconscious and not doing well. Arriving in La Esmeralda a bit before 10:00 a.m., I was thankful to hear the sound of an airplane landing, then overjoyed to hear a second plane landing, figuring that with two planes, there for sure would be room to evacuate the patient.

We rushed her up to the airstrip, but how disappointed we were when the planes took off and left our patient behind! I have no idea why she was not taken. I just don't know why anyone would not have taken a person so obviously sick and needing help. All I know is she did not go out. I waited there until late afternoon and then had to head home, leaving the unconscious girl and her father there at the airport. We were notified by radio that they finally took her out the following morning, but they had waited too long: she passed away in the airplane, while still about twenty minutes from Puerto Ayacucho.

The village was in shock and the sound of weeping permeated everything. There was literally nowhere to go in the village to get away from the sound of weeping. The girl was from a large family, so she was somehow related to someone in every home here. She was one of Keila's students, and then later a helper in her class, so Keila took this death harder than normal. My sister-in-law, Marie, was out in Puerto Ayacucho and was trying to help the father get the body released to be flown home. I had to be ready to leave our village at a moment's notice, as soon as we heard the plane was taking off, so we could be there in La Esmeralda to meet the plane to bring the father and his daughter's body home.

We got word late that they were taking off at first light with the body, so I left about five in the morning. We were down at La

Esmeralda before seven and called Marie. They were still waiting for the body to be released from the morgue in Puerto Ayacucho, but they were finally cleared to load around 10:00 a.m. They left Puerto Ayacucho about 12 noon and arrived in La Esmeralda at 2:00 p.m. We made it back to the village a bit after 5:00 p.m. We know in our hearts that death has been swallowed up in victory, but the grief is still there. The girl who had died had just turned seventeen, and she left behind a husband, a three-month-old little girl, and a large extended family.

In Mark Ritchie's book, *Spirit of the Rainforest*, he wrote about a Yanomamö girl named Yawalama who had been brutally chopped many times by her jealous husband. When Gary brought her down to our village, she was more dead than alive. I don't think many people thought she was going to make it, but my brother Gary and wife, Marie, and our two sisters, Faith and Sharon, spent hours patiently sewing her back together. I don't know how else to say it: She was a mess. Gary, Faith, and Sharon carefully bound everything back into place, but she had so many severed bones and tendons that the MAF airplane was called in and Marie flew out with her the next day to Puerto Ayacucho. Dr. Valverde did twelve hours of surgery and surprisingly, Yawalama did make a complete recovery and regained the use of her almost-severed limbs. She did not go back to her brutal husband, however, and each of them married other people.

Things have come full circle: the man who so brutally chopped Yawalama died the same day Yawalama's family paddled downriver with a very sick kid about ten years of age. I was almost positive he had TB; he looked like he had a very advanced stage. I was afraid it was too late, but we are going to try. I wish we had had the medicine to treat him here, but it can only be gotten from one government agency and the last patients we have taken out have not been given the treatment because there is a shortage of that medicine.

While loading the patient and the family, I realized I had been wrong. When the father asked me for help, the little kid looked so small, I thought it was the younger boy of about ten, but then I realized it was the older sister who is about thirteen. She had lost so much weight I did not recognize her. I knew that unless the Lord did a miracle for her, the child was not going to make it. Just too sad!

The village where they are from, Coyewäteli, has lost many people in past two or three years to tuberculosis. From the weight loss I saw in both the mother and the father, I was pretty sure they probably already had it as well. It was heartbreaking to take them down there and leave them. The doctors at the clinic don't have any medicine either, but they did tell us they were going to try and get one of the government airplanes up there to take the sick people out to Puerto Ayacucho, where, we hoped, the hospital would have TB medication.

The desperately sick little girl was flown out to the hospital in Puerto Ayacucho a few days after I took them down to La Esmeralda, but the family with a little coffin were flown back into our village a week or so later. She had died out in town just a day after getting there. Because of everything that was going on, the earliest they could get a flight back up to La Esmeralda was almost a full week later. Our hearts went out to this family. In the past year, they have had multiple deaths from TB and it is not close to ending.

In spite of all the bad news, God continues to show Himself strong in our behalf. We have prayed and continue to pray that God will give us His wisdom during these days. We know we are safest when we are in the center of His will but, at the same time, do not want to find ourselves in a position where we are presuming on His will. It is our desire that our lives reflect His love, reflect His peace, and that we may act as a testimony, not only to the Yanomamö but also to the Venezuelan national people we have to come in contact with.

◈ ▣ ◈ ▣ ◈

We lost air support in February of 2006 when then-President Chavez gave an order expelling New Tribes Mission from all indigenous areas. Although the order specifically named New Tribes, most mission groups, seeing the handwriting on the wall, accepted it and all pulled out at the same time. Our decision to stay is documented in my second book, *I Can See the Shore*.

We knew it was going to be difficult without air support, but we could not fathom exactly what it would mean to suddenly have nothing available. We quickly learned our greatest challenge was the continued operation of a mission outpost almost three hundred miles from the nearest town and hospital. We go three months or longer without any fresh food. We never know when we will get our food delivered. Mail service is nonexistent. Nevertheless, the greatest challenge is medical.

We had to make an annual pilgrimage back to the United States because Keila has to be physically present in the USA for at least two months a year to keep her green card current. Because I love aviation and anything to do with it, we offered to represent our mission at the annual Experimental Aircraft Association (EAA) Air Venture Convention in Oshkosh, Wisconsin. That way, we did not feel so bad about the time and the funds that had to be spent to fly back to the USA just to keep a green card current.

In 2007, while we were getting ready to pack up for our annual trip back, we had another death in the village. We lost so many people to very preventable deaths because there was just no way to get them out to medical help. After this death, the village met together, then approached our family, asking, "What are you all doing? This is really serious. Why can't you get an airplane?"

"Why is it only up to us?" I responded. "We are doing all we can. We are as affected by the lack of air support as you are. But you all can help too." Key point to keep in mind: The Yanomamö are poorer than church mice. In fact, they would eat the mouse if they ever caught it. So it caught them off guard that I was asking what they could do about an airplane. This was a new concept for them. In their minds, airplanes were unattainable.

After much discussion, nothing much was accomplished other than to reinforce how difficult it was going to be to get an airplane. The fact that the government was extremely hostile and had by this time closed our airstrip and all the other airstrips across the state of Amazonas did not give us much room for hope. We did, however, decide to continue praying about the situation.

The next day, in Keila's school room, the empty desk of the little girl who had died prompted the conversation to turn to the need for airplanes. Keila challenged her preschool kids to make beaded necklaces and bracelets so she could take them to the United States and see if she could find a market for them with our friends. The kids were immediately caught up with enthusiasm for the project.

When Keila told me about the children's plan, I was skeptical. Sorry, I was not convinced they could make a difference. I mean, how many beaded necklaces could they hope to make?

The Lord rebuked me for my attitude. I remembered the little boy bringing his lunch to Jesus. In Christ's hands, the little boy's five loaves and two fish were not only enough to feed the multitudes, but there were twelve baskets of leftovers to be taken up. It is not what we have, but Who we give it to that makes all the difference. So, I went from being skeptical to being their biggest supporter. We encouraged the Yanomamö schoolchildren to continue making their necklaces and bracelets. We found American children who were willing to partner with the Yanomamö children and help them by doing fundraisers and selling the beads for the village. Our prayer was that this might take off and be a blessing not only to the Yanomamö, but to all who heard of their determination. Over the time of our fundraising for an airplane, those determined kids with their beadwork helped raise almost $30,000 toward the price of the plane.

It is impossible to know how many lives an airplane would save. How many lives are going to be transformed by the message of peace that this plane is going to bring to this still warring people?

Starting a project of this complexity, it is hard to know exactly where you are going to end up. It was at the EAA annual week-long convention that I met with Dave Voetman, the visionary behind the Quest Kodiak. I was fascinated by this airplane, as it had been designed from the ground up to be a missionary aviation craft. Although it was much larger than the Cessna 206 (ten passengers to the Cessna's six passengers), and it used a turbine engine instead of the piston-powered 206 engine, it could still operate on the same length runways with a larger margin of safety than even the 206 could claim. This was impressive because the 206 has been the workhorse of mission aviation for decades.

At that point, even a 206 was beyond what I thought we could raise. I figured we would start small with a Cessna 182, which would be a good compromise airplane: only four passengers, but it had good range to make the long flights into the jungle.

Dave had heard that lack of air support was affecting our work and he wondered what our plans were. I explained to him that we had never, as a family or as a mission, ever done fundraising, but we were praying about a Cessna 182. He grinned at me and inquired, "What about the Kodiak, Mike? Sounds to me the Kodiak would be a perfect fit for you all."

I shook my head. "No, it's way too expensive for us. We are looking for a used Cessna 182. We think we can find one for about $150,000 and that will be hard enough for us to raise."

Dave frowned, but his eyes were twinkling. "Do you think it would be harder for the Lord to raise the $750,000 for the Kodiak or the $150,000 for the Cessna?" I had to admit, either amount was probably pretty insignificant to the Lord. "Listen," Dave told me, "you have until the 31st of December to raise $375,000. If you can raise that, the Quest Foundation will match you dollar for dollar to make up the rest of the funding. So if you can raise $375,000 by December, that is in effect raising $750,000." Well, that sure sounded good, but I was heading back to Venezuela on August 7, and it was already the end of July. Although I enjoyed my talk with Dave, and felt very encouraged because it all sounded so good, I was not sure what we could do to take advantage of this amazing offer from the Quest Foundation.

It took us two days to get to Front Royal, Virginia, and we stopped overnight in Pittsburgh, Pennsylvania. The next day, I called the airlines to confirm our return tickets and to ask about luggage restrictions, as this is something that changes with the seasons. For some reason, Keila started looking for her green card. It was gone!

She frantically looked through everything, but it was really gone. We had had it in the car driving down and Keila was sure she had had it at the hotel. The only possible conclusion was that someone had stolen it from the hotel room when we went for breakfast.

This was terrible news so close to our return!

I called the immigration department and asked them what we could do. I explained that we were flying back to Venezuela in just four days. I could not believe the agent's next words.

"Under no circumstances should your wife leave the United States. If she leaves without a current green card, she has to start the entire process over. If you apply for a new card from outside USA territory, you are getting a new card. You are not even guaranteed you will get a card. I am sorry, if your wife wants to keep her immigration status, she needs to stay in the United States and make an appointment to have her card replaced. It normally takes about six months to have a new card issued."

Well, that answered *that* question. Dad and Mom were traveling with us and already had their tickets. That evening, at the kitchen table with Keila, Dad, and Mom, we went over our options. We decided that I would take Dad and Mom back to Puerto Ayacucho and then return to the United States, where Keila and I would deal with her paperwork. It was not exactly what I had wanted to do, but in light of what the immigration agent had told us, it seemed like our only option.

I had already told everyone what Dave Voetman had explained to me about having until the 31st of December to try and raise funds for a Quest Kodiak. Dad looked at me. "Mike, maybe the Lord is giving you the time you need to try and raise the funds. Think about it." I nodded. Fundraising was also not something I wanted to do, but I would at least see what God had in store for us.

Dad was planning on going over to one of his supporting churches in Winchester, Virginia, the following Sunday. He and Mom asked Keila and me to drive them over. We gladly agreed. I loved traveling with Dad and Mom and listening to Dad share his heart in churches. I have never tired of listening to him talk and share about his passion for the Yanomamö and seeing them come to the knowledge of the Lord and grow in Him. When I said that, Dad told me that he was not scheduled to speak. He only wanted to greet the church family there, as they were such dear friends and, due to his age, he did not know if he would ever get back to the States.

We got to the church about fifteen minutes before the evening service started and walked in and sat down. Dad was still greeting friends, but Keila and I were already seated. Dad walked up with a gentleman and introduced the pastor to me. "Mike, the pastor has asked me to share a bit tonight. I have asked him if you could share in my place. I think this would be a good first place to share what the Lord has laid on your heart about the airplane."

I stared at him. If the pastor hadn't been right there, I probably would have tried to make some excuse. I mean, *Fundraising? I can't get up without any preparation and try to do fundraising!* Dad smiled and nodded. So I hesitantly agreed.

After a few songs, the pastor asked me to come up and address the congregation. I slowly walked up to the front and took the podium. Talk about not feeling prepared! But I swallowed hard and began.

After giving a brief history of the changes in our work due to the political difficulties and loss of air support, I said, "Geographic isolation has been a huge obstacle in getting the Good News to the Yanomamö. Aircraft cut travel time from days to hours or even minutes. But now, we find ourselves with no air support at all. We are trusting the Lord to allow us to reestablish air support for Amazonas state in Venezuela. Everything related to aviation is expensive. Even the aging aircraft used by mission agencies, while used and old, are still prohibitively expensive. In spite of the expense, we are asking God to give us wisdom as we seek to set up our own flight program. Up until just a few days ago, we had decided we were going to try and raise $150,000 for a used airplane that's more than thirty years old, a Cessna 182. But just a few days ago, we were challenged to set our sights on a Quest Kodiak, the next-generation missionary aviation airplane.

"Quest Aircraft's new Kodiak runs on readily available jet fuel. It was designed for the short, rugged airstrips in remote tribal locations, has lower maintenance requirements, and compared to the commonly used Cessna 206, can fly 35 percent faster while carrying almost three times the payload.

"Aircraft are lifelines for missionaries who are in the jungle working in remote tribal villages. Your donation will further the eternal impact on the indigenous people in Amazonas, emergency transportation for missionaries and tribal people will be provided, vital supplies will be brought in. This plane will make it easier for the ones working in these remote locations to continue working.

"Quest will sell the Kodiak to selected mission agencies at cost. Tentative price has been set at $750,000, but this is expected to go up to $900,000 for mission agencies. Commercial price on the Kodiak has been set at $1,450,000 per airplane. The Quest Foundation has already promised us $375,000 in matching funds if we can raise this same amount before the end of December 2007. We will also get an additional $75,000 for matching funds to finish out the base plane cost of $900,000. Once we match the funds that the Quest Foundation has given, we will get our serial number and our production slot, and additional required options to make the base aircraft field-ready are estimated to be $180,000 per plane."

I finished up with a plea: "Join us as we trust the Lord to make this vital tool a reality as we continue to pierce the darkness of the

Yanomamö." I turned back to the pastor and thanked him for the opportunity to share the vision we had of the work.

He walked up and shook my hand. "Thank you, Mike." He then turned to the congregation and did something I have never seen happen in a church. "We can have a business meeting anytime someone wants to officially call for one. I think we should have a brief business meeting. Can I have someone make a motion that we have a business meeting right now?" Immediately, someone made the motion and someone else seconded it. The pastor went on. "Now, we have heard the need of the Dawson family serving in the jungle. We have funds in our savings account right now. I think we as a church should be the first to donate to this cause. Is there any discussion before we vote on this?"

You could have heard a pin drop. "Good. No discussion, we are all agreed we need to do something. I propose that we donate $10,000 from our savings account toward this airplane. Could we have a motion?" Again, the motion and second were quickly made. The church voted immediately, and before we left the church that night, we had our first $10,000 toward the Quest Kodiak! Wow! I remember thinking. Just wow!

A few days later found Dad, Mom, and me in Puerto Ayacucho, but only one day after arriving there, bad news! Mom and Dad had gone downtown in a taxi and got out leaving Mom's purse on the floor of the taxi. In the purse were both Dad's and Mom's passports! This was terrible news!

We frantically thought of everything we could possibly do to retrieve those passports, but because they had no idea of what type of car they had been in, what color it was, nor any details on the driver, it quickly left us with no options and we were left without much hope. The only thing we could think to do was go to the local radio station and ask them to announce that we had lost two passports. Disasters drive us to our knees, and believe me, losing your paperwork is a disaster that seemed pretty huge. So we prayed and asked others to pray with us. Secretly, I hoped someone was praying with more faith than I was able to muster. In fact, someone was, and God granted us favor because—praise the Lord!—a miracle was announced with a phone call from an old lady telling us that her son-in-law had gotten in a cab and found two passports, and were they the passports we were looking for?

As soon as we could get directions, we headed over to their house. The further out from town we went, I found myself hoping we were not being set up for a robbery or something even worse. We arrived at the lady's home only to be told that the passports were not there: her son-in-law had found them and they were at his house. By then I was really worried, but the lady's daughter was there to go with us, so away we went, even further from town. You can imagine how grateful and thankful I was to finally get to her house, and after she went in, to see her actually come back out with the passports in her hand. Up till then, I guess I half expected her to come out with guys toting guns or worse.

How my heart sang with praises to our Lord! Our God is still in the miracle business, and I consider myself so blessed to get to see one every now and then. I don't mean to sound flippant, or to sound like I don't have faith, but it is so refreshing to see God do special favors for His children even when our personal faith grows fragile and weak. Dad and Mom were singing louder than I was and were most thankful for all who joined them in prayer.

My sister Sandy wrote a poem about the lost passport incident. It is included here with her permission.

> I sat on my chair and I bit on my thumb
> And I wondered oh wondered oh what had they done

My parents were sitting with
Their heads slightly bowed
I think Mom was crying
But Daddy he smiled?!

Our God is able
Dad said with a grin
Our God is able! He said it again
So why do we worry and why do we fret
I've lived a long time and God's not dropped me yet!

You see let me tell you what had gone on before
While riding in a taxi
Mom left her purse on the floor
Oh, but that's no crying matter
I can just hear you say
But their passports and visas
Were in there, that day.
And really without them the outcome is grim
For without passports or visas you can't live in this land
It's not like the US that has illegal's rights
And people to yell and scream and put up loud fights
in this land it is scary without papers to prove you really can
be here
So, what would they do?

Dad patted Mom's hand
It's okay, dear, he said.
God's in control so let's go get us some bread.
The chicken at Pobre Domingo surely smells good
Let's walk over and get some.
I think that we should.

Oh, Joe, how can you be hungry at a time like this?
And I don't want chicken

I'd rather have fish
So, grumbling, Mama ... she gets to her feet
And still chewing on my thumb I watched them leave.

It's crazy ... I pondered
It's crazy, I said aloud.
But there is no hope in this world
They'll find the passports now
Oh, Michael, hurry
Dad says with a shout
Stop being a Jonah ... stop living in doubt
Anyway, I'm hungry so get on a move
Let's go to Domingo's and get us some food.

We posted flyers and posters on the lights in the street
if you find 2 American passports
Won't you return them please.
We asked the radios to announce it
And they did with a shout
"Old Don Pepe lost his passports and he wants them
back now!"

Day 1 it passed slowly
Day 2 dragged along
Mama half-crazy and well my faith was gone
it'll never happen, I couldn't help but say
Need to contact the embassy and let come what may.

Then ... what was that? For in the distance
I hear the phone ring
And running I grabbed it.
"Yes?" I was so excited I nearly screamed.

Good sir, let me tell you ... a trembling old voice did say.
My son-in-law found some passports in a cab the other day.

if you come out to my house
You can have a look.
And don't forget the reward that was promised.
The old voice said, and it shook.
Yes, madam. Thank you, madam!
I said with a grin. I could hardly believe it
Thank you! I said again.

But as we drove further and further ... out to the countryside
it was wild desolate country and my fear I tried to hide.
What if this was a ruse ... some kind of scam.
to trick the rich gringo ... and oh, let me tell you, I chewed
my thumb again.

Finally, we got there
The old lady kind of sweet
Oh, the passports aren't out here, and her voice trembled weak.
And frightened, my eyes darted about to and fro
Searching the shrubs and bushes for some kind of foe
But then she continued ... my daughter will go
She will take you to the lugar [place] and soon you will know
if the passports are yours and I trust that they are
You will remember, and her lip kind of snarled.
The radio ... the posters and flyers did say ... you promised
a reward,
So, I hope you will pay.

The daughter she climbed into the car with a smirk
Let's go that way, she says with a jerk.
Oh, you can bet I was nervous
Nervous as can be
I looked at the barren dark country
As the car gathered speed
Frantically chewing on my thumb by then.

She's gonna take us to some spot where she has a friend
And they will rob or kill us ... ohhh maybe do both
I was so frightened I nearly choked

But soon we pulled up to a tiny little house
And the girl climbs from the car, as meek as a mouse.
I'll be back, sirs ... madam ... says she.
in the blink of the eye
She returned and whoopee.
The passports she had them there in her hand
And we were so happy we danced in the sand.

And let me tell you I was humbled, humbled as can be
That our Father in his heaven takes care of you and me
And in his gentle mercy he smoothes out the way
Gives us the things we need and the strength for each day.
And now with more faith I can return to the States
Where my wife hides in the basement
Afraid of no escape
For she lost her green card in that foreign land
And she is now one of those bad people
An illegal alien ...
So, I say to my father ... My God, with a yelp
Only one word ... and that word is:

HELP!!!!

I did return to the USA, and Keila and I went to Washington, D.C., to the immigration office and put in an application for a replacement green card. I had already notified everyone we were going to be stuck in the United States for possibly up to six months and were open for meetings. In my phone calls and correspondence, I explained about the fundraising we had agreed to do for our mission. All who know me and have ever heard me speak know we never mention money unless put on the spot with a question or something. That's why I wanted to make sure everyone knew what was going on.

Our first church service was a supporting church in North Carolina. Again, we were blown away by their response. After the services, the offerings totaled more than $43,000! It was becoming more and more obvious that this was a God thing; we were only along for the ride. But by the time December 31st arrived, we were still $21,000 short of our goal of $375,000! I called Dave Voetman. To be honest, I felt badly that we had not been able to make our goal and wondered what we could have done differently.

Dave was not put off, however. "Mike, the board does not meet until after the middle of January. You have until then to make up the difference!" To make a long story short, we did raise the full amount and we were given our production slot. We were number twenty-two of mission "at cost" airplanes. With hearts full of praise, we left for Venezuela encouraged by what God was doing for us and for the Yanomamö. How excited I was to tell the village that we were going to get an airplane!

Our son, Ryan, wanted to be our pilot. He got his airframe and powerplant mechanic's (A&P) licenses, which allows him to work on both the airplane and the engine. He enrolled in Moody Aviation for his pilot training, figuring that by the time he finished the three-year course, our airplane would be ready. Ryan did graduate from Moody with his commercial and instructor pilot's licenses, but our plane was still not ready.

While at Moody Ryan was offered a position with Spokane Turbine Center to instruct on the Quest Kodiak. Because Venezuela was still basically closed and we did not have an airplane yet, we figured: What better way to build time and experience on the airplane he would eventually be flying than to be an instructor on it? So our mission, Mission Padamo Aviation and Support (MPAS), gave Ryan its blessing.

Sad to say, due to many factors beyond anyone's control, we did not get our Kodiak. Before our number could come up, due to a struggling economy the Quest company had to be sold. Because of their commitment to missions, the owners of Quest had tried to keep the company as long as they could, but the harsh realities of this economy finally forced them to sell.

I will be the first to tell you that I was disappointed. Disappointed, but not discouraged. God has a plan for this country, this ministry, and our precious Yanomamö and the many other tribes in Amazonas State that have been abandoned. We continue to seek God's favor as we make adjustments to our plans and goals to provide air service, not only for our missionaries and our tribal church brothers, but also for anyone with medical emergencies and other needs. God has a plan and we only desire to fit into His will.

At the time of the sale, the funds donated specifically to MPAS by our donors for an airplane came to just over $400,000. MPAS received $408,000 in cash from the sale of Quest! We were able to use these funds to purchase a used Cessna 206, and still had enough left over to do all the short takeoff and landing (STOL) modifications that were needed to make our plane the mission aviation workhorse that it can be.

Our prayer going into this endeavor of starting a flight program has always been that God would do this in His time. We only want to make sure we are ready to walk as He guides and provides. Our motivating verses are from the book of Joshua, where Joshua commands the priest to pick up the ark and march. The Bible goes on to say that when the priest carrying the ark walked into the water, the water split before them. We praise the Lord for

His goodness and His omniscience. Losing the opportunity to purchase a Kodiak was not our will, and not as we would have done it, but every step taken was bathed in prayer. We watched God do miracle after miracle in our fundraising efforts, yet for some reason God has closed this door. Because we know beyond any shadow of doubt that none of this has happened without His knowledge, we rest in Him.

At the time of this writing, the Cessna 206 is getting the final phase of modifications and Ryan and family are finishing up Spanish language school in Costa Rica. We look forward to what the Lord has in store for this aviation program. Please pray for His guidance as we proceed. We want to do nothing outside His will and everything for His honor and glory.

We look at all the needless deaths and believe in our hearts that one day God is going to allow us to have our own flight program running so that, when emergencies happen, our son Ryan will fly in with our beautiful airplane and bring these dear people the relief they need, and at the same time carry in supplies and missionaries to tell them about a God who loves them so much that He sent His own Son to die for them. And He lives now, and desires that we might live with Him.

14

BIBLE SEMINARS

Every time we start planning a seminar, we always wrestle with the same questions: Are we going to have enough fuel? Are we going to have enough food to feed the students? and all the other myriad questions and doubts the enemy throws at us. Thankfully, God always gives us the peace we need and this time was no different.

◈ ▣ ◈ ▣ ◈

As I wrote this, about twenty guys were walking three days out from Parima to come here for a week of Bible teaching. The day after they left Parima, Abraham and Nando left from here with a boat to meet them. They had to travel for two days to get up to where the trail from Parima comes out to the Buta River. So, in all, it is a five-day trip for the guys to get here and a five-day trip to get home. When I think of all the dangers in the jungle and all the enemy villages they have to somehow get by without problems, I find myself worrying for the people making this long walk. I find myself praying for their safety and that the teaching they get here will encourage and sustain them after they get home. Frankly, the fact that they are willing to travel for more than over ten days round-trip to get a week of teaching is amazing!

Abraham and Nando finally met the people of Parima. It took them a whole day longer to get out to the river than we had anticipated: they made a long, hard six-day trip to get out. One of the reasons for the extra day walking was that they decided to go past enemy villages during the night rather than chance meeting their enemies on the trail or encountering a hunting party.

Another reason it took them longer than anticipated by boat was that there were more of them than we had planned for and Abraham and Nando had to do three shuttles from where the trail is down to the rapids where they had left the big boat. Nevertheless, they got here, so after giving our guests a day to rest up, we went right into the Bible classes.

We finished our seminar with a simple observance of our Lord's supper on their last night. The fact that we had watched the "Passion of the Christ" movie in Yanomamö the night before made it all the more solemn, as we each contemplated what Christ had suffered for us to purchase our salvation.

After our seminar, we began preparing everything to get the participants home. From here, they would travel about two and a half days by boat, and then take three days on foot to get home, so it did take a lot of preparation to make sure their trip home went smoothly. Finally, everything was ready and we were all down at the port ready to push the boats out. Suddenly, Gonzalo asked Gary and me if he might be able to go up and say goodbye to my dad before he left.

Dad's physical condition had really gone downhill in the past few months. I realized that Gonzalo knew Dad was very weak and that this would be his last opportunity to see Dad this side of heaven, so we agreed to take them up to say goodbye.

We headed up to Dad's house. Dad was no longer able to talk, but he seemed to understand that Gonzalo had come up to say goodbye.

Gonzalo took his hand and told him he would see him in heaven. Dad nodded his head. With all of us standing around, Gonzalo prayed, thanking God for Dad and his willingness to come down to the Yanomamö. He began to weep, but regained control and continued, saying, "God, this man came down as a young man. He made an offering of his life to the Yanomamö and now, You are getting ready to take him home. We thank You for his offering and we know we will be reunited in heaven one day. Many Yanomamö will be in heaven because of my friend's offering."

Not surprisingly, Gary and I and the other guys who were with us in the house were all crying. Each of the other Yanomamö guys prayed in turn. As I listened to each one pray, I found myself encouraged in the Lord by their words, in spite of my tears. Because of how weak Dad had been and how uncertain we were of how much time he had left, we had debated whether it was a good time to try to do a seminar, but we had decided to go ahead with it. We praise the Lord for the way He used our brothers from Parima and surrounding villages to encourage us!

Knowing the dangers they faced, we were relieved, six days later, to hear that they had finally made it all the way home. We pray that the teaching they received will continue to encourage them during their times alone. We were encouraged by the spiritual commitment they had all demonstrated.

◈▣◈▣◈

We had people here from many different villages. We had asked each village to send only their Christian leaders, so it would not require as much fuel to pick them up or take them home. I shook my head, remembering how close we had come to canceling, but a traveling merchant had come through at the last minute, as it were, and we had been able to purchase enough fuel to do this seminar. The classes went well and the leaders seemed to really enjoy it.

On our last night, during testimony time, one of the leaders shared how refreshed he was and now how excited he was to get back to his village to share what he had learned. All the various students who spoke mentioned how difficult it was in their villages to maintain a good attitude when everyone was against them and against the Gospel. "We feel so alone all the time, so we are really happy to be able to come and get encouraged," they said.

Although I knew what they meant, I was gratified to have one of the last students direct his comments to the other students. He said, "Yes, it is difficult, but we have to remember what Christ said. He said, broad is the way to hell, and narrow the trail to heaven. We Yanomamö know a trail gets wide because of many people walking on it, whereas a trail that does not see much use gets overgrown and narrow. What was Jesus telling us? He was telling us that most people are not going to accept the way of salvation but are going to go on to hell. This should cause us to work harder, not get discouraged."

Amen, I thought to myself. *He really gets it!*

Because our fuel situation kept getting progressively worse, we decided to take teams out for teaching and encouragement instead of sending our boats around to the villages to pick up and drop off people. We always make every attempt to keep our partners at home as involved as we can, as we so desperately need their prayers. Thanks to Facebook and a satellite link, it is easier to do so now than it was even a few years ago. The following is a series of posts showing why we so desperately need the prayers.

April 5, 2017 at 1:44 p.m.

We are leaving in about a half hour to head over to a village on the Orinoco right at the mouth of the Mavaca River. We had tried to show the Jesus/Passion movie up there a few months ago but we had gotten rained out. We are praying for ready hearts and clear skies. Thanks for joining us in prayer.

April 5, 2017 at 9:38 p.m.

We left on schedule, but I kept feeling like something was not right. I listened closely to the motor: sounded fine. I checked our fuel: we had enough. Then I started cataloging all our equipment: Projector, check. Speaker, check. iPhone with the Jesus/Passion movie, check. Little doohicky that allows me to connect my iPhone via an HDMI cable to the projector, check. HDMI cable... Bummer!

So, we turned around and headed home. By the time I realized we had left the cable, it was too far to head all the way back, pick up the cable, replace the used fuel, and still get to the village before dark, so we will try again tomorrow. I am just super thankful we realized we did not have the cable before getting all the way to the village. Then we would have had to deal with a bunch of very disappointed Yanomamö to make us feel worse.

April 6, 2017 at 12:56 p.m.

OK, we are off again! Prayers appreciated. I have tried to think through everything. Got my list made, checked it a bunch of times, and Lord willing, this time we will be able to show the video and share with everyone. With no communication with anyone, pray they will be home, as we have no way of knowing.

April 8, 2017 at 7:56 p.m.

We showed the Jesus/Passion movie and it played flawlessly. The Passion part is such a powerful piece that many times while showing it, you can hear people crying, and this time was no different. A young lady sitting in a hammock off to the side of where I was sitting broke down and started crying as the men were beating Jesus. The next morning, some girls came over and I overheard them asking the young lady why she had been crying and she said, "I just felt so badly for Jesus as the men were hitting him and laughing…" Her voice trailed off and I did not hear any more of the conversation. My prayer is that the Holy Spirit would continue to bring the reason for His beating and sacrifice to her mind. At the end of the Jesus movie, a real clear plan of salvation is given. Most of the audience are unsaved; pray these words will come back to them.

◈ ▣ ◈ ▣ ◈

Some of our guys were on a missionary trip way upriver at a village in which we had never done a work. I personally had actually never even been in the village, as it is not only way up our Padamo River and then up the Cuntinamo River (which would be bad enough, as these rivers have more rocks and rapids in them than water), but then getting to this village requires a two-day walk inland! Our people were very surprised to find a small group of believers there. Our guys asked who they had heard about Jesus from and an old man told them that years ago, when he was still an adolescent boy, his people had visited a village where there was a missionary named Dani. This missionary told them about God sending His Son to die for them. "I believed it and accepted Him as my Savior," the old man told them, "and now, my wife and my children and a few others here are saved and we meet together and while we don't know a lot, we know that God loves us and has provided a way of salvation for us."

Amazing that the light of the Gospel is shining in this far-off village because of the lives and sacrifices made by missionaries who took the Gospel to this forgotten peoples—and they never even knew anyone had listened. I share this story to show that many times, even when we don't know it, God is doing a work. It is always God who gives the increase. The missionary mentioned was Danny Shaylor.

On May 22, a group of six men from our village of Coshilowä—Timoteo, Lanzo, Alfredo, Nando, Victor, and Agustine—set out to take the Gospel up to the headwaters of this river. This is the area where the original missionaries, including my parents, started working so many years ago, but the Gospel was not received very well. They returned late on the 31st, tired but exuberant over the reception they had been given, the people who had accepted their message, and the fact that to them, it was obvious there were many, many people praying for them. They had been privileged to watch the Lord work in so many different ways. Here are just a couple of the stories they told upon their return.

May 23–24: They arrived in the village of Yamajuteli. While still hanging their hammocks, they were told of a young boy, probably fourteen years of age, who was on his deathbed. Timoteo and Agustine went over to see if they could witness to him. They got to his hammock and found him asleep. They decided to just sing a few songs and see if he might wake up. While they sang, he did in fact wake up, so they started sharing the Gospel with him, specially stressing the part that Christ defeated death, not only for Himself, but for all of us.

The boy, in spite of being in obvious pain, listened attentively. When they were finished, he asked for help to sit up in this hammock. He acknowledged the fact that he was a sinner and he was dying in his sins. "I don't want to go to hell. I know now, I don't have to go to hell, Jesus already took my place in hell. Help me pray so that I might be able to go to heaven to share heaven with Him. I believe that Jesus did die for me. I believe He was raised from the dead for me." By this time, he had tears running down his face. Timoteo and Agustine joyfully led him through the sinner's prayer. Before they left this village the next afternoon to head up to the next village, a total of fourteen people had accepted the message of hope and had followed the Lord in believer's baptism.

May 29–30 in the village of Majaraña: "We found a hunger for the Gospel in this village that was hard to believe." The guys told me, "We had meetings from the time we arrived to way into the night and then all the next day and the entire village was right there hanging on our every word. Many of the young people of the village came forward to give their lives to Christ as soon as the invitation was given, and even one of the village witchdoctors came forward and gave public testimony to his desire to accept Christ."

"This is a message of hope, with a future. The demons offer me neither hope nor a future. I want to accept the gift that Jesus is offering me," the witchdoctor said.

Over and over as our guys were giving us their report, they emphasized their desire for me to please thank everyone who had been praying for their trip. They said the prayer support was such an encouragement. They also asked that everyone keep praying for these villages and the new believers.

◈ ▣ ◈ ▣ ◈

We reflect on the many blessings God has given us, especially our health, our team, and the fact that we can always count on God's protection. This truth was once again brought home this past week. We were returning from our six-day hunt for the upcoming conference. There are a number of rapids between our village and our hunting area and we have gotten used to having to portage through and around them. On the Walidima Rapids, there is a small chute on the left that works really well for dugout canoes, but is too narrow for a speedboat. So, I have gotten used to taking my speedboat right down the main falls, making sure we have both front and back tied with ropes so that the boat can be held tightly against the inside of the waterfall and not get caught in the current.

This portage started as all the others had. We had the boat snubbed down and were allowing the current to push it down, with us controlling the speed of the descent. I have no idea what went wrong: One second everything was under control, and the next second it was obvious we were losing the boat. I yelled to let the ropes go, as I was afraid someone was going to get dragged into the falls. Nando refused to let the rope go. He knew if he did, the boat would be destroyed, but as soon as the boat went another few feet, I could see that the danger that Nando himself would be pulled into the falls was increasing by the second. I kept yelling, "Just let it go!"

Finally, after what seemed a lifetime but I am sure was only a few seconds, Nando did let go of the rope, and we watched my beautiful new boat flip over and disappear! It resurfaced about a hundred yards downriver and crashed into the big rock wall on the other side. It hung up there and the current kept repeatedly slamming it into the wall. It was hard to watch, but we were grateful that no one had been hurt. It was a good time to give a short lesson on what the Bible means when it says, *Lay not up for yourselves treasures upon earth, where moth and rust doth corrupt, and where thieves break through and steal: But lay up for yourselves treasures in heaven, where neither moth nor rust doth corrupt, and where thieves do not break through nor steal: For where your treasure is, there will your heart be also.* Matthew 6:19–21.

I pointed out that on this earth, we can lose things so fast that there is not even any time to have moths or rust have a chance at it; in less time than it took to tell it, a shiny new boat was a shattered, beaten-up hull.

We were miles away from anyone and it looked like we were going to be stranded on this hot rock for a long time, so after we contemplated our options, we decided that our best chance was to swim across and see if we could get what was left of the boat freed from the rock wall. It was a hard swim, but we finally made it and were in fact finally able to get the boat loose. We bailed it out and decided we could tie up the backboard to strengthen it enough to put the motor back on it and start home. To be honest, the boat actually drove very well in spite of how bad it looked. We made it home fine. Again, I am very thankful no one was hurt!

Our conference went well. Timoteo and Samuel helped me teach every day and I was blessed as I sat in the class and listened to them bring out the truths of His Word. Keila, Sandy, and Sharon worked with all the younger children, giving them activities and a good midmorning snack: a strategy that allowed their parents to listen to the Word with a minimum of distractions.

A week later, we were invited to the village of Seducudawä to hold another meeting. The young man in charge of the little body of believers up there sent word down that he had been holding meetings with his village, telling them all he had learned during the conference, and he wanted us to come up for the last day, which was Sunday. To be honest, I felt a little put out. When the invitation was delivered, they told me they had also invited other villages to come down *and* they had told those villages that I would give them the gas needed to go home plus the gas they needed to send hunters to go hunting for a meal. Well, gas is hard enough to come by when the travel is *my* idea. To have someone else volunteering what tiny little bit I had left was almost too much.

But I bit my tongue, and we went up after our church service on Sunday and I was — well, I was totally blessed. We had a meeting from 11:30 until almost 5:00 p.m. It was not that Timoteo or I were that long-winded, but after we both finished, first one, then another stood up and either asked the Lord for salvation or prayed to get back in a right relationship with the Lord. I sat there almost the entire time, shaken at how close I had been to making an issue of someone having the nerve to volunteer my fuel. Praise the Lord, He continues to work here, sometimes in spite of ourselves.

I might add it was so refreshing to hear their testimonies. But the best thing for me was listening to the closing prayer. "*Jabe Yai Bada* [Father God]," he started. "We sitting here, having listened to Your Word today, are so happy to be here. We here, just recently, were all of us in Satan's bondage and in his service, but because of You sending Your Son, and He willingly laying down His life for us here, we now all have been snatched away from Satan's grasp and now we have a part with You. For this we are really *bujidoblao* [happy]!"

Well, I was pretty *bujidoblao* listening to his prayer (and to be honest, feeling a bit guilty), so I had to rebuke myself for mumbling about my quiet weekend being busted and my precious ration of fuel that I am going to have to dip into to get all these people home. It is easy to float downriver, but it is very difficult to get back upriver to their own villages, especially because there were very high flood waters at that time. But God continues to provide so we can.

Speaking of gasoline, a man who had promised me a few barrels of gasoline let me know he was back in La Esmeralda and I could come down and get them. Mia had been hounding me to take her on an overnighter, and because her two cousins were here visiting, we thought it was a good time to take them with us, and give them their overnighter sleeping on a sandbar out in the mighty Orinoco River.

The problem is, she was been raised on my stories of the way it used to be up here, when Amazonas was still wild and wooly: stories of fish literally jumping into the boat by the dozens and animals coming down to the beach and seeming to dare anyone to take a shot at them. Why, I have even had alligators sneak into my boat as we lay up in our hammocks sleeping on the bank—not just sneaking on board either, but committing grand larceny on my fish. Once they have filled themselves to satisfaction, they slide back over the side of the boat and, as a final and lasting insult, leave behind a smelly, stinky, slimy calling card.

On one trip, we even had a tapir brazenly swim across the river, get out on the bank beside our canoe, climb into our canoe, and commit a huge, horse-sized indiscretion right in our boat! You are probably thinking, *Come on, Mike, how do you know that?* Well, I will tell you. You could read the tracks plain as day: where he got into the river, where he got out, and where he stepped into the boat—and his indiscretion was still there for all to see and smell. Then, as if that were not enough, the crazy animal thundered through our camp, bouncing us out of our hammocks like so many shucked peas, and then disappeared into the jungle, leaving us fumbling in the dark for our guns and ammo.

Well, those were the stories. But for Mia, the reality of the trip was that the river rose and the sandbar we were going to sleep on disappeared, so we tied up alongside the jungle in a rainstorm and Mia and her cousins finally fell asleep under a table with a tarp thrown over it to keep them dry. We fished this morning, but the only thing biting were the gnats!

"Be of good cheer," I told my complaining little daughter, "as the mists of time slowly erode the harsh reality of your life today, you can use my stories!"

◈ ▣ ◈ ▣ ◈

After we were finished with our conference and other responsibilities, Keila, Mia, and I flew out to Puerto Ayacucho on our way to the USA for a short break. Our flight was fine, but we arrived in town to find that the airline we use to get to Caracas had canceled flights and was rescheduling. That meant we didn't have a flight and so were going to have to go by bus.

This literally added insult to injury: I had hurt my wrist on our conference hunt trying to hold my boat in the rapids. I had even posted on Facebook about it, somewhat tongue-in-cheek. Well, I should have taken it more seriously. It continued to bother me, so, after arriving in town, we went to the hospital where I had it x-rayed. My crazy wrist was broken, so then I had to be traveling with a clumsy cast on my wrist. Bad enough to have to wear it, but I could just imagine what the TSA would want to do to me, because, of course, they were going to be positive I had something illegal or improper in it. Well, should be an interesting trip.

15

PRAYER OF JABEZ, YANOMAMÖ STYLE

We never know who our lives are going to touch. The rule of thumb for missionaries is: "Don't dare try and tell anyone the Gospel until you can speak well enough not to confuse people." Praise God, some people don't follow man's wisdom, but they follow the leading of God's Spirit.

❖ ▣ ❖ ▣ ❖

Admiral Chester Nimitz took over as commander of the Pacific Fleet after the bombing of Pearl Harbor in 1941. In *Reflections on Pearl Harbor*, he recounts three mistakes the Japanese made that morning. First, they attacked during a time when many crewmen were on leave, or the deaths would have been tenfold. Second, their attack was limited in scope, leaving the dry docks untouched. Finally, the Japanese totally missed the storage tanks of fuel.

I've never forgotten what I read in that little book. It is still an inspiration as I reflect on it. Any way you look at it, Admiral Nimitz was able to see a silver lining in a situation and circumstance where everyone else saw only despair and defeat. President Roosevelt chose the right man for the right job.

I will add another reason: Only hours away by ship, minutes away by air, from Pearl Harbor was sailing a ship loaded with soldiers. One of them was the man who would one day become my dad. If the Japanese had seen this ship and sunk it, the death toll would have been much higher, and I would not have been born.

After living in Majecototeli for a time while trying to learn the Yanomamö language, my parents were disappointed when the mission leadership announced they were going to pull all personnel out of the Yanomamö area and concentrate on learning the language in a central area before returning to the tribe. By this time, my folks had started making some friends and had tried in a limited way to share and show God's love. Down through the years, I often heard Dad say sadly that he always felt his first years, especially the time spent in Majecototeli, had been a waste of time.

I forget the exact date, but it had to have been sometime in the beginning of 2005. The political landscape was changing for the worse, and there were a lot of questions about what this government might try to do. I had given Dad a small booklet called *The Prayer of Jabez* and he was really excited about all he was reading.

One day, over early-morning coffee, he announced to all of us that he had decided to ask God to increase his territory. Having just finished the book myself, I knew what he was talking about, but was quick to point out the reasons his prayer was not only unrealistic but also downright impractical.

"Dad," I said gently, "this government is going to pot and we can't get more missionaries in. And frankly, we have all we can do now. Please don't ask God to increase your territory, we can't handle what we have now." Dad just shook his head.

I tried a different tactic. "Dad," I began again, "you are eighty-five years old, how much more do you think you can do?"

Dad was not put off. "Mike," he said gently, "Caleb was eighty-five years old when he asked for his mountain and he conquered it. My God is not hindered by my age." So, he kept praying that God would increase his territory.

In August of that same year, 2005, a commission came up and effectively ended our missionary activity by revoking our fuel permit, which basically shut us down. In my human viewpoint, our territory was shrinking fast, not expanding, and I brought that fact out to my ever-praying dad. He was not shaken.

In November of that same year, then-President Chavez ordered New Tribes Mission out of all indigenous areas of Venezuela. Although we were no longer with New Tribes, but instead ran a separate mission, the powers that be were sure that we too were going to leave. They sent commission after commission to prepare the Yanomamö against us. They also came to do inventories of all we had on the base, including measuring our houses and listing all assets: boats, motors, tractors, and anything else they could count. The days were dark. Dad was not shaken.

On January 12th, my own world was severely shaken by the death of our five-year-old Mikeila. I thought this would deter Dad. I remember him going up to her little coffin and, with tears in his eyes, telling his little granddaughter to be watching for him, as he would not be far behind her. But his faith was not shaken.

In April of that same year, the powers that be figured they could not make us leave, so they would try another tactic. They decided to put a military base right in the middle of our mission base. To my way of thinking, this was terrible news! The last thing we needed was an overbearing presence here forever looking over our shoulders ... and on and on my talk to the Lord went. Dad was not shaken, but continued to pray, asking the Lord to increase his territory.

The funny thing was, these military personnel were young men, some of them still in their teens, and for many of them this posting was their first time away from home. These were lonely boys who easy to befriend. As we got to know them better, they opened up to us, admitting that the only reason this base had even been established was to harass us. In fact, we were their only source for anything. They had basically just been tossed out here with a tent, which only lasted until the first torrential rainstorm of the rainy season, so we loaned them one of our buildings. Then we hooked them up to our generator, then to our well, then to our satellite Internet link.

So many times, they would walk up and start talking with us. Finally, as they were getting ready to leave, I would hear one of them whisper to Keila, "Señora Keila, we have not had anything to eat..." So we were able to show God's love in a real way to these lonely boys. I even became friends with one lieutenant. He shared how they had been taken in for special instructions before being sent up here and they had to study a file. Holding his hand above the table about ten inches, he said, "Your file is this thick." That was sobering. When I told the family about our file later on that day, Dad was not shaken.

Over the years, we developed friendships with many of the military guys as they rotated into and out of our village. Many of these friendships really became a blessing to us later. Case in point: We had to be up in Caracas for some paperwork of some kind. Once again, the dratted airline serving Puerto Ayacucho was not flying at the time, which means we either had to take a bus (much the cheaper route) or hire a taxi (more expensive, but worth every dime). We took the taxi. At that time, the major rivers still did not have bridges, but there were flat barges that served as crude car ferries. The longest one was across the Orinoco River: If you got caught with the barge on the far side, it could mean a wait of up to three hours or more while it filled up over there and made its slow way back over to your side, where it then repeated the process.

Our driver must have had a sixth sense, as he was driving like a maniac, but it was all for naught. We screeched to a stop in a cloud of dust but were disappointed to see the barge, filled with cars, already about thirty or fifty yards out in the river. The inside of our car filled with the dust that seemed as disappointed as we were, as it slowly settled down, clouding everything with a powdery film. I got out, partly to stretch my legs and partly to figure out where to use the restroom. I knew we were looking at a long time in the hot sun waiting for the barge to come back over to our side. As I walked up to the river's edge to look over the water, I heard a man running up behind me calling my name. Surprised, I turned around. I didn't know anyone over here; could someone really be calling me?

Sure enough, it was a guard who had been stationed in Cosh for a couple of months or so, and he seemed happy to see me. "Hola, Mike," he said, thrusting out his hand. In Spanish he asked me what I was doing. I shrugged.

"Trying to get to Puerto Ayacucho but the barge left without me," I said smiling. I was, of course, only making small talk and had no idea he was going to take my words as a mission.

Pulling a whistle out of his pocket, he began to blow it frantically and at the same time waved his arms over his head in the generally recognized sign to return. I was even more surprised when the barge started swinging in a big circle to come back.

"*Gracias, amigo*, but I can't leave my taxi here. There is no room on the barge for another car," I explained smiling. He was not deterred. The barge settled back against the muddy ramp carved into the steep bank of the river. Climbing down, my guard friend got up on the barge and started motioning to all the cars to move forward. Each one obeyed until they had opened up enough space that there was room for our taxi, straddling a few feet of the main

225

barge and the rest on the rampway. Smiling broadly, he gave Keila and Mia hugs, shook my hand, and walked back off the barge, signaling to the operator that he was free to go. I looked around at everyone staring at us with expressions of "Who are these people?" on their faces.

This is just one such story. Things like this happened many times. The friendships we had forged with the guards came in handy for us when we had to be out in the cities for whatever reason. For the most part, we have gotten along very well with them and, as I mentioned, we try to show God's love in our daily actions and interactions.

Sometimes, though, we do feel stretched. Case in point: My brother Gary and his wife, Marie, flew into La Esmeralda and two guards there gave them a hard time. I did not know either of these guards and did not see anyone that I recognized. *Great! They are all new ones here now*, I remember thinking to myself.

A number of times I had to bite my tongue to keep from saying anything, because these guys were being so obnoxious going through Gary's and Marie's stuff. There was a long boat trip still to go to get home, so it about broke poor Marie's heart to see all of her carefully packed stuff strewn all over the runway there in La Esmeralda. They finally finished and, leaving the stuff still strewn all over the rampway, they walked back over to their command post, leaving us to pick up everything and repack. We finally got it all packed back up and the priest there offered to carry our stuff to the river in his truck. I think even he was embarrassed by how rough the guys had been.

Three days later, I had to be back down in La Esmeralda for something, and to my surprise, one of the two guards who had gone through Gary's and Marie's stuff came down to the port asking me for a ride up to Cosh. He had just received his transfer orders and, to his deep disappointment, he was being transferred up to our village. My first thought was to make some excuse and just say no, but I thought *What's the use of acting ugly?*, so I agreed.

Two days after he got up here, he apparently developed a wicked toothache. Gary and I were down by the generator house. The house we loaned the guards is near there, so this guy came out holding his jaw and asked Gary if he had anything for a toothache. I saw Gary's eyes widen when he recognized the guy, but he didn't say anything, instead telling the guard to come on up to the house and he would treat him—which he did.

Shortly after getting back up here with the obnoxious guard, we had another of the unending commissions in from Caracas, asking questions and trying to trap us into something they could use as a basis to order us out. These inquiries have gotten really old, but what can you do? We have to be polite, and all we can do is try and answer every question to the best of our ability. This time, after we had had to listen to and answer questions of this newest commission, this same guard followed Keila and her mom home and sat at the kitchen table talking with them, asking his own questions (more just out of curiosity than anything else, I am sure). But one thing led to another, and before long, Keila and her mom were witnessing to this young man.

To make the tale of a very long afternoon short, he accepted the Lord as his personal Savior. This young sergeant started witnessing to his fellow guards, and the joy of his salvation was real. Three or four of his fellow guards came up to the house and they too were led to the Lord.

A few days later, another new guard arrived. By this time, Keila and her mom, who was still up visiting with us, had started a Bible study with two lady doctors who had been sent up here to take over the medical work. The new guard and the young man who had gotten saved earlier asked if they could sit in on it, and the one who had not yet made a profession prayed the sinner's prayer, asking Christ to forgive him of his sins. PTL!

That was on a Sunday. The following Friday, four guards from his command went swimming and one of them drowned. We spent all that afternoon and then all the following day looking for him. His body was found on Sunday morning around 7:30 a.m. I had thought we would take the body on down to La Esmeralda right away, but the captain who had come up to help in the search assured me that he had already called for a helicopter. So we returned to Cosh and waited for them to show up.

Finally, around 2:00 p.m., that captain asked me if I would take the body on down, as it didn't look like the copter was coming. By this time, the days in the water and the hot sun had taken their toll on the poor man's body: it was not a pleasant trip down.

The young guard who had accepted the Lord had to go down with the body to be there for the autopsy and investigation. He was very concerned, but we assured him we were all praying for him. He told us he had spent all morning witnessing to the boy who had drowned and how he wished the boy had accepted the Lord before they went swimming. Our prayer is that before he breathed his last, he had called out to the Lord for his salvation, but we of course have no way of knowing.

After we left with the body, Keila and her mom had an opportunity to talk to the guards who were left here and, praise the Lord, two more of them accepted the Lord. The next day, four more of them got saved! So, of the group of nine young men stationed here, seven got saved, one drowned, and one other one went out with the sergeant and has not yet come back. We don't really consider ourselves to be missionaries to the armed forces, but God knows!

◇回◇回◇

Fast-forward to 2011. We went ahead with our plans to hold a Bible seminar for our students from faraway villages. (We had wrestled with whether to even hold it, as fuel was scarce and the fact that Dad had just passed away was still a raw wound.) We had students from eight villages. Many of them brought their wives and children along, so we had a full house at mealtimes, but we never ran short of food! We left the last day open for testimonies, and how they blessed our hearts! It is obvious that God's Holy Spirit was working, continuing to draw people to Himself. We had twenty-one visitor students get saved, and twenty-three of the young people and kids from Cosh also went forward to get saved as well.

So many great testimonies were shared that space does not permit me to reproduce all of them, but I would like to share the testimony of Rojelio Lulubewä. His testimony stood out for a number of reasons. I think one of the biggest reasons it affected me so powerfully was that this was the first seminar we had had since Dad passed away. I wished he could have been here to listen to these testimonies, especially Rojelio's. I know it would have blessed him!

Rojelio is a boy from Majecototeli, the first Yanomamö village Dad and Mom had worked in so long ago. Rojelio married into this village. He had asked if he could attend the seminar and we agreed. He had gotten saved about six months ago, but he is such a shy young man, I had never really spent much time with him. Here is his testimony:

> My father is in hell now. I am sure all my uncles and my brothers are also in hell. They never accepted the message of someone dying for their sins. Now, my mother, I know she is in heaven. Back when she was a little girl, some missionaries

came to our village and even though, she said, they could not talk our language very well, she understood what they were trying to tell her and she believed what they said and asked Jesu Cristo to forgive her sins. She was just a young girl, but it changed her life.

By the time I was a young boy, people knew my mother was different. She did not participate in the rituals and wild living that all the other women and girls took part in. Most of the village teased her, but by the time I was old enough to understand anything, she had accepted their teasing and to be honest, the village in fact respected her. I never really understood what made Mom different, and although she tried to tell me, she knew so little herself, she really could not explain it. All I understood was that because of what some *nabäs* had told her, she lived differently and knew she was a child of God and one day was going to go to heaven to live with Him. She always fascinated me, but she died while I was still a boy and I never knew what she was talking about. But the way she lived always impressed me.

I came to Cosh and was surprised to find the missionary family that my mom had talked about living here. The man and his wife were now old, but it was obvious they still loved their God and the Yanomamö. I was fascinated. I went to church every time I could and when I found out there were Bible classes every morning, I started attending them as well. Then not too long ago, I prayed and asked God to cleanse my own heart and to make me His child. I finally understood what my mom had tried to tell me.

I am so thankful that missionaries went to my village and told my mom about God's Son becoming a man and dying to save us. I wish my dad and uncles would have accepted the message, but they did not want to hear it. I am so thankful my mom did accept it. I know I will see her again and I am so happy that I was able to meet and get to know the missionaries who talked with her when she was just a little girl. They probably never even knew they had changed her life and now have changed mine. Now, I want to follow the Lord in believer's baptism tomorrow.

After saying all this, Rojelio sat down with a big smile on his face.

I was so surprised to hear this! I know, from having talked with Dad and Mom and others of the pioneer missionaries who had first worked among the Yanomamö, that they considered those first years to be a waste. I am not sure exactly how long they worked up in Majecototeli (Platanal, as it is now called), but I know Dad and Mom went there in December of 1953, and had already been moved out of there quite a few months before I was born in August of 1955, so they were not up there very long. But God used their time up there to touch the heart of a young girl and change her life and this blessing extended to today and continues on. Praise Him, His Word will never return void!

This reminded me of another story about Dad and Mom. Late in the 1960s and early 1970s, we were stationed in the village of Mavaca when another village that lived way inland visited them. The village had fled their own *shabono* because of a raid they had gone on during which they had killed someone. They knew it was now their turn to have raiders come in retaliation. Their nerves had broken and they fled to the safety of a larger village away from the beaten path of their enemies.

Not having anything better to do, they came to a church service Dad was holding. It was an interesting time as they came flooding into the small church hut in their feathered finery and paint. Most of them were as naked as the day they were born, except for strings around their waists and the paint and feathers—and because most of the feathers were sticking out of holes in their earlobes, they could hardly be thought of as much of a covering. But I digress.

They came flooding in and took seats on the rough benches. I was a teenager of about fifteen years of age and had a hard time not staring, but then we started singing. Listening to native Yanomamö singing is enough to take your mind off most things and before I knew it, I was not concerned about naked people; I was just trying not to laugh out loud. There were probably about a hundred people in the hut, and there were close to that many different versions of the song being sung at the same time. Again, I digress...

The message was preached and Dad said at the end, "If anyone wants to come forward and ask me more about *Yai Bada* and the penalty He paid for you, and ask me to pray for them, I will." He no sooner finished speaking than a young lady, probably fifteen or sixteen years old, stood up and almost ran to the front of the church. Everyone stared, most of them surprised that any visitor, let alone a girl, would go forward that fast. But I am sure that a few of them, us included, were staring because the young lady was not wearing a stitch of clothing. She was completely naked! I don't remember much more about that night, but Dad and Mom did pray with her. The next day, early, she was at the house. "Milimi, could you give me some clothes, I don't want to be naked anymore," she confided. Mom found her something and while the girl was getting dressed, she told Mom that her village had decided to head home. After talking for a while, the young lady left. We never saw her again. About a week later, word came back down that on the way home, the village had run into raiders and the raiders had shot someone: The person shot and killed was the girl who had gone forward that night. Again, you just never know how much time you have with someone, and there is never a better time than right now to tell someone about God and His love.

The older I get, the more I respect Dad and Mom, because they saw that young woman not as a naked young girl but as a girl who needed Christ. To me, this is one more story that describes who they were and their ability to see a people for whom the only answer was in Christ.

◈回◈回◈

During all this time, Dad had continued praying his prayer asking God to increase his territory. In reality, I had almost forgotten he was even still praying that prayer until I looked back and thought about all the young men and commissions who had come through our village from every part of Venezuela. With just the eight or ten guys rotating in and out of our base from all parts of Venezuela every forty-five days or so, well, wow! God enlarged our territory!

So often in this work I am reminded of what Joseph told his brothers: You all meant it for bad, but God meant it for good! All things really do work together for good; Romans 8:28 ... if we could just truly believe this verse! We serve an amazing God! Praise Him!

16

STYMIED IN LA ESMERALDA

Have I ever mentioned how proud I am of my wife, Keila? When thieves ransacked our house, one of the items stolen was my razor. I did have an old disposable razor, but it was so dull it was like trying to shave with a kitchen knife. Keila took the old razor, cut the blade off it, and, using tie wraps, fastened my razor blades to the handle. She did it in such a way that the blades still swivel! I think I am going to keep this girl!

◈▣◈▣◈

In April of 2008, Dad took a serious turn for the worse. We did not think he had many days left with us, so we sent word to our siblings in the United States that if they wanted to see Dad, they should make plans to come to Venezuela, and we would do all we could to get them permits to come up to Cosh.

Gary and I agreed that Keila and I should go out to meet them in Puerto Ayacucho and then travel on up with them. How great it was to see them arrive there! In the group was my oldest brother, Steve; then Joe and Jerald, my two youngest brothers; and our youngest son Stephen. Susan and Gerald Lee were also traveling with them, although they had only been back in the States for a furlough and were returning to their field of service.

Just about the time they were to arrive in Puerto Ayacucho, the little air taxi company we use had its permit revoked. Keila and I looked at each other. *Now what?* we wondered. Our group did not have enough days scheduled in country to make a long wait for a plane out in Puerto Ayacucho feasible, so when Keila mentioned calling a general who had given her his card, we thought it was worth a try.

Two years earlier, while we were waiting for a flight in Puerto Ayacucho, Mikeila had wandered into the general's office. We were surprised and more than a bit apprehensive when we saw him carrying our little one to us. He would not have been considered a friend to the missionaries. But he was matching Mikeila's contagious smile as he handed her off to us. "You need to watch my little *catire gringa* [blonde gringa]," he told Keila. Keila thanked him and Mikeila waved a cheery goodbye to the general as he walked off.

Less than two months later, and only one month after we said our goodbyes to our precious little Mikeila, the military started putting pressure on us because we had not left the country with the other missionaries. They seemed quite surprised that instead of being a bunch of North American missionaries, we claimed to be Venezuelans by birth. Well, it was not our fault they had not done their homework! As we had become an embarrassment to the head general, he flew in to see what our issues were. We watched him climb out of the big helicopter and walk toward us. When he recognized Keila, his first words to her were, "Where is my little *catire gringa*?

With tears running down her cheeks, Keila told him what had happened only a month earlier. His face changed; I actually thought he was going to start crying. He got control of his emotions and asked, "Why was she not taken out of here to medical help?"

"We tried and tried to call, but no one answered the radio. Everything happened so fast," Keila told him. He slowly shook his head. Taking a business card out of his pocket, he handed it to Keila. "If you ever need help again, you have only to call me," he told her. Retrieving the card, he wrote another number on the back and, showing her the new number, told her: "This is my personal cell number, call this one and I promise you I will answer." Giving Keila a hug and shaking my hand, he turned and went back to the helicopter, and we watched it climb back up into the sky. For those of you who are interested, I recount the entire story in *I Can See the Shore*.

Two years later, that general has been transferred to a higher command in Caracas. We had not seen him since our conversation with him on our airstrip at Cosh, when he had given Keila his card. Finding his card, Keila dialed his number. I think we were both surprised when he immediately answered. Asking what he could do for us, he listened as Keila told him about Dad and how near death he was. He offered to send a Cessna Caravan up to Cosh to bring him out. Keila explained that Dad's problem was not so much an illness as it was his age, and Dad had asked us not to bring him out. He had told us many times that he had given his life in the jungles to the Yanomamö and wanted to be buried there in our little cemetery. The general listened quietly as Keila explained that Dad was asking for his children to come see him before he passed. She told him about the air taxi's problem and how we did not know how to get the family up to Cosh in time to see Dad.

The general immediately offered to provide us transportation. "Let me work on this and I will get back with you," he promised. Keila hung up and we thanked God for His constant faithfulness to us and His provisions for our every need. When the general called back, he informed us that there was a C-130 cargo flight heading up to La Esmeralda on Friday and he could get us on that, but it would only be to La Esmeralda. We accepted, knowing we could get someone to come and meet us there by boat.

He directed us to be at the air force base there in Puerto Ayacucho at 7:30 a.m. Arriving there, we were met and directed to the VIP waiting room on the base, and were treated extremely well. The plane arrived at about 11:30 and a soldier came in, took down all our identification information, and told us we would be boarding shortly. A bit later, we were led out to the giant cargo plane and climbed in. Once we were seated, they began to allow the rest of the passengers on. Soon thereafter we lifted off and sailed out over the vast Amazon rainforest. In this much faster airplane, we began our descent into La Esmeralda after only thirty-five minutes of flight time. So far, very good!

Imagine our surprise when, just as we got off, a national guard there told us to move out of the line of Venezuelans and form a line of "foreigners." I explained that we *were* Venezuelans except for my older brother and a brother-in-law, and that although they were not Venezuelan citizens, they were residents of the country. He did not care, and continued to yell at us. His next comment just about floored me, as he told the guard next to him not to allow us off the tarmac, but to make sure we were sent back on the plane when it took off. I again tried to talk to him, to explain that not only were we Venezuelans, but I lived in the area, and my brothers had permission from the highest authority for the entire area.

"Show me your authorization," he demanded. "Who allowed you to come up here?"

"Our authority came from the general of the 52nd brigade," I told him. "He doesn't give letters, he spoke with us, then called the air force general in Puerto Ayacucho on the phone and told him to put us on the plane. He expects that his orders are going to be carried out. By the very fact that we flew in here on a military plane should tell you we have high connections. How else would we be able to get on a military plane?" He refused to listen to me, telling me that his orders were to stop us.

I asked him to step aside with me so we could speak in private. I think he thought I was going to offer him a bribe, but instead I told him, "Don't make me call the general. I really don't want to get you in trouble, but we were put on this flight by the general himself. This entire trip has been authorized and put together by him. I really don't want to bother him with this insignificant detail, but I will if I have to."

I was shocked by his response and, yes, even a bit dismayed. "Call anyone you want, call the general. You can call the president for all I care, but you are getting back on that plane and leaving here!"

Praise the Lord for cell phone technology, because, with a sat link, it has even gotten up this far in the jungle. So I quickly dialed Keila's phone out in town, explained what was happening, and asked her to call the head general as we were being shipped back. I then tried yet again to talk with the guard there, asking him to at least listen to us, as I hated to see him get in trouble, but we were not going to stop calling until it was just too late. Keila called me right away, saying she had spoken with the general and he was calling the superior for the military base in La Esmeralda.

Just then we were ordered to get back on the plane. I quickly called Keila again and told her we were being ordered to board. By this time, we had a huge audience of native people there in the community and it was obvious they were bothered by how we were being treated. We have known all these people all our lives and they knew Dad was sick and we were trying to get home for a last visit. In the meantime, Keila called back and said that the general had told her to tell me "under no circumstances are you to board that plane."

"Easy for him to say," I told Keila, "but this guy has a huge AK-47 pointed at my belly." Figuring it was time I took a more proactive stance, I called the air force general out in Puerto Ayacucho to explain what was happening. He also told me not to get on the plane. As soon as I hung up, I saw one of the air force pilots receive a phone call, and a minute later he walked over and told the guard that no one could board yet, as they were not finished loading cargo.

Finally, a bit of a reprieve! I tried yet again to explain to the guy what my brothers were doing, but he was, if anything, even more rude. He began to yell at me and I attempted to answer his accusations.

In the meantime, Keila called back and gave me the head general's phone number to call, which I quickly did. The general explained that he had finally located the commanding officer for the guard base and that this person should be arriving in a couple of minutes. He again told me, "Do not board the plane. We are getting it straightened out." I thanked him and a few minutes later, I was gratified to see a man speeding up in a military jeep. He quickly came over to me, apologized, and promised that it would be taken care of in three minutes.

Looking around at the huge crowd of people still milling around, he asked if I would take my group across the runway and wait in the commando. "I will let you continue your trip as soon as I get this straightened out here," he told me. We agreed, and as soon as the huge cargo plane took off, he was over, once again apologizing and telling us we were free to go.

Some friends from Cosh had come down in a canoe with an outboard motor to pick us up, but they had paddled down hoping we could find enough fuel to get home. So, we spent the next two hours trying to find twenty-four gallons of gas to get home. God granted our desires and we found the fuel. One guy charged us about ten times what gas is normally worth for the first twelve gallons and the other guy gave us his twelve gallons for free, so all in all, not bad!

At 5:08 p.m., we headed up the mighty Orinoco River. The sky was black with a huge storm approaching, and I briefly wondered if being made to leave would have been the better option. This was going to be a long night. As soon as we started making headway, the spray almost totally drenched those who were sitting near the front of the long canoe. I kept trying to move to present as small a target as possible to the spray, but I shouldn't even have bothered, because it began to rain in earnest; the six hours it took us to get to Cosh seemed like an eternity. Waking everyone up when we finally arrived, we spent the next couple of hours just enjoying being together. We started out telling everyone how great our God is and how He had done miracle after miracle for us to allow us to get there. How we praised Him!

The small air taxi company was regranted its permit, so when it was time for the family's return flight, it was not as traumatic as when they had flown in. Thanks to the general, the air taxi company was allowed to fly direct to Cosh to pick us up so that my brothers and youngest son Stephen could start their long trip home. We had hoped our strip would be left open, but after that one authorized flight, it remained closed.

◇▣◇▣◇

Then there was the time we had to head down to La Esmeralda to try to clear up a situation with our fuel ration. Why in the world a country sitting on the world's largest reserves of petroleum would have to be rationing fuel is beyond me, but that is the reality of socialism. I remember laughing one time when a friend of mine quoted someone as saying, "If you put a socialist in charge of the Sahara Desert, in three years they would be rationing sand." Little did I know how true that was! Now we are living the reality. I had gone down there two days before and had gotten it all set up, but when the guys got down there with the barrels, they were turned down. So, I was not in a good mood about having to make the trip twice.

Another reason for my bad mood was the fact that at the last minute, we had to take along a lady in hard labor and her mother. Thus, on top of my bad mood over the fuel ration not being honored, I was worried for two reasons: first, the chances of her having the baby in the boat were so high it was almost a given; and second—the most important reason—I did not have quite enough fuel to get down to La Esmeralda. When it had just been us heading down, I figured it would be fine if we had to float a bit, but that thinking was thrown out the window (or rather, out of the boat) when we put the lady in labor in with us. To say that this occurrence changed the dynamics a bit would be a huge understatement. As we were about three gallons short of what I normally use to get down there, you can bet I was really praying. By the way, three gallons translates into about thirteen miles or about twenty-six minutes of running time. Now, if we run out of gasoline and have to float... I did the math in my head as we were roaring down the river and I was not happy. According to my calculations, it would take us about five hours to float that thirteen miles! By then I was *really* praying!

I suppose if you did a global search and auditioned for a finalist, you could not find two more inept people, medically speaking, than my nephew, Jody, and myself. And there we were, careening down the river with our patient in hard labor! I was glad I was driving, which meant no one expected me to do anything besides drive and watch the river. My nephew tried his best to appear occupied with watching the river, but as it was still really high, it was obvious he was not needed in that capacity. He was not happy and made that apparent to all. Finally, his whining got so bad I just could not take it; I had to tell my nephew to get a grip on himself and shut up. It was hard enough being worried about a lady in labor without having to put up with his whining (just kidding ... sort of)! Thankfully, we made it down there before the baby put in an appearance. Among us, the patient, and her mother, I'm sure Jody and I were the most relieved when we actually did make it all the way down there without running out of gas!

We got the patient up to the little government clinic and the doctor checked her out. He told me she was having twins and the one to be born first was breech. Whew! Glad we had brought her down. I was extremely happy to leave her there to wait for an airplane the next day. I felt bad for the poor girl, as it was obvious that she was in a lot of distress.

We started working on the fuel problem and that took the rest of the day, so we had to spend the night. We have a house (actually more of a hut) that we keep in La Esmeralda for the times when we get stuck in the village, and that is where we went to spend the night. The mosquitoes that attacked us are worth a story in themselves, but suffice to say that if a doctor had examined me the next morning, he would have checked me into an emergency room for a blood transfusion.

I was awakened around 11:00 p.m. by a commotion around me. Sharing the house were about ten families from Cosh who had come down to La Esmeralda for one reason or another, and the commotion was being made by the women. They were talking about the girl in labor, but because I had left her with a doctor, I figured I had done about all that I was capable of doing. So, after slapping myself silly trying to reduce the cloud of mosquitoes *inside* of my mosquito net with me, I went back to sleep. Upon awakening in the morning, I remembered the commotion and asked what had been going on.

The ladies started laughing and told me the baby had been born and was fine. I said, "Well, good thing we got her down to the clinic where she could get good care."

Teresa, one of the ladies in the house, said, "Yeah, she had really good care. There were a bunch of doctors working on her all night. You should have seen them! There was Dr. Teresa, Dr. Gypsy, Dr. Diana with Davey and Bernabe assisting, and the doctor in charge was Marcos Perez."

"What do you mean?" I asked, confused. Everyone she had named were Yanomamö, and all were from Cosh, and I knew none of them were doctors. I realized she was pulling my leg, but I did not understand her slant.

"Well, we were called last night, and somehow you missed the call, but we all went up there and the girl was doing really badly. Davey and Bernabe ran around to the doctor's residence, and even though they banged on all the doors, they could not get any one to come out. They ran back to tell us they did not know where the doctors were. By that time Gypsy and I had begun to help the girl and I was somehow able to turn the baby and get it situated right. It was born a short time later, so then I sent Davey and Bernabe to try and find some scissors to cut the cord. They frantically ran through the entire clinic trying to find anything with which to cut the cord but the only thing they found, which they brought to me, was a pair of tooth-pulling forceps! 'What can I do with these?' I yelled at them, and it was a good thing the doctor did not show up then, 'cause I would have given him a piece of my mind. Well, they finally found something, and we cut the cord. Mother and baby are fine." Teresa finished with a smile, "You should have come up."

"That is OK," I told her, "I got a whole lot more enjoyment out of listening to your story than if I would have had to be there. So anyway, Teresa," I told her, "next time there is a lady in trouble, just tell them to call you Yanomamö doctors. The service is better and closer and I don't have to scare myself silly driving a lady in labor down in the boat!"

It is a good thing God has given us humans a sense of humor, because the situation in every respect was deteriorating at an alarming rate, but the Yanomamö can always see a funny side to anything. I am just thankful no one insisted I get up and help. By the way, my nephew Jody slept through it as well.

Remember the doctor who had examined the girl and told us that there were twins and the first one in line to be born was breech? I guess the doctor was wrong on that one. I asked Teresa about the twin when they were telling me about all that had happened and she assured me that only one had been born, and only one needing to be born. No twin.

For further icing on the cake, I was able to get the needed fuel! For us, this was a huge "Praise the Lord" and a huge answer to prayer. We were able to get 1,320 gallons of diesel fuel for the generator and 475 gallons of gasoline. The gasoline was about half as much as we were hoping for, but we were grateful for what we did get.

◈ ▣ ◈ ▣ ◈

A few weeks later, the silence of our early Sunday morning was shattered by the blasting roar of two fighter jets streaking low over our little jungle airstrip (which was still closed). I thought they would come back by and give us a little air show, but after only one pass they roared off into the distance. I figured some commission would be right behind them, but no one came, even though we finished breakfast and went on to church. Then, while we were still singing, we heard choppers. I figured the distraction would empty the church, but the song leader kept going. We lost a few people, but most stayed seated and singing. One of the church elders and pastor of the church, Timoteo, got up and said, "All foreigners know that Sunday is a day where people meet together to worship the Lord. Let us finish our service, then we can go listen to what they have to say to us." As I was not that excited to run out and get in the spotlight anyway, it sounded good to me. Timoteo preached a good message about our battle not being against flesh and blood, but against principalities and powers, and wickedness in high places. It was a good message and the Lord used it to calm my heart. Timoteo was still speaking when, about twenty minutes later, we heard the first of the three choppers take off, then the second, and then the third.

After our church service was over, we found out that the delegation had been the vice president, along with about a dozen ministers, including many generals and all the people who normally travel with a delegation of this size, including television cameras and crew. At first, I felt badly that we might have been rude to the vice president, but after hearing all that had been said, I think it was the Lord who kept us in church.

The lieutenant told us that the vice president had been very friendly; the general traveling with him ... not so much. He told us that the vice president, noticing the electric lights, commented on how pleasant it was to have the niceties of civilization even up in the jungle. The general hastened to assure him that the military command tried to make their bases as nice as possible.

I am not sure why or how our lieutenant got so brave, but he said, "Excuse me, but our electricity is courtesy of the missionaries." The vice president went on to comment on the clean water, and again he was told that the water too was courtesy of the missionaries. This went on and on. Finally, the general asked the vice president to send someone over to the church to tell the missionaries they had to come out. The vice president was emphatic: "We did not come up here to bother someone in church. I have seen enough," he said. "Let's go!"

God continually uses such times to show us that it is *not by might, nor by power, but by My Spirit, says the Lord of Hosts* (Zechariah 4:6).

17
TRAVELS AND TRAVAILS

We were supposed to leave at daybreak to take my sister and her family up the Ocamo to the mouth of the Iyowei River, where their son, Joe, was waiting for them with a dugout to take them the rest of the way home. They had a hard twelve-hour trip ahead of them. My speedboat won't fit up their small *caño* (creek), or I would have taken them all the way home. But it started raining that morning at about 2:00 a.m. and was still coming down hard. They *had* to leave that day, so I was not sure how much longer we could wait for it. Mia was going with me. When I asked her if it might not be better if she stayed, as it was going to be a wet and nasty trip, she declared, "Dad, to us adventurous types, the harder the better!"

"Well, to us 'older' types, the softer the better," I told her. "So, just so you know, I am praying the rain stops."

❖ ▣ ❖ ▣ ❖

When all else fails, take the bus ... NOT!

Shortly after one of our seminars, I needed to head back to the United States for talks having to do with the movie *The Enemy God* that we were involved in with the Caleb Project. It was just a very quick trip: I actually left here on Monday and was back here on Saturday morning.

The small airline that services Puerto Ayacucho was not flying due to governmental problems, so I got a flight out with New Tribes to their main hub out in Puerto Ordaz, where I was able to catch the late afternoon flight to Caracas. I had hoped that the airline would have its act together by the time I needed to fly back in, but that was not the case.

As soon as I arrived back in Caracas, I called Luis Bravo in Puerto Ayacucho to ask for flight information, but he told me they were still not flying: actually, no one even in the company knew when they were going to be allowed to start flying again. I looked at my watch and saw it was three o'clock. I knew that the buses for Puerto Ayacucho leave at around 6:30 p.m., so I grabbed a cab and took off for the bus terminal. Too late I remembered I was not carrying that much cash on me. I normally use a credit card for traveling with the airlines, and after having been the victim of a holdup a couple of years ago, I try to keep as little cash on me as possible. Anyway, I looked in my wallet, and saw that I had 105,000 bolivares (bs) on me. *That should be enough*, I thought.

I arrived at the terminal, paid the cab driver his 50,000 bs, and ran in to see if I could get on the bus. They did have a few seats left, so I paid the 35,000 bs for the ticket, which left me with 20,000 bs. Having traveled by bus before, I remembered how cold I had gotten. The buses travel at night and they always have the air conditioning cranked all the way up, so much that it almost snows in there. So I ran around to all the little stores in the terminal trying to find a blanket of some kind. I finally found a store that had a beach towel, which I purchased, leaving me with 2,000 bs in my pocket. Not wanting it to burn a hole there, I immediately bought myself a cup of *café con leche*, and then I was broke.

Why all the details, you might be asking? Well, it was a contributing factor to the utter misery in which I found myself all night long. At the risk of sounding a bit like a whiner, I would like to recount the story. Not to gain your sympathy, but so that in the event you are ever in a foreign country and wondering if you should just take the bus, maybe my experience will bring you back to sanity. So, if me whining a bit helps you make the right decision, it should be worth it in the long run, and is in keeping with my decision to live my life as sacrificially as possible.

I looked at my watch: 3:55 p.m. Well, it was going to be a long wait till 6:30 when we were to start boarding the bus. As I sat there, I suddenly realized that the constant rumbling I was hearing was my stomach. I remembered that the only meal I had had was the airline dinner on the jet. Though I am sure some nutrition expert has verified that airplane meals meet all the daily nutrient requirements of the human body, they lack a bit in filler. I was getting hungry. I looked at my watch again: 3:58. This was going to be a *long* afternoon. I looked around, and everyone I saw was eating something. When I had money, my hunger was just there, minding its own business, gently letting me know I should start thinking of something soon, but it basically just left me alone. As soon as I was broke, however, it began to demand and exert pressure on me to take care of it. It was only through the most determined efforts that I refrained from going out and begging in the street. Slowly the afternoon sun went down ... building the Brooklyn bridge could hardly have taken so long!

We finally were called to board our bus. We ticketholders fought our way through the swirling crowd and finally made our way inside. Gratefully I settled into my seat. I had decided I would try to fall asleep as soon as possible so that the night would go fast and the trip would be behind me. The air conditioning was going full bore, and in spite of my towel, I was shivering in my seat. Suddenly, there was a person tapping me on my shoulder. "Sir, you are sitting in my seat," she told me.

"No, ma'am, here is my ticket." Well, it seems we both had seat number 25. The bus attendant was quick to help.

"Just sit back there," he told me, indicating a seat several rows back. I moved all my stuff and once again made myself comfortable. Again, another tap: "Sir, you are in my seat." Again I had to move, this time to the last row of seats. Thankfully, no one tried to move me off of those seats. After spending the entire night bouncing around back there like a ping-pong ball in a milk jug in a hurricane, I know why: they were *miserably* uncomfortable! Words can't describe it.

I wish human words could describe how it feels to hit a pothole almost big enough to swallow the entire bus while careening down the mountain in a rainstorm. In trying to write about this trip, I have decided not to tell you about the incessant squeaking of the window right next to my ear, nor about the time I finally dozed off, and the agile driver was able to swing the rear of the bus so that he could manage to catch not just one hole, but a second one as well. The first thump partially dislodged me from my seat, but the second thump was able to catapult me off the back of the seat in front of me in such a way as to bounce me off the roof and deposit me back in my seat without me even dropping my towel.

I won't even go on about the cold anymore, but two things I will mention. Have you ever noticed how the sight of food, even when you are not that hungry, can get the ol' juices flowing? Well, try watching people eat when you are about starved! Puts it in a whole new light, I'll tell you. Every place we stopped, they were selling food and people were buying and eating! What a time! Something else everyone did at the bus stops was use the restrooms. Too late, I remembered there was a charge for the restrooms. This night was beginning to get long ... the rise and fall of Rome's civilization had scarcely lasted longer. No, I am not going to go on and on whining about this trip. In closing, I will only say what I heard the cat Garfield say one time in one of his cartoon TV shows: "There would have to be two of me to feel worse."

Finally the night ended, and we arrived Puerto Ayacucho hardly the worse for wear, though mental trauma is hard to detect. I briefly contemplated falling to the ground and kissing it upon exiting the bus, but was able to control myself.

◈ ▣ ◈ ▣ ◈

Unless you want to walk, which almost no one does unless it is someone running away with someone else's wife, most times we travel by boat. It used to be almost always by dugout canoe with an outboard motor on it, but a church in Florida had mercy on me and gifted me a beautiful Boston Whaler speedboat, so now my trips are a lot more enjoyable. Most of our river trips are on the upper Orinoco River and its tributaries. We don't do much traveling between Puerto Ayacucho and TamaTama by river if we can help it.

Because the Yanomamö all live on the upper Orinoco, there really is not much need for us to be on the lower river. Every once in a while, though, we do have to do it, and it is normally cause for concern due to the many military guard checkpoints you have to go through. The last time I did this trip was in 2008 and I figured we were going to have problems at every outpost. There was so much hostility from the government against the missionaries who had decided to stay working in Amazonas State, but the Lord took care of the details like you would not believe! There are three guard checkpoints just to get to our port from Puerto Ayacucho, and though we had no problems, it did takes time. I figured that it was only going to get worse once we actually got away from civilization and were really at their mercy, but praise God, He treats us as if we all have the faith of an Elijah.

It was after 2:00 p.m. when we finally got to the port, and while I was backing up to put the boat in the water, a guard started toward me. *Oh, great, here we go, I thought* (oh ye of little faith).

When he got closer, I recognized him as one of the guys who had been stationed at Cosh. We chatted for a bit, then he asked, "Where are you going?" I told him I was headed home. "Could you do me a personal favor?" he asked me next. "My lieutenant is here and has to get back to his post in Puraname by tomorrow. He sent me down here to find him a ride. Could you give him a ride?"

I quickly ran through the list of stuff I was taking to figure out what I could leave as the amount of fuel we have to carry to make a trip like that is substantial and weight is a big problem. "Yes," I told him, "I can take him *if* he has fuel in Puraname. If I have to leave here with full fuel, I can't put any more weight on. Might your lieutenant be able to replace fuel at his base?" He assured me the lieutenant could and would be happy to. The guard ran up to tell his lieutenant the good news.

I frowned as I realized that the boxes and bags they were bringing down were his cargo and then, to make matters worse, he also had a private with him. At that point, I had a lieutenant, a guard, and about fifty kilos of food to accommodate! We had to leave twenty-five gallons of gasoline and some of our cargo just to get the boat to plane on the water, but as it turned out, it was well worth it.

In fact, the smartest thing I ever did on that trip was take that lieutenant! At every guard outpost, he went up and got the papers stamped himself. I never even had to get out of the boat! He thanked me profusely as we dropped him off at his base the next day. By that time, I was wishing he was going all the way to La Esmeralda, as that way he could help us get through the last guard posts, which were also the worst ones. But I should not have worried, because as he was replacing our fuel, he asked me if I could take one of his solders on up to Las Esmeralda. That was the last checkpoint! So, not only did God give us a good trip,

He also gave us a military escort the entire way!

We had one scary incident. There are some bad rapids on the river, and there are places where there are wild whirlpools. We were approaching one such place and all of a sudden, about fifty feet ahead of us a huge log popped up out of a whirlpool. I panicked and stopped the motor, but we still hit the log. I did not think it had done any damage, but I wanted to check my propeller, so I hit the tilt button to bring the foot of the motor out of the water. I was looking back to check the prop when suddenly I became aware of a speedboat coming at us hard from the Colombian side of the river.

I quickly lowered the motor back down into the water, and had it started before the foot was even totally submerged. I was just ready to jam it into gear and take off when, without warning, the boat approaching us suddenly veered away as hard as it could. About then, I remembered the lieutenant and his guard were in the boat. I am pretty sure that the reason the would-be interceptor veered away so hard is that they saw the military escort and decided we were not worth the trouble. I am convinced this whole trip was a huge answer to prayer!

To be honest, the most dangerous part of the entire trip was when I got home and discovered I had forgotten my keys to the house. Keila always locks stuff up like Fort Knox, because of a few boys in the village who love breaking into people's houses for who-knows-what reason. Anyway, I figured I could break into our house myself. I thought, *Really, how hard can it be?* It seems the thieves run in and out as if it were a public restroom or something. Anyway, I figured out my best route to gain entry. Remembering a section of ceiling over the bathroom that Gary had fallen through earlier in the year while installing some wiring (a place that Keila had been hounding me for months to fix, but I had not gotten repaired yet), I figured I could climb up into the attic and gain entrance into our bedroom from there. Sounds easy enough! I eyed the hole, even peering in below to make sure there was a foothold down there. Lowering myself carefully, my foot found the towel rack, and I chuckled to myself at how good I was! Suddenly the towel rack gave way and I fell crashing down, further enlarging the hole Gary had made. I knew that now I had really better get to it and get it fixed!

◈▣◈▣◈

Some days you just wish you had stayed in bed. We headed down-river in the rain, deciding not to wait it out because we wanted to make sure we got our place in line for fuel down in La Esmeralda. They only allow so many people a day to purchase fuel, and we wanted to make sure we were one of the ones to get some. Getting fuel is a process to begin with. You have to push your fifty-five-gallon barrels up to the tanks, as there are no vehicles to get the barrels there from the port.

My nephew Jody had gone down the night before, so I was pretty sure he would have put my name on the list, but I still wanted to be down there in good time. We actually made it down there before the office opened, just a bit after 7:00 a.m. Jody had put my name on the list, so we were in good shape. He had been the first in line, no less! All was good! The main guy showed up only a little bit late and greeted us all with jokes and handshakes.

Great, I remember thinking, *he is in a good mood!* Well, not that good a mood, it turned out, because the next thing we realized was that he had started from the back of the list, so instead of being first in line, we had become last. Bummer! *Oh well*, I thought, *forget it. We can still get our fuel and get started home before noon, anyway.* Wrong! It was almost noon by the time he even got to us. We got in line with our barrels and the next thing we heard was: "Pump is shutting down until two, come back at two."

I realized just then that not only was I feeling badly about this ordeal, but I was coming down with something. I ached all over, so I went to my boat and just sat there waiting for 2:00 p.m. I didn't even feel like talking with anyone. I dozed off in the sun and awoke to a terrible headache, so I decided to wash my face. I bent down over the side of the boat, and too late, remembered my glasses in my shirt pocket. The last I saw of them was them sinking out of sight in the strong current. I could have cried. My backup pair was still in the States waiting for a ride down. Oh well, what can you do? Like I said, I should have stayed in bed.

Eventually, we put the fuel we purchased on the fuel barge, and most of us came home by speedboat, leaving the barge to come on behind. We expected it to get in around noon, but it did not arrive until 8:30-ish, and then we had to unload it even though it was night. I backed the trailer down the bank and locked the brake on the tractor. We put the first barrel on and were rolling it up to the front of the trailer when, all of a sudden, the trailer came off the trailer hitch ball.

I was hanging onto the tongue, yelling for more help while being pulled, slipping on the muddy bank, into the river. For a minute, I was afraid we were going to have to go diving for the crazy trailer, but once the whole thing was in the river, it slowed down enough that we were able to stop it and hold it while I backed the tractor down and got the trailer hooked back up. Whew! Funny, I hardly felt sick at all while that panic was going on, but then, if a doctor had been present, all he would have had to do would be fill out the paperwork and they would be shoveling dirt on my face! Mercy!

In the midst of the chaos and turmoil and scarcities of everything, we continue to watch God provide above and beyond our wildest hopes. We had just gotten word—well, a rumor really—that the barge with bottled gas had arrived in La Esmeralda. Here is the thinking process my mind went through: *What to do? If I wait until the rumor is verified, the barge will have come and gone before we get down there, leaving us with no gas. If I run down there on a rumor, I will use one hundred liters of our carefully hoarded gasoline, and if the barge is not there, that's a really bad waste of the precious fuel. Do I flip a coin?* It goes without saying that we were praying about it, but there had been no clear answer … probably going to wait until noon and just go.

It is strange how much life here changed under the form of government we have now. Before, the guy with the barge would just leave our gas cylinders with friends and we would pick them up and I would turn in our empties when we saw them again. Now, if we are not there, we don't get any. Many times, even when we are right there, we still don't get any because we are with the wrong side politically.

We decided to go ahead and head down. We arrived in Esmeralda about 3:30 p.m. and found the barge there. It had just arrived about 3:00 p.m. that same day, so they beat us there by only thirty minutes. Nevertheless, we were informed that they would not start dispensing the bottles until the next day, as there was a big discussion about who would receive them. It seems they were about forty bottles short of the amount needed for each of the people waiting to get theirs.

Well, that leaves us out, I remember thinking. *No way we will get the five we have coming, one for each of the families on our base now.* "Well, God," I said, "we are here, we need Your help to get this very needed gas for the stoves." We went on up to where the meeting was being held and stood there listening to people shouting and yelling at each other. Finally, the military guy who was trying to bring order got fed up with the whole process and left the building. I followed him out, knowing he was going to be in charge of the distribution and also knowing he had to be in a foul mood after that meeting. I breathed a silent prayer. "*Teniente*, we heard they were already giving the bottles out so we frantically drove down from Cosh and did not bring anything to sleep in. Is there any way we could get ours this evening, so we can go ahead and head on home?" I asked.

I was surprised at his answer. "Well, I don't see why not. Come on back in and let me ask everyone if anyone has a problem with it," he said. I followed him back inside and, to make a long story short, half an hour later, Keila and I were heading back upriver with the five very necessary cylinders of bottled gas.

Living in the Amazon rainforest means there is an accent on *rain*! Mercy, it rained as we shoved off and rained the whole way home. Have any of you been roaring up a river at night in a pouring rain, when you can't see your hand in front of your face and all of a sudden have a lightning bolt split the air above your head? When the flash and the explosion merge into one catastrophic explosion of light and sound and you realize that even as you are ducking your head, that if it were going to get you, you would be gone? Well, if you have not, lucky you! But still, WE GOT OUR GAS! Praise the Lord!

Missionary work involves an awful lot of traveling, for one reason or another. Villages are far apart and our supply center is also a long way away. Because there is so much that can happen on a trip, I am always happiest when getting back home. For instance, there was this trip to Las Esmeralda: All in all, a good trip, which means that, in spite of the difficulties, we made it home.

I won't bore you with the trivial facts that we left Cosh at 10:00 p.m. and arrived down there at 5:30 a.m., of how long it took to load our boat with the building materials, and how we set off for home at 1:30 p.m. and finally arrived home at 4:59 a.m. Which, if I haven't already bored you to sleep with all the numbers, you have added it up to be one heck of a long trip in a boat.

Nor will I make much of how my hammock rope broke and dumped me, my hammock, and blanket into the dirty bilge water at about 3:00 a.m. while still heading downriver; or how in spite of it being high water and there probably being only one sandbar in the entire distance between La Esmeralda and Cosh, somehow our driver ran us up on it. Or about how, because of how loaded we were, the boat hit before the foot of the motor did and due to how slowly our overloaded boat was going and it being night time, none of us in the boat realized we had even stopped … the driver least of all of us, and blithely drove along not realizing that he was just pivoting off the pegged prow and was not actually making any headway. Because none of us realized we had pegged, we don't even know for sure how much time we lost! And I certainly won't try to bore you with details of the freezing rain that tried to extinguish the last vestiges of life from our quaking bodies. No, what I do want to tell you about is our attempts in the night—not once, not twice, but *five* times—to try and make an assault on rounding a point and all five times we were thrown out of the channel and crashed into the bank.

The first two times, I was a bit nervous watching both motor drivers fight to keep the prow of the boat heading into the current. We were running two fifteen-hp outboards, one on each side of the huge overloaded boat. It was truly nerve-wracking to watch the guys struggle to hold the boat, only to have it swing into shore regardless of how they turned the motor handles. The third and fourth times, I found myself standing, as I was getting quite worked up. This does not usually happen! It seemed there was something in the water that would just slam the prow over to shore, whereupon we would back out and try again.

After the fifth time, I motioned for the guy in front to hold us into shore. Then I asked everyone if any of them was seeing an angel with a flaming sword, as our battle with the current reminded me of Balaam's donkey running away from Balaam's desired route. I asked both drivers if they wanted someone else to spell them. I was afraid we were getting to a place where we would start taking the dangerous point for granted and we would find ourselves broadside against some rocks and all be swimming.

Now, don't get me wrong: Personally, I would not mind seeing an angel, and I even enjoy a good swim, but 2:00 a.m. seemed to be stretching it to get psyched up to enjoy partaking of this pastime—not to mention sinking—in that area. Plus, it would be guaranteed that we would lose our cargo and not get any of our materials back, so I wanted to make sure our drivers thought they were up to the task. They assured me they were and neither seemed suicidal, so we pushed back out to try again. That last time, we made it around the point and were able to continue our trip home. We never did figure out what was causing the boat to crash into the shore those five times. That has never happened to me before. But we did make it home with our supplies, praise God!

◈ ▣ ◈ ▣ ◈

Some times our traveling involves large jet airplanes rather than a dugout canoe or speedboat, but it seems we are always asking God for traveling mercies and asking people to be praying for us. I still bow my head in wonder at all the miracles we have been so blessed to watch God do for us.

We had started packing on Tuesday for our Thursday flight out of Orlando International Airport. With the medicines and other donated items, it was obvious that we were going to be well beyond the six suitcases allowed. So, I called the airline and asked them what we could do and what additional bags would cost. The lady was very helpful and after she found out how many bags we had, we discussed different options, including upgrading to first class. We finally decided that paying the additional cost for the four additional suitcases was the cheapest of the various options. We got to the airport at 6:00 a.m. for our nine o'clock flight and unloaded the bags from the rental van. A porter came out to help and offered us curbside check-in, but when he saw the quantity of bags coming out, he asked if we were aware that there was a luggage embargo to Venezuela. This was the first we had heard of it, and because we had just been discussing excess bags on Monday, I was hoping the porter was mistaken.

He assured us he was right and that it was not the airlines, but rather the country that had initiated the embargo. My mind raced. What to do? We had to drop the rented van off by 6:30 or incur additional charges for it, so I left Keila and Mia with our bags there on the curb and rushed to meet the rental deadline. While driving to the dropoff, I was frantically pouring out my heart to the Lord. *What can we do?* I prayed. *We can't just fly off leaving four of our bags.* Especially since when Keila packs, she never puts things that go together in the same bag, figuring that if someone tried to steal something, they would have to go through every bag to find the other shoe, or the cable for equipment, and so on. But, now, what to do? To be honest, my first thought was to demand my rights. We had called, we had talked to an agent, so it was not our fault we were stuck at an airport with too much luggage.

I dropped off the van and, while seated in the shuttle to go back over to the airport, I was still praying. "I honestly don't know what to do," I told the Lord, "but You do, so I am just going to leave it with You. We have asked people to pray, so instead of worrying and yelling, I am just going to accept whatever You have for us today." To be honest, I still did not know what was going to happen, but I felt better.

The shuttle dropped me off and I walked over to where Keila and Mia were still sitting with all our luggage like two evicted tenants with all their stuff on the curb. I smiled in spite of my worry and fears. "Well, let's see what God is going to do here," I told Keila. She nodded. "We might just have to cancel going and repack everything," I told her. She agreed, so once again, leaving her with all our luggage on the curb, I walked in to find a supervisor. "God, please direct me to someone in a really good mood who will be willing to help," I prayed. I stood in line, but then, glancing at my watch, I realized I didn't have that much time, so I walked up to the counter to one side and just stood there, hoping to ask for a supervisor when I could catch the agent's eye. My heart sank as I heard the man she was waiting on giving her a hard time. She looked over and mouthed the words, "Be with you in a minute." I nodded.

She finished up and called me over. I explained our problem and she shook her head. "I am really sorry, but there is nothing we can do. It is not American Airline's embargo, it is being put on by Venezuela," she explained. I nodded. "I know that now, I just wish I would have known before we came here with all the bags."

"Yes, you should have called," she said. I nodded again.

"Well, to be honest, we did call on Monday, as we knew we were going to have too many pieces. We spoke at length to a lady and we even had her check on whether it would be cost-effective to go first class, but after running the figures, she told us that first class would cost $1,300 and just paying for the four extra suitcases would cost $800. We told her we would just pay for the four extra pieces. That is when we should have been told there was a cargo embargo. We stated at that time how many pieces we had and she did not say anything about an embargo. But at this point, what are our options?" I asked.

The agent tapped her computer keys. "Would you be willing to go tomorrow? I could switch your flight with no penalty and would even put you in first class so you could have six seventy-pound suitcases instead of fifty-pound suitcases in economy."

"OK, that would work," I told her.

She once again tapped her keys, frowning. Looking up, she said, "Not sure why, but that is not working, I need to see the supervisor." She walked off and about five minutes later came back with her supervisor.

She had me repeat the whole story. The lady supervisor listened closely. She asked a few questions, but oddly, though not knowing what God was going to do, or how the day was going to turn out, I just felt a real sense of peace. I honestly felt encouraged knowing how many people were praying for us. Saying she would be right back, the supervisor walked away. She was back in five minutes.

"They have waived the embargo for you. She is going to finish checking you in. Is the excess going to be a problem?" she asked.

"No, we budgeted for it," I assured her. By this time, it was after 8:00 a.m.: our flight was supposed to leave just after 9:00 and we still had to check all the luggage in and make our way through security. I rushed out to the curb and found that the porter had piled our stuff on his cart. "They are going to let it go!" I told him.

"All of it? Are you sure?"

"Yes," I assured him. We hurried inside. While the lady finished up our check-in, the porter loaded our bags onto the conveyer belt as if he was afraid someone would change their mind.

We got to our gate with minutes to spare and all our luggage checked in. Praise the Lord with us! In all the times I have flown, I have never heard of anyone being allowed to take more than the embargo allows. How my heart sang to the Lord! How my heart was humbled knowing how many friends, brothers and sisters in Christ, took time out of their day to pray for us. Thank you.

When we got to Caracas, everyone else's luggage came in and ours did not. I told Keila that maybe the Lord figured that, since there is an embargo, the best thing would be to just let our luggage trickle down. While we were waiting, two guys walked up and started talking to us. Seeing the four carts we had, they asked how many pieces we were bringing in. Hoping they were not going to make an issue of it, we told them.

They edged closer. "If we help you with your luggage through customs, would you tip us?"

"Yes," I assured him, "we would be willing to tip if our luggage comes up. So far, only one piece has come up and the belt is almost empty." Just about that time, all the rest of our luggage came up. They took each bag off the belt and loaded our carts. I wondered what it looked like having airport officials loading our carts. Asking us to wait for a minute, they walked off, but quickly returned pushing two wheelchairs.

"These will help," they assured us. Telling Keila and me each to climb into a wheelchair, they pushed us toward the customs booths. They pushed our suitcases through the machine, and then reloaded our carts. Not a single suitcase was unpacked. In less than ten minutes we were through and loading our bags into the pickup truck that had been waiting to pick us up. What an amazing day! Like I said, I think to have a cargo embargo waived is way harder than splitting the Red Sea. After all, the sea is only nature, whereas man is stubborn and obstinate. But we serve an AWESOME God! Praise Him with us!

18
Hunting and Fishing Stories

You know, I just hate it when I am out in the late evening, taking a leisurely walk with Keila, and just about the time I think of something really romantic to say, I open my mouth, and some fool bug, with nothing else to do but commit mayhem and chaos, dives past my teeth and lodges behind my tonsils! Wouldn't you just hate that?

I had a guy working in my yard. The gnats were terrible—I mean, just *terrible*! I noticed him waving around a large piece of cardboard that he had covered in oil, flailing it around his head. "Stop playing and get back to work," I chided him.

"I'm killing gnats," he responded.

"Well, you can't kill them fast enough, more just come to take their place," I told him.

"Yes, but revenge sure feels good!" he told me. My question was, should I leave him with his revenge, or make him get back to work? He did seem awfully happy out there.

❖ ▣ ❖ ▣ ❖

I was sitting out in our cookhouse with a bunch of the guys shooting the breeze. Suddenly Keila yelled at me from the house that she needed my help with something. Tongue in cheek, I told the guys, "You all are the ones called the fierce people. Now, if I were fierce like you Yanomamö, I would ignore her yells and keep talking, but I am afraid of her, so I had better run."

Pedro looked at me and with the straightest face said, "Heck, it is because I am afraid of my wife that I am still sitting out here."

I was able to finish doing Keila's job quickly and rushed back out to my cookhouse to continue listening to the stories being told out there. It has become an almost daily ritual for the guys of the village to gather over at my cookhouse in the evening: We try and find enough coffee and sugar to brew up a big pot of coffee and we sit and swap stories until the coffee is ready. The Yanomamö are awesome storytellers and normally you would be hard pressed to award a Best Story of the Evening prize, but that night the prize would have been awarded to Antonio Mejia, and there would have been no runner-up. I will try to tell you Antonio's story.

Andrez and I were paddling up the river, when suddenly we saw a huge snake swimming across the river and we quickly took chase. This snake was huge and we could already picture our return to the village with all this snake meat on board. Our frantic paddling quickly allowed us to catch up to the snake. For some reason, it was swimming with its head held high. I took careful aim and was gratified to see the snake slump down, twisting and turning on itself as a dying snake will. The water was deep, so we grabbed it by the tail and began to haul it into the boat. It is normal for a snake of this size to continue to twist and quiver even long after it is dead, but after a long time, Andrez and I seemed to be no closer to getting the snake in the boat than we were before I shot it.

I knew it had to be dead, though, as I had aimed right for its head from hardly a few feet away from it. So we continued trying to get it in the boat. But every time we got a few feet in, it would pull the same amount and a bit more out of our hands. My hands ached and I finally had had enough. I let go and sat down.

"Just forget it," I told Andrez. "I am too tired; furthermore, it is pulling us downriver and we will have a harder time getting home.

Just forget it," I repeated.

"No, I have had my hands on it for so long, I already feel like it is mine. I have to take this snake home!" insisted Andrez. "Come help me, I can't hold on much longer!" He was right; by this time, he had his hands wrapped around the very last tip of its tail and his arms were hanging out over the boat, almost in the water.

I finally started helping him again, although by that time, I would have gladly just cut it loose, but Andrez insisted I help him. So, with the both of us tugging on it we were finally able to get over two meters of the huge snake back in the boat. But my hand got a huge cramp in it and I could not hold on any longer. "Andrez, I can't hold him," I gasped. "Just let go!"

"No!" he insisted. By this time, we had lost all we had gained and Andrez was once again stretched out over the water, hanging on for dear life to his tiny little piece of the snake's tail. Looking at his desperate eyes, I couldn't help myself, but grabbed ahold of the snake again and started frantically tugging on it. During all this time, we had yet to see the snake's head, but the snake, instead of ceasing its pulling, seemed to be increasing in strength.

Finally, I told Andrez, "Listen. I am going to pull a bit more in the boat, then I am going to just cut that much off. That way, if we have to let go of it, we can at least have some of it to eat."

Andrez reluctantly agreed. We tugged and tugged; finally, figuring we had enough, I grabbed my machete and before it could slip back through our hands, I chopped hard, trying to sever its huge backbone. This got its attention. *That's funny, this snake is dead*, I thought. The next thing I knew the snake had reversed direction and the head came flying toward me. I still did not realize the snake was alive, but just thought I must have hit the right nerve.

At least the part that was chopped was no longer trying to slither out of the boat, so we were able to pull another three meters or so into the boat and I again picked up my machete. Telling Andrez to get a good hold, I chopped down hard again. This time the results were violent! The snake again came flying at me. Closer this time, allowing me to get a much closer—too close, actually—look at the snake's head. Expecting to see bullet holes and much damage, I was surprised to see no damage at all.

"THIS SNAKE IS ALIVE!" I yelled to Andrez. At that time, all I wanted to do was let the other half of the snake go. We already had enough. But Andrez refused to let go.

"Chop it again but be ready to shoot it this time!" he told me.

The snake finally must have gotten tired, too—either that, or it missed about half of itself—so the head was coming up more often. Finally, I got close enough to have a chance to swing at its neck and thankfully, my machete was sharp and severed the main bone running down its spine behind the head. The fight was over. We pulled the rest of the snake into the boat and collapsed. We were quietly drifting downriver and neither of us had the strength to paddle to shore so we could tie up and rest. Finally, realizing we were getting further and further away, we paddled to shore and rested some more.

Finally getting my breath, I began to examine our trophy! What a huge snake this was! There was going to be good eating tonight! Remembering the untouched head that had flashed past me twice, I moved over to where it lay, barely still connected. I picked it up. My eyes bugged out as I examined it again. There was not a mark on that head! Wait, right on the tip of the nose, it looked like a bullet had barely broken the skin. I HAD MISSED! We had been wrestling with a live snake! The bullet hitting its nose must have just stunned it for a bit. Good thing we had not known that earlier. I don't care what Andrez wanted, I would not have held on to a live snake — not one that big!

◈▣◈▣◈

Of course, I have my own stories which I will throw out there against anyone else's stories. Mia was looking at a scar on my arm, which, although it doesn't look like much now, ran across my entire arm when I was a skinny ten-year-old. Obviously, Mia did not realize how dangerous it was to ask an outdoorsman about scars. After forty-five minutes of listening to me expound on it, all glassy-eyed, she told me she had to go help her mother teach school. (Actually, she seemed downright excited to go.) The funny thing was that normally when she has to help with the 107 preschool kids, she looks like what I look like when the dentist tells me I need to have a root canal redone. Such are the side benefits of telling someone about your scars.

Fran Cochran, Gary, a new missionary (Simon iTuni), and I were night fishing on a sandbar across the river from TamaTama. Nothing was biting, and we had mostly given up and were just sleeping with our lines still out. My line was a brand-new roll of 100-kilo line, 220-pound test. If you are not a fisherman, you should know that this was a big enough line that I was ready for some serious fishing. As I said, nothing was biting, so I was using the large wooden float the line was wrapped around as a pillow and had the line lightly wrapped around my hand two or three times so that the slightest jerk would wake me up.

Around 2:00 a.m., I did wake up, but not with a slight jerk. The round piece of wood that the 330 feet of line had been wrapped around was banging me on the back of the head so hard I feared it was going to knock me out. Then, I realized my right arm was stretched almost to the pull-off point and that my huge line was burning itself across my hand, scoring into my hand in such a way that I forgot all about the log hitting me on the back of the head. I tried to get my other hand around so I could pull on the line and get some slack, but my body was being pulled in such a way that I couldn't reach the line with my other hand.

I started shrieking at Gary and Fran to come help, and they woke up trying to figure out what was happening. By that time, the 330 feet of line was all out and the fish had not even slowed down. I was being jerked closer and closer to the river's edge and could not free my hand. I was praying the fish would break free. Finally, Gary and Fran grabbed the wood the line was wrapped around and Gary tugged on the line, giving me enough slack to get my hand loose. They both hung on to the piece of wood, but the fish never slowed down. The line snapping in the night sounded like a rifle shot echoing across the river.

My hand was badly burned by the line. Sad to say, because that fish was one of the ones that got away, he has never been able to continue growing, unlike the many monsters I have caught that continue to grow to this day. However, that one remains in my mind as one of largest fish in the Orinoco. I trust he continues to swim free, since I could not be the one who caught him.

The ravages of time and sunspots on my hand have even reduced my deep scar to a few puny little white marks across the width of the back of my hand; if you squint just so, you can almost make them out. It might have been Mia's trying to squint just so that convinced her it was time to go help her mother in the school.

◈ ▣ ◈ ▣ ◈

Speaking of time passing, some time ago, while hunting with some Yanomamö friends, we came to a land-locked lagoon that was drying out. The size of the original body of water was evident from the dried-out mud, decaying leaves, and other swampy debris in a wide circle around the small water hole that was left.

We carefully picked our way up closer. Large anacondas love to hide in the dried leaves and grass of a swamp and I had no desire to wind up as snake lunch. It was just too nice a day for that.

As we walked closer, our eyes were busy cataloging all the different tracks of animals that were coming to the water hole, either to find a drink or to get a meal from the ever-dwindling water hole itself. There were agouti paca tracks, wild boar tracks, capybara tracks, and even tapir tracks. A small flock of wild turkeys had come down at some point, as evidenced by their tracks. All of a sudden, though, they were no longer important, as the large paw prints of a hunting jaguar got all our attention. They so fresh that the mud still oozing back into the indentations! I once read that we only have so much room for worries. It must be true, because seeing those fresh jaguar tracks totally made me forget all about the anacondas. We all peered off in the direction the tracks went, I guess to make sure he was not still skulking in the underbrush hoping for lunch. It was way too nice a day to wind up as jaguar lunch!

Suddenly, with a huge splash, every fish in the pool of water jumped out of the water and hung suspended in the air, glistening in the sunlight, then fell back into the water with another splash. *Wow, that was cool,* I thought. We forgot the jaguar and continued to approach the pool. I had never seen that happen before, and had no idea what could have caused hundreds, perhaps thousands, of fish to all leave the water in unison.

While we were watching the water, it happened again! Every fish in that small body of water (it must have been something like a fifty-foot circle) suddenly flashed into the air again—and there were some nice fish in the bunch! We began to make plans to take advantage of the large number of fish and the small water hole. We hesitated about jumping right in, however, because we had no idea what was causing the fish to act like they were. Then, yet again, the fish flashed into sight, hung in the air, and splashed back into the water.

Now my Yanomamö friends were frantic: They just had to start getting some of these fish! It was as if they were being teased by the fish. They each got a long pole and began to poke around in the water, trying to flush out whatever in the depths was causing the fish to go crazy. One of my friend's poles had gotten wet all the way up to where his hand was. His yell coincided with the next group flash of all the fish. I looked at him. He had dropped his pole and was rubbing his arm. We all started laughing at him. We knew what was in the water now: a giant electric eel. But I had never seen an electric eel affect fish like that before. What was going on?

We pulled vines down and used them to tie hooks on our long poles. Using them, we began to pull them through the water, trying to catch the eel on the hooks. Suddenly, Ramon let out a yell. It was obvious he was taking an enormous jolt, but he was unwilling to let go. Slowly the giant began to come out.

From the other side of the pond, Pablino yelled, saying he had hooked it as well. *Wait*, I thought, *there is no way they could have hooked the same eel, their poles are not long enough.* Sure enough, Pablino had hooked a different one! How many were in there, anyway?

Before we were finished, we had seven huge eels drawn up on the bank. All of us had sustained more voltage than I thought was possible and still be walking around, but the fish were no longer flashing in the waning sunlight. We had cleaned the pond of eels! Now for the fish!

I learned a few things from my experience in that pond. One, if you are distracted you can take a heck of a lot of pain; and two, if you work together as those eels were doing, just a few of you can make a huge number of others jump to your bidding.

◈ ▣ ◈ ▣ ◈

This reminds me of another encounter we had with eels. This happened back when I was in grade school in TamaTama. Our teacher taught all twelve grades in a little one-room schoolhouse, and us little guys listened in fascination as she was teaching the high schoolers science. I don't remember her lesson; I just remember her talking about electricity, something I did not know that much about because we did not even have a generator on our base at that time. She talked about lightning and other things that produce electricity. She challenged the high schoolers to capture an electric eel and said if they did she would show them how to light a light bulb.

Because my older brothers, Steve and Gary, were in high school, I tagged along with them that night as they searched for an electric eel that could be pressed into service for their science experiment. They finally found one down in a deep hole surrounded by huge rocks. Earlier they had made a tool to capture the eel. It consisted of a long pole with a wire loop at one end with a nylon rope tied onto the wire loop to draw it closed. Eels breathe air, so they come up about every ten to fifteen minutes or so to take a breath of air before heading back under. When you are standing there in the night, keyed up to capture one, those ten to fifteen minutes seem to last a lifetime, but finally the eel's head rose out of the murky water — and we were ready. The head of the eel came up right in the middle of our loop and so (I think it was my brother Gary holding the rope) he jerked it tight and the eel exploded. The rest of us clung to the pole and slowly started pulling him out of the river. He was not happy. Just then we learned another fascinating fact about electricity: Water conducts it just fine. Our pole was wet and all of a sudden, we were feeling shocks like you would not believe traveling up the pole and whamming into our hands and our bodies. Wow! This was great!

We put the eel in a large tub of water and then brought the tub up to the little schoolhouse the next day. Our teacher showed the guys in her science class, with all the rest of us hanging on her every word, how to rig a 12-volt light bulb on two wires. These two wires ended with two blunted probes. Touching one of the probes to the forward part of the eel and the other one toward the back end of the eel, we watched in fascination as the light bulb did in fact light up. We laughed in appreciation as a few of the high schoolers took enough of a shock to dance around for our amusement. I have always appreciated those guys taking the time to suffer shocks to bring a little amusement to our rather drab lives.

◈▣◈▣◈

Some days are such that you count the victories, no matter how large or small. Well, I am not sure whether this should really be listed as a victory, but after my past three weeks, I will count this one as a large victory. Just wish it were mine. You be the judge.

I noticed a large, ugly, offensive, and way-too-smart cockroach in our bathroom. Way too smart, because it would stand still on the wall above the commode tank and wait until I was inches away before making a mad dash to safety behind the tank. First, I was disgusted and beat the wall behind him in frustration, but as my nightly hunt remained unsuccessful, I plotted ways that I might exert the superiority that I knew I had … but to no avail. That crazy roach had me timed to perfection and my frantic beatings were always inches behind him.

First, I hated to walk in and spot him on his place on the wall. Then, I began to look forward to the challenge of possibly winning the round—which of course, as he was only a roach, would be the end of the fight. But either I was slowing down, or that was one smart roach! Timing! Mercy! Well, the fight dragged on and on and on. I began to give Keila early morning updates on the previous night's battle. She took the updates in stride and I don't think she was all that interested or impressed with me, or the roach for that matter, until one night when she had to get up. Wouldn't you know it? She gets up, spots the roach, takes a can of insect killer, and the war is over. Victory! Really, the thing that bothers me is … insect killer? Doesn't seem fair. I almost miss him.

◈回◈回◈

There was another drawn-out struggle with an evil rat that insisted on chewing through the water line running to our kitchen. Here are the entries from my Facebook page to bring out the drama—or maybe it's the trauma—of this struggle.

Monday, September 8

Well, another sleepless night for Keila and myself. We have been fighting in almost hand-to-hand combat a rat that somehow got in here a few weeks ago. I started out with nonchalantly baiting my traps, confident this was not going to be much of a contest. But I was, unfortunately, sadly mistaken. The rat wanted nothing to do with my traps. I moved up to foods that should have caused the entire rat population of the Amazon to start on a forced march to our house, but the rat would not take the bait. He was happy, it seems, with chewing through the water line running to the kitchen.

Now, this might seem a small thing, but we have our water in a reservoir so that even when the generator is off, we still have running water. But if a stupid rat chews through our water line when the generator is off, we no longer have running water in the morning, but rather a mess! So, although Keila started out blaming the rat and being very angry at it, she has now moved from blaming the rat to starting to hint that my hunting abilities might be wanting. This was too much for me, so I, again to no avail, starting lying in wait for said rat. But he would never show until I had given up and gone to bed. Then he would run out and gnaw on the pipe and retire to wherever he retires to, chuckling over the mess he was once again draining out on our kitchen floor.

This was too serious! I called in a team of culinary experts, then used ingredients imported all the way from the United States (our stash of peanut butter), and again baited my traps. Nothing… but the pipe was bitten through again. Again, a mess. Now Keila is not only hinting at my hunting skills, she is downright rude! I then remembered we had some rat glue. Spreading it around on a lid, I balanced it right under the place the rat has to stand on to get at his favorite gnawing spot. Nothing! He bit the pipe at two separate places that night and got away scot-free.

Friday, September 12

I have to go on an outreach trip today, so am leaving Keila in charge of rat patrol. She is not a happy camper.

Tuesday, September 16

I am back! had a great time! One old, old man asked me to lengthen his life, as he was not ready to die. I had to explain that I was only a man like him and could not lengthen anyone's life. From there, I shared the Gospel with him at the top of my voice, as he was about deaf. He said he heard me and understood.

Keila was fine. No, she did not get the rat. She and Mia set the traps again, including the glue one. All they caught was a poor unfortunate frog, which has us a bit concerned. Not that she caught it, but as soon as I got home, Keila showed me the frog. He was a *very* stuck — hopelessly stuck — frog. I had to finish up some other stuff and when we went back to take care of the frog, it was GONE! Now, that frog could not have moved himself. Something moved him. The big question is, what in the heck moved the frog? All kinds of questions now!

Thursday, September 18

Agahhhh!!! I broke a tooth! Not to mention, the rat bit through another water line, causing my wife to pronounce an ultimatum: "Either the rat goes, or you go!" So you know who is going to be down there standing guard tonight, although I did offer to return after she got the rat. She was not amused.

Sunday, October 5

Traps set again! So far, Mike, 0; Rat, 10

Monday, October 6

This is one smart rat! I have baited the traps with everything from chicken and meat to other fruit, including papaya, bananas, cashew, and other miscellaneous jungle fruits, and nothing! I have even baited the trap with some of our hoarded peanut butter and he sneers at me while still chomping through some piece of PVC pipe. So last night, I even baited the trap with PVC! Nothing! My sister returned to Cosh from the U.S. yesterday and brought Mia a goody bag of chocolate bars, Skittles, and whatnot, so today the trap is baited with a Skittles. Trust me, it is not easy to talk an eleven-year-old girl into giving up a Skittle for a rat! We'll see what the Skittle does though, but after this, I am out of ideas!

Thursday, October 9

I hate to keep boring you all with tales of my ongoing battle with this rat, as one-sided as it has been so far. Well, the rat ignored the wasted Skittle and chewed on my wife's garlic! Go figure! Probably is a health nut rat. Well, we'll see ... I baited the trap tonight with garlic. I do have to admit, I feel like I am playing catchup with this rat, like I am only reacting instead of acting decisively.

I almost got into hand-to-hand combat with the rat and the score turned. It was Rat, 12; Dawson, 0 until this morning at 2:20. The final score was Dawson, 1 pellet; Rat, 12 robbed traps. But a pellet trumps robbing traps all blind! You heard right. The rat is dead!

◈ ▣ ◈ ▣ ◈

Years ago, when I was just a kid, my dad went hunting with a group of Yanomamö men. He was excited to be included on this hunt and hoped he would not make a fool of himself. He was so trying to make a good impression on these lords of the jungle. To be honest, he was still fairly new to the work and was barely able to communicate, but because he had been raised a Virginia hillbilly and then trained as a sharpshooter in the Pacific, he figured he should at least be able to hit what he shot at.

About an hour below the village, in trees along the river bank, they spotted a large troop of spider monkeys. If the Yanomamö had trophy walls, the spider monkey would claim a prime spot on those walls, as that species is extremely difficult to catch and shoot. They can make jumps of more than thirty feet to another tree, and in order to catch a troop that is in flight you have to be able to run as fast as you can with your eyes on the trees to keep sight of your prey. Unfortunately, the sound of the boat motor alerted this troop and they were in full flight even before all the men had exited the dugout canoe.

The Yanomamö, with their long bows and arrows, were like shadows in the jungle and almost as quiet. Within fifteen minutes Dad was puffing like a freight train and he could barely make out the guy he was following. He gamely kept running, but the jungle was so thick, he tripped on a large vine and lay on the ground panting. *Forget it*, he decided. He looked around. The jungle was so thick he could barely see any distance in any direction. Not even sure how to get back to the boat, he decided he would just rest up there and wait for the hunters to finish chasing the monkeys and make their way back to the boat; then he would get back with them. His heart and breathing finally slowed down and he grinned to himself. *And here I thought I was in good physical shape. Man, but those guys are good in the jungle!*

Still ruefully chuckling to himself, he all of a sudden became aware of a crashing and swooshing in the branches coming toward him. He jumped up. Not sure what was approaching, he wanted to be ready. He couldn't believe it! Coming right to the tree under which he had been sitting was the entire troop of spider monkeys, and he was ready for them. He took aim and began to fire. Five times he shot and five times he watched a large monkey come crashing down. He gathered them up and put them all in a pile and once again sat down on the log where he had been resting when the monkeys came.

He was still sitting there when the hunters came running up. Their eyes bugged out as they saw the pile of monkeys. They looked at Dad with eyes filled with respect. As they tied up the monkeys, Dad quietly listened to them talking. Although he could not understand everything they said, he understood enough to know that they were impressed by his speed. Over and over he heard first one, then another one say they had really thought he was way behind them. "How did he get ahead of us?" they kept asking each other. Dad never said a word.

Years later, when I was in my late twenties and had already returned to Venezuela as a missionary, a group of the men were over at Dad's house with us and people were swapping stories. One story led to another and finally one of the guys brought up Dad's impressive speed in the jungle. "He outran all of us!" he exclaimed. "We thought we had left him way behind, then we heard all this shooting, and since he was the only one with a shotgun, we knew it had to be him, but man, we never did figure out how he outran us!"

Dad grinned. "So, you think I am really fast, right?

"Yes!" they exclaimed. "You even outran Lobema!" (*Lobema* in Yanomamö means fast man.)

"Do you want to know the truth?" Dad asked sheepishly. At their nods he grinned again and told them. "I ran out of breath and stopped. You all left me, but while I was still sitting there waiting for you to come back, the monkeys made a big circle and came right to me. I did not run at all. I shot the monkeys and then just waited for you all to come back. When you found me, you just assumed I had been chasing monkeys."

❖▣❖▣❖

This final story should be filed under "Mysterious and Unexplainable." A group of guys and I had just finished up our Bible class, and someone got to telling a story. We were hunting up this long, eerie swamp about 2:00 or 3:00 a.m. and we were only paddling enough to make headway.

I was whistling, making the sound a tapir makes and was really hoping one would answer. Tapir meat is the best meat in the jungle. For those of you who don't know, a tapir is South American's largest animal and is scientifically classified in the horse family. Of course, science being what it is these days, I'm not sure if that means anything; I only bring it up because I am reminded that the Native American Indians claimed that horse meat was way better eating than cow meat. So maybe the scientists are right and the tapir is a long-distance cousin of a horse, because, mercy, their meat is delicious! Anyway, most of the guys in the dugout canoe were either asleep or half asleep, and Gary had been arguing for a while about just forgetting the tapir and just heading back to camp, as there was nothing out. Suddenly, my spotlight reflected back on a pair of eyes! Huge eyes, as a matter of fact, big enough and far enough apart that I immediately figured we had found our tapir.

Everyone sat up and we bent to our paddles with a will. Our dugout canoe leaped forward in the water. I jacked a shell into my 12-gauge and was ready—but right in front of my eyes, the animal no longer looked like a tapir. I held my breath, squinting my eyes through the early morning fog, and realized that I was staring into the eyes of a huge jaguar! Every spot was in vivid relief. By this time all had quit paddling but our canoe continued to move forward. I had the gun up to my shoulder, but was not sure I was going to shoot. The Yanomamö do eat jaguar, but it is not a favorite meat. I don't much care for it either, but I kept my aim on him just in case he decided to make it personal. Suddenly, again a drastic change: Instead of a jaguar standing on the bank snarling at us, it became a huge buck deer with a glorious antler rack. Now this was more like it. I squeezed the trigger and the buck leaped into the air. I knew exactly where I had hit it, so I was confident of my kill. We were going to eat good! We all climbed out of the boat and walked up to where it had been standing.

"I first though it had been a tapir, then a jaguar. I saw the jaguar so clearly!" I said. I was surprised when everyone in the boat echoed what I had seen. Now I was really spooked! What was it? We looked around, but from the tracks it was obvious we were going to have to head into the jungle after it. Remembering the jaguar, there was no one who wanted to push our luck in there. What if the buck became a jaguar? Maybe a wounded jaguar? Thankfully, Gary again brought up how sleepy he was and suggested that we could come back in the morning and track it down.

"Did you all see how big it was?" I kept asking. It was huge, they all agreed. We headed back to camp and the next morning early started back up the river to our swamp to find my trophy deer. We got to the spot and Ramon took the lead tracking the deer. "This can't be right!" I told him, pointing at the tiny little tracks. "My kill was huge! These tracks can't be right." We lost the tracks and Ramon began casting around to find the tracks again. The jungle was incredibly thick right there, so instead of all of us tromping around, we left Ramon to work out the trail. We heard him start laughing. *What in the world?* I wondered.

He called us over. Lying dead at his feet was a tiny, little, midget spike buck. It was hardly bigger than a large rabbit. "This can't be right!" I kept insisting, but we took him home and ate him anyway. Now you might be wondering, what happened to the tapir? Then to the jaguar? Then to the huge trophy buck? Well, let me tell you. No one wonders more about that than I do. It would have been one thing if I had been the only one to see them—I could have explained it by the shadows, the fog, and an overeager mind—but all of us in the boat saw exactly the same thing. Another Amazon jungle mystery.

19

OUTREACH TRIPS

Technology is grand! I can play the Jesus movie off my iPhone and show it on a tiny battery-operated projector. Even my speaker is battery operated. Amazing… When we first started showing movies to the Yanomamö, we had a huge projector, huge reels of 16-mm film, and it took a huge generator to run it all. Now it has really gotten portable. Good thing, too: I'm getting too old to be hauling those heavy crates around!

◈ ▣ ◈ ▣ ◈

For the past few years, I have concentrated on the outreach aspect of our ministry with the Yanomamö. We know that a New Testament church has to be self-governing, self-supported, and self-propagating. This is harder to accomplish than it sounds. Because there are just too many Yanomamö villages scattered throughout this jungle for missionaries to reach by themselves, I have endeavored to teach and train Yanomamö believers to reach their own people. I would like to bring you along on our trips, so to speak, to give you a front-row seat on what it takes just to get to these forgotten little villages scattered through the jungle; then, to allow you to listen firsthand as many come to a saving knowledge of Jesus Christ. So, sit down and enjoy the ride.

On our first trip, we left Cosh and headed south toward the Brazilian border. It would be a long way: One hundred fifty miles by river, which is a *very* long way by river. I really appreciated my Boston Whaler with its 100-hp outboard pushing us upriver at thirty-five miles an hour in spite of the fact we were very heavily loaded with fuel. This side of eternity, no one will ever know how many times I have said a heartfelt *thank you* to the ones who gave to make this boat possible for us! We arrived up at Samuel's village at about 5:30 p.m., but he was not home. He had gone hunting so as to have something to feed us and had not gotten home yet. He arrived about thirty minutes after we got there, and, sad to say, he was empty-handed.

We had a meeting with Samuel that night. The next morning, about 5:00 a.m., Samuel got up and went hunting again so he could feed us. We told him not to worry, but he said he would only go for an hour or so and would be back before 8:00. Well, he did make it back and he had had a successful hunt. He came back with a large *basho* (spider monkey). We ate well that noon, but although it was tasty, it must have been an old monkey, because it was tougher than shoe leather.

We started a service that lasted until almost 1:00 p.m. We broke for a few hours, as it was just too hot to do anything. That evening we talked about things of the Lord with him way into the night. The next day, Sunday, we had a very good time in the Word with them.

Samuel shared that when he had moved from Cejal to get away from witchcraft and witchdoctors, he had allowed his brother and a brother-in-law to move down from another village. They had promised they wanted to hear about God. However, once in the village with their houses built, they began to do witchcraft, and Samuel was discouraged. "This was not what I had in mind. I wanted to get to a place where my children would not have to listen to witchcraft all the time; now, my brother and brother-in-law are doing it right in our midst! What can I do?"

I knew firsthand that he spoke the truth, because during our entire time there, we could hear them chanting. The only times they were quiet were the times we were actually talking about the Lord. It was eerie: every time we would start, they would take off into the jungle, and then return when we finished; once they were back, they started chanting with a vengeance. Saturday afternoon, while resting after our long morning meeting, I could not help but overhear a session where the witchdoctor started out in the spirit world, intending to go to a faraway village and attempt to kill the young son of an enemy witchdoctor.

Knowing that he was dancing in a tiny area right next door, it was hard to believe he was actually heading out to kill someone. It seemed unreal. I lay there in silence and listened as he approached the village, looking for his prey, then listened in horror as the shaman began sounding like a little boy. As the little boy became aware of the witchdoctor's presence, he began to scream in panic. His mother ran to assist him but was unsuccessful in freeing her son. Her wails of grief were almost more than I could stand to listen to. Remember, the only chanting and speaking was the witchdoctor right next door, but his powers of mimicry were so incredible, you would have thought there was a whole cast of people in that hut. Next, the witchdoctor, once more in his own voice, began to sing his song of conquest as he headed home to his own body and village. Unreal! How true Ephesians 6:12 became once again: *For we wrestle not against flesh and blood, but against principalities, against powers, against the rulers of the darkness of this world, against spiritual wickedness in high places.*

Before we broke up to come home, Samuel told us that he had been so discouraged that he felt like a person out in the middle of the river with no paddle in a sinking boat. We had arrived just in time to push his sinking boat to shore. He broke down and began to sob.

It is incredibly rare to have a grown Yanomamö man break down and cry in public, and it took us all by surprise. He sobbed for a long time, and while he was sobbing, one of the guys that were with us, Agustine, said, "Let's sing a song to encourage him while he is so sad." Agustine led us in singing "Trust and Obey." Samuel continued sobbing and walked around and hugged each of his children in turn, then his mother, his wife, and then made his way over to us, still being led in yet another verse of "Trust and Obey," and hugged each of us in turn. By this time there was not a dry eye in the house. It was obvious that God was in our midst just then. We felt truly blessed to be there.

◈▣◈▣◈

Not all trips are as great as the one to Samuel's village. Some are downright hard. Concerning this next story, I am not even sure where to start except to say I am glad we are back. I read something that Patrick McManus wrote about a camping trip he had done and he commented that only bad trips are worth writing about: "No one writes about a smokeless campfire, no bugs, etc." He called his trips "a fine and pleasant misery." If that is the case, I will be able to write about this trip for a long time. There was enough misery in this one trip that I had better just tell the story.

It almost goes without saying that it was raining. I have no idea why I was on an overnight trip in the rainy season with no rain gear and no extra set of clothes, but the misery factor kicked in early. We finally pulled over to see if the worst of the storm might pass, as large raindrops hitting your face at thirty-five miles an hour just plain hurt. The cloudburst did finally pass, but the storm caused us to get to our destination village with just enough time to unload and set up the movie equipment before dark. I was asked if we could run up and pick up people from two villages just upriver who also wanted to see the movie, so we roared upriver and picked them up. My teeth were chattering in the cold wind and my wet clothes in the extremely high humidity of the rain-forest, but we made it back to the village where we had set everything up. I eyed the high, steep, muddy, and extremely slippery bank and remembered thinking it was going to be a real treat to come back down that bank to take everyone home after we had finished showing the movie. My poor boat was so overloaded. I waited for the twenty-five plus people to make their way up the bank before it was my turn.

Once again, the equipment worked flawlessly and the movie played really well. My two friends and I continued to shake because of how cold we were in our wet clothes, but we were gratified to see everyone hanging on every word. We finished up at 11:20 p.m. and Antonio and I herded the group back to the river to ferry everyone home. The bank finally cleared and Antonio and I started down. It had been muddy and slippery enough before, but given the number of bare feet that had just used it, it had become treacherously slippery, so I decided to lighten people's hearts and inject some levity into the night by slipping and plunging down the steep, muddy bank. Thankfully, there was a little beach at the bottom, so I did not add insult to injury by falling down the bank and plunging into the cold, muddy water of the Orinoco — although, on second thought, the water would have been softer to land on and thus would have saved me some bruising, but why quibble?

Everyone really appreciated my efforts at humor and showed it by almost laughing themselves sick. Worried for their health, I threatened to leave anyone still laughing on the beach. I started the motor and we took everyone home. After we got back to the host village, the bank was just as steep, just as muddy and slippery, but somehow I made it back up to our sleeping place around 12:30 a.m.

I would like to point out a few things about my falling down the bank. You can pout and cry (or maybe it would be cry then pout), or you can try and laugh it off. Wait! A third option is to try and write about it to make you, our partners, smile as if you had been there to watch me tumble down the bank, teeth clenched to make sure a tiny indiscretion did not slip out (although, because the only ones around me were Yanomamö, they would not have known… but you understand). Anyway, happy smiles.

We hung our mosquito nets and warmed up with a huge pot of coffee and spent the next two hours talking with the guys from the village about the movie and about Jesus and what He means to us today. It was a relief to finally get out of my wet clothes and into my hammock. At my age, tinnitus is a pain, but the loud ringing in my ears was absurdly irritating until I realized it was a chorus of mosquitoes singing high opera in my ears.

Somehow, I had allowed almost the entire village's population of mosquitoes to get under my mosquito net with me. I briefly thought it would be in keeping with my desire to live sacrificially to help my brothers by keeping the mosquitoes inside my net, so that the rest of the village could get some needed sleep. Then I realized that this was taking things a bit far, so I spent a large portion of the rest of my sleeping time trying—unsuccessfully, I might add—to evict them.

I put our belief in the preventative benefits of drinking neem to a serious test that next week, because when I woke up the next morning, there were at least thirty *Anopheles* mosquitoes filled with blood, *my blood*, against the inside of my net this morning trying to get out. I wondered where the fine and pleasant part of our trip would be, because we had had the misery part in spades!

It was all made worth it this morning, because after our service with everyone in the village, four guys made a public profession of faith in Christ! We were invited to the next villages upriver the next weekend to show the movie to them. There was our "fine and pleasant!" God is good!

The next weekend found us once again showing the movie in some forgotten little village with the same mosquitoes and the same steep, high, muddy bank (just in a different location), so I wrote: "I do realize it would be in poor taste to whine again about things previously whined about, like the mosquitoes, muddy banks, etc., so I will try and keep this update only on bright and cheerful happenings."

After five minutes sitting there trying to think of something bright and cheerful, I came to the sad realization that if I were to share only bright and cheerful happenings, this would be an extremely short update and would fall far short of the strict rules of honesty and objectivity that I hold myself to. Not to worry, though: I can still share woe and misery and never mention the worrisome mosquitoes. For any of you wondering, after getting home, I did take a double dose of the neem tea we drink as a malaria preventative and am tempted to go downstairs and drink another dose, but that would probably be overkill. Whatever! Here is a brief, factual account of our trip over to the village of Widocayateli.

We fooled the storm that normally waylays us by announcing in advance that we were leaving at a certain time. We then left two hours later and the amount of water still falling off the leaves into the river gave us stark evidence that the storm had, in fact, made a major effort to drown us. We ran through a few modest late showers, but they were nothing compared to the deluges we have been subjected to on our previous trips.

We arrived at Widocayateli and navigated the steep, muddy bank that is always a given at a Yanomamö village. We were shown the little roofed shack we would be using as our sleeping quarters, which was also going to double as a place to show the movies. Thankfully, there were no walls, so most of the people could sit outside and still have clear sight of the movie screen.

I am sure you all realize that I always comment on how grateful we are that the equipment works. Well, this time, that almost did not happen. I had everything hooked up, but for some reason the projector would not recognize the HDMI connector. I kept praying and fiddled with it for about twenty minutes, stopping and starting it, connecting and reconnecting everything, and was about ready to admit defeat when all of a sudden it connected to the phone. Whew! Such a relief. But then the iPhone would not play the movie! This has never happened before with this setup, so after trying and trying, I finally realized we might be having something more serious than just equipment jitters. I began to ask God for special protection and a shield for our equipment. Again, I was very close to admitting defeat, but I kept looking at all the expectant faces of the villagers sitting around waiting for their special movie. Many of these people had never seen a movie in their lives and this was a big deal for them. We did not want to disappoint them, especially because this was the Jesus/Passion movie and we wanted them to hear this message. I could have done a handstand when, all of a sudden, the iPhone started playing the movie. Thank you, Lord!

We finished up around midnight. Thereafter, we left to take people home whom we had brought down from three different villages to the central village for the movie; then, it was back to our steep, muddy bank up to our little host village to hang our hammocks. Now, in a normal update, that would be the last entry for the night, but unfortunately, during the night there came such a roaring noise from the direction of my friend Timoteo's hammock that I was afraid he was being mauled by some ferocious jungle cat. I braved getting out of my hammock to face the mosquitoes for the short walk to Timoteo's hammock where the wild noise was coming from. Come to find out it was his snoring! I shook his hammock about four times, hard, until he woke up, then asked him to stay awake long enough so I could get to sleep before he started up again.

Sad to say, he beat me to sleep and started up snoring again right where he had stopped. I had no desire to brave the mosquitoes again, so started calling him: *Timo, Timo, Timo* ... well, you get the picture. I called and called and called. Finally, Jaime from the next hammock over told me to save my breath, that Timoteo was making so much noise on his own that he could not hear me calling him above his own snores. Finally, the long night was over. The rise and fall of the Roman empire was hardly as long.

We had a good meeting with everyone, and from their questions and comments, it was obvious the people had been given lots to think about. We brought three guys home with us, as they asked us for more teaching. We had special teaching sessions with them for a week and then took them home when we went back up to the same area for our next outreach trip.

During our one-week seminar, we had many of our villages' young guys sit in on the meetings, and one of them made a public profession of his faith in Christ's finished work. Another one of our young guys, who had lost a twelve-year-old daughter about six months ago, came forward to rededicate his life to Christ. He admitted that after his daughter died, he did not believe Jesus really loved him, because if He did love him, Jesus would have healed his daughter. I was able to share again with him the story of Mary and Martha and, yes, even my own story. With tears on both our parts, he was restored to his faith. The students we had here from other villages did really well and while they are going to continue to need teaching, at least they have the basics. Pray for the men who live in villages where witchcraft and demon worship are the norm.

Our next trip was a great trip. Up and back, we had no problems with the motor, which is always a real answer to prayer. I do have to put one qualifier on our great trip, though. We gave a new believer a ride back down to his own village, situated about four hours by our boat from the village where we had been teaching. The young man sat right behind me. We no sooner started out than he started singing his version of the songs he had just learned at the top of his lungs. I smiled at his extremely off-key rendition of the song. After one hour of the same song, I was no longer smiling. The four-hour trip until we dropped him off was about the longest four hours I have ever had, but he was still singing at the top of his lungs, just as off-key as when we started, and had the biggest smile on his face when we dropped him off.

On our next trip, the roof of the house we were in was broken and almost falling in. I was afraid the crazy thing was going to fall on us that night. It creaked and swayed every time someone moved in their hammock. Again, our equipment played flawlessly and attention was incredible. We probably had between sixty-five and seventy-five people present, and we talked and showed video until almost 1:30 a.m.—and I don't think anyone went home. The next morning, in our meeting before leaving, one of the witchdoctors told everyone that he knew what we were telling was true. "I have seen heaven. I have seen this place. I have seen God's light." I kept waiting for him to take it a step further and admit that he wanted the new life we were talking about, but he did not. After he sat down, I asked him if he might want to ask God for His salvation, but he did not wish to. I could not help but think about 2 Corinthians 4:3-4: *But if our gospel is veiled, it is veiled to those who are perishing, whose minds the god of this age has blinded, who do not believe, lest the light of the gospel of the glory of Christ, who is the image of God, should shine on them.*

On our way home, we stopped at a friend's village, where the witchdoctor's wife had personally invited us to come teach them. We agreed, not really thinking it was going to be that profitable of a trip as the witchdoctor was very opposed to the Gospel. When we got over there, we found out there had been four deaths right upriver from the village where we were going to be showing the video. All the people in those villages are related, as they used to be one village. When we heard about the deaths, we were sure the people would not want any visitors during this grieving time and would ask us to leave, but surprisingly, they welcomed us.

The entire village turned out to see the Jesus/Passion movie; sitting near the front (no chairs, just on the floor) was the witchdoctor! The movie is long, about three hours and forty minutes the way we do it, but not a single person left the house during the entire time. Then, at 8:00 in the morning, we met for a meeting and again, the old witchdoctor was there with his whole family. Our meeting went until a bit after 12 noon. Ten people got saved and I was shocked to see the witchdoctor get up.

Although he himself did not get saved, he did tell the whole village to make their own decisions. He told the villagers he would not fight the Gospel and asked the new believers to learn all they could so they could teach him. He ended by saying, "I really like what I hear. I want to know more. So, you new believers, don't just play at this but be serious!" I was gratified to see that one of the first people to get up and get saved was the witchdoctor's wife who had invited us!

We praise the Lord for this incredible time! After such a time, I hesitate to even mention the grief and misery that I endured. But I have to let you all know that somehow, I forgot my hammock bag! In it, of course, were my dry clothes, blanket, and mosquito net along with my hammock. I almost yielded to temptation and went home after the movie, but our talks way into the night are some of our most profitable, so, when the witchdoctor's son offered me his hammock, I took him up on it and he shared his wife's hammock. Not that I got much sleep with Timoteo snoring. But we all have our crosses to bear.

This next story is about our trip up the Padamo and Cutinamo Rivers to the village of Wasareco. We had been invited to their village to help them inaugurate their little church building. Knowing we were coming to show the Jesus movie, a guy with relatives in a faraway village went to tell his family about it. We arrived there about 4:30 p.m., just a short time after he got back. He had brought three people from his village, two young men and a young woman. All three accepted Christ as their personal Savior! The next day, they followed the Lord in believer's baptism along with five other new believers from Wasareco. No foreign missionaries had ever been to this very faraway, deep inland village. Pray for these new baby believers. Because I had a commitment to show the Jesus movie in another village on Monday night, I left at 3:00 p.m. and headed back downriver. Our team was in two boats, so some of them decided to stay up in the Wasareco area and continue teaching in other villages.

After I got back home, I updated my praise and prayer list with this comment: "Really good trip. Just a few thoughts tonight. Every time I do a trip up there, I have to say I respect my parents more and more. I can't imagine traveling up this terrible whitewater river with seven kids, the oldest being nine. Also, there really must be something to all this global warming stuff because the trails are now longer, the hills steeper and the boat heavier."

While visiting a distant village, I watched as four witchdoctors tried to cure a woman using their witchcraft. First, each one had an assistant blow repeated blasts of powdered drug up the witch-doctor's nose, one nostril at a time. The power of the drug was enough to cause the one getting the blast to grab the back of his head and scream. This was repeated until each of the witchdoc-tors had enough to push them from this world to some far-off place known only to the initiated. As they began to chant, first softly and then with more urgency, summoning the demons they wanted to help them, I was impressed again at how, as each witch-doctor began to channel a certain spirit, his moves, his features, and his actions took on the aspect of the spirit that had control of him at that time. It is uncanny and scary to watch such a person, knowing that he is no longer in control of his actions, but has given himself totally to this evil power.

How my heart was burdened as I realized again the depth of blindness that holds these people bondage to their rites of fear and hatred. Later, I had a chance to speak with two of the witch-doctors and shared with them the fact that there is a God who loves them and that even though we as humans fall way short, this God of love sent His only Son to us, and He became a Yano-mamö that He might make a way for them to His land. The only way to make this way was to take on our sin and bear the punish-ment for this sin: The Son of God had to die to secure our salva-tion! No other way was possible!

"The fact that you call God *Yai Wanonabälewä*, the Enemy God, is because there is enmity between God and Satan. God did all He could by taking sin and death and putting them over onto His own Son; but now, it is up to you to accept His gift or reject His gift," I told them. They listened intently, but I left their village burdened that my words had not penetrated the darkness that blinds their minds. Their darkness is so dark, their bondage so intense, that sometimes when you are face to face with such spiritual blindness it is easy to get the mistaken belief, or fear, that the Gospel is not powerful enough to cut through the impenetrable darkness.

Then, praise God, God's word comforts my heart with the precious verses found in Hebrews 2:14–15: *Forasmuch then as the children are partakers of flesh and blood, He also Himself likewise took part of the same; that through death He might destroy him that had the power of death, that is, the devil; And deliver them who through fear of death were all their lifetime subject to bondage.*

My sister Velma wrote this poem and I just love it.

> He thought he'd won
> the devil smiled
> And rubbed his hands with glee
> The maker of the world was dead
> Hanging on a tree.
> "The world is mine
> I own it now,
> I finally won," he cried.
> He didn't know he'd lost it all
> The day that Jesus died—
> Two days he smiled
> His heart was light
> Now man was his alone—
> Then words that echoed through the years,
> turned his heart to stone
> "For God so loved
> the world, He gave
> His only Son to die—
> But on the third day He would rise,
> give man eternal life."

That Sunday morn
He waited there
As darkness changed to light
Then terror seared his burning heart
And anguish filled his eyes ...
The empty tomb —
He's risen!
It can't be true," he cried.
He finally learned, he'd lost it all
The day that Jesus died ...

We had made a commitment to get to every village on the Ocamo, Orinoco, and Padamo Rivers to show the Jesus movie at least once. Shown together with the Passion, this is a very powerful tool. That's why we were heading off again to visit another village way up in the jungle. Wait a minute! I guess at almost 300 miles from town, I am already pretty far up into the jungle; nevertheless, these guys are even further up than we are.

The village we were going to was the village of Shashanawä. This has been a difficult village, as they have not only been resistant to spiritual truths, but they also have a deep hatred for people in our village. As a matter of fact, they killed a man from our village and his family killed someone from their village a few years ago, and things have been really strained since that time. While I was down in La Esmeralda, I saw the guys who had killed the man from this village, and started speaking with them about the Lord.

They invited me to their village to show the Jesus/Passion movie to them. We asked the Lord for prepared hearts and that our projectors and equipment would work well. Although we were invited, there must have been people in the village who did not want to reopen relations with our village, because they did not even acknowledge our presence. We were not fed, which is, cultur-ally, a real slap in the face. But as I told my companions, we did not go to eat, we went to feed.

We acted like there was nothing wrong, just set up our movie equipment and waited for night time. There was a huge crowd, so as soon as it was dark enough to start, we turned it on. I can't tell you how impressed I was with the equipment! It worked flawlessly! The movie is really long: it is most of the Jesus movie and about an hour of the Passion of the Christ. The two together are a powerful tool! Even though the projector only has a two-hour battery life, with the use of a small solar charger/inverter, it worked really well!

When the movie was over, the main guy who had invited us told us that he had too much on his mind to talk right then, but wanted to talk in the morning. We told him, "No problem." He was there first thing with another man who lives downriver from the village. We talked with them until they had to leave, and we left at the same time. I never did figure out why the village had treated us so strangely. I had been really careful who I brought with us so as not to jeopardize either the relationship or some-one's life, but as I said, they really treated us oddly.

Then, on the way home, while traveling down the Ocamo River, I had my headphones on, listening to the group, The 2nd Chapter of Acts, singing the song "Holy, Holy, Holy." I especially love the third verse: "Holy, Holy, Holy, though the darkness hide thee, though the eye of sinful man Thy glory may not see, Only Thou are holy, there is none beside Thee, Perfect in power, in love and purity ... ."

I had just finished listening to the song when we stopped at the village of Jishiyobä. I have a really good friend there, Antonio, who has, sadly, walked away from the Lord. We used to enjoy such a deep friendship and he went with me on so many missionary trips, but after losing his son to a horrible fire, he and his wife were never able to resolve their issues; they broke up, and he turned his back on the Lord and has not wanted to have any more to do with the Gospel or, for that matter, with us. Still, when possible, I always stop and visit with him as time permits. He was home, so after the usual gourd full of plantain drink, we visited for a bit.

An old man walked up and Antonio introduced him as his father, which means the man was Antonio's uncle. I know this because Antonio's father is dead. I started talking with the old man. He was from a faraway village and I had not met him before; as a matter of fact, the old guy had had very little contact with any missionary. But when I looked at his eyes, I saw he had the unmistakable look of a witchdoctor that displays his hatred and animosity toward us.

During the conversation I got around to telling this man about God and His love for him. The old guy's reaction stunned me, I guess mostly because the words he used were so much like the words from the third verse of "Holy, Holy, Holy." He said, "Oh, you are talking about the One who can't be seen!" I nodded my head. I stood there for a while longer talking to them and finally had to leave. As I walked back to the boat, I could not help but think about the words from Ecclesiastes 3:11 that say, *He has placed eternity in the hearts of man* .... The Yanomamö know so much about God, so much about His beautiful land, but so little about the true character and heart of God. So little, in fact, that they call Him the Enemy God. How sad!

I really enjoy our outreach trips to share the Gospel of Jesus Christ, but sometimes it also breaks my heart. In one of the villages, we had the Lord's Supper. Remember, these are very poor people and any kind of implements to use for drinking or anything else are in short supply. The church leaders decided to use just one cup for communion. This was not the first time I have done this, but in this particular village, there was so much tuberculosis (TB), I found myself trying to figure out a way to avoid drinking out of the common cup.

When I realized I could not come up with any reason that would not sound totally selfish, I found myself counting people ahead of me in the drinking line. I was number forty-seven! I then noticed that the guy giving the cup was almost always giving the same side toward the person drinking, so I decided I would turn the cup to drink out of a "clean" side when it was my turn. Then, at about number twenty, the cup started being turned! Anyway, the Lord rebuked me for worrying about something silly, so from then on, I just concentrated on the fact that Christ died for me and what an honor it was for me to be participating with these brothers and sisters in Christ.

A week or so later, four guys and I headed up to a village on the Ocamo River to show the Jesus/Passion movie. One of the guys with us was from that village, but had married into our village. He got saved in December and it was because of his witnessing over in his former village that we got an invitation to come and speak with them. Not too long ago, this was an enemy village, but God's Word continues to work in hearts.

We had a very receptive audience for the sharing and then showed the Jesus/Passion movie. Thereafter we spent some time answering questions (by that time, it was 11:00 p.m.). It was obvious God had in truth been preparing hearts. We then had to take the people home whom we had picked up from a village below the village where we were showing the video.

We motored up to another village and picked up some other people who had sent word they wanted to come to the meeting, so we collected them in the morning and returned, started our meeting at a bit before 8:00 a.m. and going on until past 11:00. As we began to conclude the meeting, and one of the witchdoctors stood up and told us he wanted to say something. You can't script these meetings and you just never know what's coming, so I was very pleasantly surprised when he asked us if he could talk to God himself. We assured him he could.

Well, his prayer was so beautiful! He confessed his sins to God and asked God to save him! He told God that he wanted to make sure that when it was his time to stand before Him, he wanted to make sure his name was written in His book! As you can imagine, this totally made our day! After he sat down, another man also stood up and publicly accepted Christ as his Savior.

After the last service, we moved on down to the river and the ten new believers followed the Lord in believer's baptism. The ex-witchdoctor from Jishiyobä gave a clear, beautiful testimony of his trust and faith in Christ. He asked us to remember to pray for him and the rest of the students. I assured him we would!

As we climbed back up their steep, muddy bank (almost a given at any Yanomamö village), I remembered how difficult it used to be climbing those banks with the huge carrying cases of the film projector, big generator, and speakers. As it was, I almost slipped back down with my tiny backpack carrying our current equipment, and I realized we had gotten the smaller stuff just in time. Good thing, too: I never could have made it up the bank now with the old equipment.

We showed the movies and then sat and talked far into the night. Looking at the seating facilities (a hard log) the next morning, I hoped our meeting would not go long, but after a few hours, I could see the handwriting on the wall and just got back into my hammock. (Then the problem became staying awake!) Listening to the little band of believers in this village sharing, how in spite of much difficulty they encounter, they continue to live for the Lord, so we were greatly encouraged. I wish I could end the story here, as that was the highlight of the trip, but working with the Yanomamö is always like walking a tightrope in an ice storm and today seemed like it might be one of those days.

We said our goodbyes, walked back down, and took our places in the boat. We had had too many people for my speedboat, so we were in a long, large canoe with a 50-hp outboard engine on it. Our boat driver was not at his place back by the motor, so we sat waiting for him to come down. All of a sudden, along came a crying, almost naked young lady, carrying a baby; without a word to anyone, she jumped into our boat and sat down staring at the floor, crying her eyes out.

I recognized her as a girl from our village who had married the son of Wabucosiliwä, the headman of Tumba. Soon, an older lady and the headman of the village came down, and from the agitated way they were flying down the bank, I figured they might be our side show if they slipped and fell the rest of the way down; however, they made their way down without slipping or falling.

They launched a tirade at the young lady in our boat. She was married to their son and they wanted her to stay. According to one of the bystanders, the husband beat her all the time and because two of the guys in our team were part of her family, she had taken this occasion to try and return home. It was true: she had scars from machete cuts on her back and arms, and many bruises. We did our best to mediate the whole thing, but the two parties were worlds apart. The man and his wife wanted the girl to get out of the boat and she had no intention of doing so.

This went on for about an hour, with all of us trying to figure out a way past the stalemate. By this time, the mother-in-law had jerked the baby out of the girl's arms, declaring that they were keeping the baby.

Everyone was looking at me, because it was my boat and I was kind of the leader of our little expedition. "No, you don't," I told them. "There is just no way in the world I am going to force that girl out of the boat. She won't listen to any of us. The only way anyone is getting her out of this boat is to pick her up and throw her in the river, but I am not going to do that. I couldn't! Besides, I would have no idea of how to grab a naked lady! Sorry, find your own solution." Well, I no sooner said that than I realized I really did not want them finding their own answers, as their solutions normally involve massive amounts of blood, stitches, and penicillin shots.

We could have sat there all day and not found a solution, so finally, in exasperation, I said to Wabucosiliwä, "My friend, your daughter-in-law won't leave the boat. Let her just go on home with us, then send your son over and they can figure out what to do over there. I will give him the fuel to return."

He shook his head in an emphatic no! Thus, we were basically back to everyone looking at me again. Not really knowing what else to do, I said, half in bluff, again speaking to Wabucosiliwä, "Well, this boat is leaving, so if you and your wife want to come with us, stay in the boat. If not, you all had better get out, as we have to leave now."

Rafael started the motor. Assuming that we were serious, and not realizing that I was bluffing, they hurriedly got off the boat — and we left. Due to the fact that in our team, we had two guys related to Wabucosiliwä, and two guys related to the girl, including her brother, I didn't think the matter was going to go anywhere,

Lord willing. We seek to be testimonies and shining lights to the villages we go to, so getting involved in a family squabble was not our intention, but what can you do?

20
KEILA'S PATH TO CITIZENSHIP

I have always said that Keila is bilingual. She speaks English better than I do and, well, Spanish is her native tongue. But after trying to get some help translating something one morning I realized—after twenty-four years—that I have been wrong. She is not bilingual, she is a perfect monolingual in two languages.

❖ ▣ ❖ ▣ ❖

In 1994, I married Keila Cornieles. She had a student visa to study in the USA, but once we returned to Venezuela, we went to the U.S. embassy and they granted her a multiple-entry tourist visa which had no expiration date. This worked great until 2001, after the attack on the Twin Towers. After that happened, on our next trip to the United States, the immigration officer drew a line through the word *indefinite* and wrote in an expiration date six months in the future. This was only the beginning of the troubles that were to befall us.

❖ ▣ ❖ ▣ ❖

Sunday, July 7, 2013
We got up early to head down to La Esmeralda to catch a plane out to town. From there, we are headed to Caracas on the 11th and the U.S. on the 12th. We sure are looking forward to seeing grandkids and kids again! We are also looking forward to representing our mission at the Experimental Aircraft Association, EAA, in Oshkosh, WI, which we have done ever since we have had to return to the United States every year for Keila's paperwork.

Thursday, July 11, 2013
We made it to Caracas fine today and are heading to the airport at 5:00 a.m. tomorrow for our flight to the U.S.

Friday, July 12, 2013
Bad news from here. Mia is a dual national, and her U.S. passport had just expired. We checked with the travel agent, and also drew on my own experience: as long as the passport of the country we are leaving from is current, there was never an issue. Well, today there was a *huge* issue. The airline explained that it was not their ruling, but rather was some directive from the Department of Homeland Security. They did tell us that if we could get a temporary passport, they would not charge us for a ticket change. We took off for the U.S. embassy up in Caracas.

Security did not want to allow Keila to enter. We had a hard time talking her through, but we finally made it through security and went into the section called American Citizen Services, where I explained what we needed. They were not in the least sympathetic. "It is the responsibility of each traveler to have their paperwork up to date, and"—I could see it in the person's eyes—"your lack of planning does not constitute an emergency on our part ... blah blah blah." I was finally directed to the person who might issue an emergency passport and started explaining what had happened. My heart dropped when she opened her mouth, as I could not understand a single word she was trying to say in English. I told her I spoke Spanish and would be happy to use that language if that would be easier for her. I only offended her more.

She handed me some forms and told me the fastest they could get me a passport was ten days to two weeks. I again tried to explain that we lived way up in the jungle, but she cut me off, saying that nothing I had told her constituted an emergency. I asked to speak to her supervisor and she told me no. Then I asked if I could at least speak to someone who spoke English as a first language. Pulling herself up to her just over five-foot height, she told me, "Sir, I am a fully accredited member of the U.S. diplomatic staff." At least that is what I thought she was trying to say. She never would speak to me in Spanish.

Anyway, to make a long story short, we were stuck there for ten days minimum, and never did get to speak to a supervisor. Really huge bummer! Mia was furious and finally told the lady, "I am the only U.S.-born national here, and the U.S. won't let me enter my own country!"... didn't even faze the lady a bit. I know, I know: "in all things give thanks." I wonder if the apostle Paul had to deal with bureaucrats? (I almost deleted this sentence, because one has only to think about how much time poor Paul spent in jail to know that he surely did.)

Sunday, July 14, 2013
Due to the high cost of staying in the capital city, we are going to try and fly back to Puerto Ayacucho today. We are heading to the airport to see if we can get on the flight. Thanks to the many who have sent words of encouragement!

Back from the airport: We could not get on. The flight was scheduled to leave at 2:30 p.m. We arrived at the airport and were standing in line at 11:14 a.m. Keila waited in the check-in line while I got in line to purchase the tickets, and Mia was back and forth updating us on the other's progress.

At 11:40 I arrived at the head of my line and the lady told me there were still seats available, but until the office released the waiting list, they could not sell them.

At 11:45 I ran and got in the other line with Keila. At 12:00, the ticket-counter lady told us to get the tickets from the first lady.

At 12:03, I was back in my first line.

At 12:33, I got up to the counter and was told that the tickets would not be released until 1:00 p.m. We huddled to see what our course of action should be. Having just come from the jungle, we could not resist the siren call of a nearby Subway.

At 1:03 p.m., I was back in line yet again to purchase the tickets. I was getting tired, but at least I wasn't hungry. Keila was back in the check-out counter line.

At 1:25 p.m., I was told once again that the tickets had not been released yet. I ran back to the line where Keila and Mia were still waiting. Mia had made friends with two little girls and two puppies.

At 1:45 p.m., we got up to the counter. The very unfriendly lady informed us that they were not going to use the waiting list, as the baggage handlers were having to handle the baggage by hand and were tired.

At 1:50 p.m., I spoke with a supervisor and told our same story.

At 2:00 p.m., Keila spoke with one supervisor and then found another one, but it was the same story. We waited, praying for a miracle.

At 2:20 p.m. they called the flight, so we gave up in defeat and decided to try again the next day.

Tuesday, July 16, 2013
What a difference twenty-four hours makes! It seemed like a totally different airport. We were through the check-in line in less than fifteen minutes. We had a nice flight to Puerto Ayacucho and planned to remain there until we hear the passport is at the U.S. embassy.

One would think that after all the carnivorous bugs and whatnot we have to put up with in the jungle, we could just relax and take it easy while out in the city. *Wrong!* I reached in without looking, grabbed a pair of underwear, and slipped into them quickly. I was in a hurry, so, picking up my jeans, I began to put them on when all of a sudden I realized there was trouble! Bad trouble. My pants—actually, my underpants—were afire! Mercy! I could not shed those things fast enough! I was covered with red fire ants that had somehow taken up residence in my clothes drawer, and they were just a-biting and a-clawing—well, actually stinging!

The way my wife was slapping her leg and roaring with laughter made me think she must have been at least an accomplice in, and maybe even a facilitator of, this whole macabre affair, but she swore she was innocent and the only reason she was laughing was that she had never seen anyone get shed of clothes that fast. Well, I guess I had busted some moves that are not normally ascribed to one of my age and girth, and I assume it might be comical to someone with a warped sense of humor, so ... well, I guess I believe her. But the whole incident left me with a bad taste in my mouth—not to mention the fact that I look awfully silly forking my underwear out of the clothes drawer with a long pole!

Tuesday, July 16, 2013
I love this song (sung by Andre Crouch), though I'm not totally sure I can really sing it yet. I do love trusting God and think I do ... but I'm not sure I really thank Him for the valleys. Still working on it!

> I thank God for the mountains, and I thank Him for the valleys,
> I thank Him for the storms He's brought me through,
> For if I'd never had a problem I wouldn't know that He could solve them,

I wouldn't know what faith in God can do.

Through it all, through it all, I've learned to trust in Jesus, I've learned to trust in God,

Through it all, through it all, I've learned to depend upon His Word.

("Through It All," by Darrell R. Brown & Dennis Matkosky)

Friday, July 19, 2013

Here I sit, still fretting about a stupid passport. Shame on me! My Bible reading today was on Matthew 10:28–31. So, I think I am going to go sit in the yard and watch the birds today.

Matthew 10:28–31: *Don't be afraid of those who want to kill your body; they cannot touch your soul. Fear only God, who can destroy both soul and body in hell. What is the price of two sparrows — one copper coin? But not a single sparrow can fall to the ground without your Father knowing it. And the very hairs on your head are all numbered. So don't be afraid; you are more valuable to God than a whole flock of sparrows.*

Well, I found out the birds have their moments as well. I was watching this small flock of very small birds — they were about two inches long — but there were about twenty or thirty in the grass eating seeds when I went out there to relax, watch, and learn. I was watching this one little one that had walked up onto the cement patio. There was a broken piece of coconut shell on the patio and the way it was lying, the wind was causing it to dip and kind of roll back and forth. Well, this little bird kept feeding closer and closer and its little back was to the shell. All of a sudden, the wind caught the shell just right and it rolled down and pressed the little bird to its tiny knees. Tiny it might have been, but it was feisty! It got up and beat the stuffing out of that coconut shell, and then stalked off with such an expression on its little face that I could almost hear it saying: "Mess with me, will ya?" On second thought, it was probably a her.

Saturday, July 20, 2013

We received word that Mia's passport was at the U.S. embassy in Caracas. We were trying to get on the flight the next day to get up there so we could pick it up on Monday. We were praying that we wouldn't lose our Delta tickets. Our travel agent said that as soon as we had passports in hand, he would try to reschedule us, and that because this whole mix-up was due to a new regulation, he felt all we would have to pay would be a change fee. Now, sometimes that can be substantial enough, especially since July is a heavy travel time.

Sunday, July 21, 2013

In order to have any kind of a chance of getting to the United States this week, we had to get to Caracas by Sunday to pick the passport up on Monday. We arrived almost three hours early, at 8:00 a.m., as I did not want there to be any doubt about our tickets. So many times down here, it seems reservations don't carry a lot of weight, so I wanted to make sure we were pretty much first in line. When we walked into the airport, I rubbed my hand in passing on a door that had some grease on it. There is never any water in the bathrooms, so I don't even know what I was thinking in heading to the bathroom ... but there I went. Wonder of wonders, there was actually a spigot with water running out of it! Hey, we take nothing for granted down here! I was very pleasantly surprised, and even said a silent but heartfelt "Thank you." I even remember thinking, *Well, it is going to be a good day today! Starting well!*

By 4:00 p.m., though, I was starting to rethink that. The plane still had not arrived. "At least they have not canceled it yet," I told Keila. "I sure would hate to have to go by bus!" Just about that time, I overheard one passenger telling a group of other passengers that the flight had returned to Caracas with mechanical problems and our flight had been canceled. Keila and I bowed our heads and asked God to somehow work out the details. I walked down to ask for myself and was told that it was too early to tell for sure, no one really knew what was going on. Finally, at 5:35 p.m. we were told the plane had left Caracas again. To make a long story short, we finally made it to the apartment in Catia about 9:00 p.m.! Whew, what a long day. The embassy opens at 8:30 a.m. and we hope to be there at that time to pick the passport up and head right on over to the travel agent's office.

Monday, July 22, 2013

We have Mia's United States passport in hand! Remember yesterday, while at the Puerto Ayacucho airport, when I had gone in to wash my hands and there was actually water coming out of the spigot? As this occurrence was so rare as to suggest divine intervention, I took it as a sign that the day was going to go well. Little did I know! I'll admit, at 4:00 p.m. when it was announced that our flight had returned to Caracas and was canceled, I wondered what had happened to my sign that it was going to be a good day.

Remember, I said that after we prayed about the situation to ask God for guidance, and while we were still sitting there trying to decide what our options were, they suddenly announced that the flight was back on! It did finally arrive a few minutes before 6:00 p.m. We boarded and in spite of other delays with waiting for a gate, and so on, we made it to Caracas, tired but very happy to have arrived. Little did we know the magnitude of the miracle that God had done for us! Here is the rest of the story.

On Monday morning, it was announced on the news that the Puerto Ayacucho airport would be closed to normal traffic for the next three days, as the Venezuelan president and the president of Colombia were holding a series of meetings there. Then, while we were at the embassy, I noticed a sign saying that the U.S. embassy was going to be closed both Wednesday and Thursday. So, all of a sudden, the significance of that flight being rescheduled loomed large! If we had not been able to collect Mia's passport today, we would not have been able to pick it up at the embassy until Friday!

Tuesday, July 23, 2013

We have tickets in hand for tomorrow's flight! Thanks also to Delta Airlines! They could have taken us to the cleaners, but only charged us a modest change fee!

Wednesday, July 24, 2013

Made it to the USA, though not without some tense moments! What is happening? Why the extra scrutiny? This trip was a paperwork nightmare. Now the problem is with Keila's green card. For a while there, I did not think they were going to let her into the USA! They put her passport and her green card in an envelope and had a gentleman lead her to a different room where her paperwork was given much additional perusal.

When she was finally called to the counter, they would not let me go with her. Sad to say, our U.S. immigration bureaucrats are as rude as their counterparts in the U.S. embassy in Venezuela. I could hear everything they were saying, although we were separated by a wide hallway and a number of rows of seats. I could hear them telling Keila that they could take her card away. At various times, it seemed like they were tag-teaming her, as there were two agents against my poor, very nervous *legal* alien wife.

I heard one of the ladies tell Keila that she was supposed to have a permit to be out of the USA on a resident visa, but Keila did have a printout from the U.S. government's website where it states that "If you are going to be outside of the USA for longer than a year you need to file a certain form to facilitate your return." So every time we have traveled, I have always gone to their website and printed off this sheet to make sure we have the most up-to-date ruling. Since Keila has had her resident visa, we have never stayed out longer than a year. As a matter of fact, this time we were returning just under eleven months from the date of our departure last year.

Although the lady accepted the printout with a frown, her counterpart lit in with: "You are just abusing this card! You are using it like a tourist visa. Resident means you live here! Remember, we can take this card away at any time. This card is not a right!"

I sat there frowning, trying to remember to pray. I could not help but think and wish that they would have allowed me up there to help Keila, because my first question to them would have been, "Pardon me, but doesn't it seem funny that with all this talk of legalizing twelve million ILLEGAL aliens, don't you think it is a bit crazy to be harassing your LEGAL immigrants?"

Romans 8:28 says all things work together for good, so why does it always take me by surprise? I posted on my Facebook page about our immigration problems, mentioning how this really looked like the last time we could use Keila's green card.

A good friend from Virginia, David Dingman, wrote me asking if we wanted help. He explained that his brother, Dick, was good friends with Congressman Frank Wolf, the congressman from our district, and that David would speak to Mr. Wolf if we wanted him to. Wow! Did we want him to? I should say we did!

Of course, here is where everything started working together for good. Looking back, we could see the clear hand of God guiding us so that we would get back at just that time, because my friend's brother was able to help us. We found out about a little-known provision stating that we did not have to have ten years in the United States, as we had thought, in order to apply for citizenship: We could apply right away! So we got busy. Everything worked out so that the time we started the application for citizenship to the day Keila was sworn in as a U.S. citizen was only a short three months!

Thursday, September 5, 2013
We were overnighting in Aldie, Virginia, and were heading in first thing in the morning for Keila's meeting regarding her U.S. immigration status. Serious prayers on our behalf were much appreciated! To be honest, when I hear songs like, "Got any rivers you think are uncrossable, Got and mountains you can't tunnel through," the first thing that comes to my mind is government paperwork. Praise God that the song does not end there, but goes on to say that "God specializes in things thought impossible and He can do what no other power can do."

I have always thought I was of at least average intelligence, but these forms we had to fill out for Keila just about beat me up! Mercy! We worked until 11:00 p.m. last night, and have been at it since 8:00 this morning, but there's no end in sight.

Tuesday, September 10, 2013
OK, we finally got all the dates figured out, and today we are getting all the necessary documentation together. Many of the documents have to be translated; others we are going to have scanned and sent out from Venezuela.

Wednesday, September 11, 2013
Finally finished! Mailing the package tomorrow. Pray for favor! Thanks.

Thursday, September 12, 2013
Keila's documents are in the mail!

October 3, 2013
We have been notified that Keila's first appointment with immigration officials has been granted for the 16th of October!

This was one more instance where Congressman Wolf's office really came through for us. Normally it takes months to get this first appointment.

October 16, 2013
We headed over to Alexandria, Virginia, for Keila's appointment with Immigration. As soon as she finishes there, we will resume our trip to South Carolina, Savannah, Georgia, and Florida. One of the best perks of being a missionary is all the fantastic people we have as our friends and teammates in this great job! God has so blessed us!

October 16, 2013
Keila's appointment went well; they said they would mail a letter telling her when her next one would be. This one was for finger-printing and picture-taking. We made it as far as Florence, South Carolina. We would have made it all the way to our destination, but we spent four hours stuck in D.C. traffic: it looked like two semis had overturned.

November 11, 2013
On this day I was on the phone with Delta changing our tickets. The bad thing was, we didn't even know how to reschedule because we couldn't know what would happen after Keila's next appointment nor how long that process might take. Realistically, Delta has every right to just cancel our tickets, but I am asking God to grant us favor. By the way, Keila's next appointment was scheduled for the tenth of December. We just received the notification letter.

December 10, 2013
After church on Sunday, we made a mad dash from Wauconda, Illinois (north of Chicago) to Front Royal, Virginia, so we could

be on time for Keila's appointment today. We dashed through some brutal weather, I might add. Then we found out that her appointment had been canceled due to a heavy snowfall in the D.C. area closing the federal government, so here we sit.

It is easy for me to get and stay disappointed, but God's timing is perfect and we know it. A friend sent me this quote from Dietrich Bonhoeffer; it is very timely: "Celebrating Advent means being able to wait. Waiting is an art that our impatient age has forgotten. It wants to break open the ripe fruit when it has hardly finished planting the shoot. But all too often the greedy eyes are only deceived; the fruit that seemed so precious is still green on the inside, and disrespectful hands ungratefully toss aside what has so disappointed them. Whoever does not know the austere blessedness of waiting[— that is, of hopefully doing without—] will never experience the full blessing of fulfillment." My friend then closed his note to me with these beautiful words: "Rejoicing in Jesus who came in the fullness of time." I can only say, "Amen!"

December 11, 2013
Take a few minutes and think on this verse, which truly blows my mind! "Then those who feared the Lord talked with each other, and the Lord listened and heard. A scroll of remembrance was written in His presence concerning those who feared the Lord and honored His name."

December 12, 2013
God is good! Not that we needed this as proof, but rejoice with us: Keila's appointment was rescheduled for December 16, 2013, at 8:30 a.m.! Normally, it takes weeks to reschedule anything like this! What a huge blessing Congressman Frank Wolf and his office have been! Thank you, David and Dick Dingman, for making this possible!

December 16, 2013

Keila, Mia, and I appeared at the immigration office bright and early on December 16th, as Keila was to take the test for citizenship. I was so proud of Keila: She studied hard and passed her test with flying colors! We then waited until everyone else had finished their tests and then all met in a room to participate in the swearing-in ceremony and the pledge to the flag.

Congressman Wolf's office had told us to call them as soon as Keila finished the swearing-in ceremony. We did so, and they urged us to head to the D.C. passport office immediately to apply for Keila's U.S. passport. I don't remember the exact time, although it was already past noon, but the congressman's staffer assured us that they had called the passport office and we could go right in. We rushed over to the D.C. transit system and before we knew it, we were at the stop nearest the D.C. passport office. We jumped off and raced over to the building. I had been given an office number, so once we walked in, I asked a person there where that office was. They told me to go back outside and go in a side door.

Wondering what this meant, we followed the directions and found the office. It was a small private passport office with room for about twenty people. The guard at the door almost didn't let us in, but I had a card from Congressman Wolf's office and they motioned us in, and told us to present our documents to the lady and take a seat. Before we even had a chance to get comfortable in the nicer-than-average office chairs, Keila was called up. The very nice people took her information and before we knew it, we were leaving the office with a promise that her new U.S. passport would be mailed to her no later than two business days! Can you believe that? Wow!

Thinking back on this entire process, we can see that none of it would ever have happened without God directing us to David and Dick Dingman and Dick's congressman friend being willing to help us. If the immigration people in Atlanta had not given Keila a hard time about her green card, we would never have attempted to get her U.S. citizenship. God's timing is perfect. What an awesome God we serve!

Another point which showed us that this was totally God's timing was that Frank Wolf, the congressman who had been such a great help, and whose office had streamlined so much for us, retired that same year. This had been our one window to access his help. His good friend Dick, my friend's brother, was sick. We did not know it at the time, but shortly after he put us in touch with Congressman Wolf, Dick was promoted to glory. So, looking back, we can see that God was obviously leading and directing and controlling every aspect of this entire affair, from start to finish. Now, how we praise Him for allowing those immigration people in Atlanta to harass Keila about her green card. If they had not done so, we would have been comfortable continuing to just keep going back and forth using that card. But they gave Keila such a hard time that we got shook up, so God's people stepped up, and now Keila is a United States citizen! Praise the Lord with us!

21

A Tale of Two Shamans and an Argument for Eternal Security

One day I found myself lost in the Amazon jungle with a Yano-mamö friend. Funny thing is, you can be lost, but until you are convinced in your own mind that you really are lost, no one can help you. Here is what happened with us.

◈ ▣ ◈ ▣ ◈

We had started out on a spider monkey hunt and were quite successful, but because my wife refuses to touch monkey meat, I wanted to get a turkey or something else for us. The only guy in our group who was not carrying a heavy burden of monkey meat was Lucas, so he and I left the main group and continued hunting. A huge storm came up, with lightning flashing, thunder crashing, rain pouring, and the wind blowing so hard branches and trees were falling around us. The pelting rain obscured the sky to the point that even at 11:00 a.m. the jungle took on an almost twilight hue. Most Yanomamö guys stop and wait out a rain, but by this time, we realized we had gone further than we should have, so we continued walking, wanting to get back to our main group. Finally, a huge branch fell, narrowly missing us, so we stopped beside an enormous tree — a true giant of the rainforest. As I stood beside the gigantic buttressing roots, I could not help but be awed by the sheer immensity of this jungle behemoth.

The wind finally died down, so we continued on our way, even though it was still raining and the jungle was shrouded by mist rising from the damp leaves, further darkening the dreary day. Something felt wrong to me with the direction Lucas was going.

I called it to his attention and he laughed at me. I frowned...
I had almost as much experience in the jungle as he did, and it
just felt wrong, but who was I to argue with a Yanomamö man
in the jungle?

About an hour later, perhaps a bit longer, we once again came up
to a jungle giant. I looked at it in interest, as I had spent enough
time beside the other tree to have almost established a relationship with it, when suddenly I realized it was the same tree. "Lucas!
We are going in circles. I told you, you were lost!"

In spite of the fact I hated to be lost, I was almost happy to have
this proof of my own ability in the jungle verified. "How do you
know?" Lucas asked me.

"See that tree, that is where we took shelter," I told him. He
looked where I was pointing and nodded his head. My joy at
being proved right was short-lived, though, banished by a rather
pressing question: Now what do we do?

Lucas quickly looked around. "Let's head that direction to higher
ground," he said, pointing. "I will climb a tree and see if I can
find the river."

We went that way, and once we were at the top of a hill, he
selected a tree and began to climb. Passing through the second
and into the third canopy of the rain forest, he disappeared from
sight, then at last came sliding back down. "I could not see the
river, but the land generally slopes downhill that way, the river
must be that way," he said.

We took off running. About an hour later, we suddenly came to
a place where we could see the tracks of what looked like two
guys running. At first we thought they were tracks left by other
members of our hunting party, and were happy to see they had

been made since the hard rain. We started following the tracks, but suddenly both came to the same realization that we were following our *own* tracks. We were going in circles again!

Then, off in the distance I heard an airplane flying toward us. Now, back in that day and time, missionary aviation had the only airplanes flying in the jungle, and I knew the schedule for that day! "Listen," I told Lucas, "let's get a bearing on where that airplane is coming from, because I heard last night on the radio that it was flying to TamaTama and then on to Parima; then this afternoon, it is flying back to TamaTama, so that airplane crosses the river right below where we parked our boat. All we have to do is head in the direction it is coming from and it will take us back out to the river. Let's hurry before it gets dark!"

We took off running: now, with the sure confidence that we knew where we were going, we really ran like crazy, thinking we could at least make it out to the river before nightfall. Well, it did get dark and we did not find the river. We took stock of what we had ... which did not take long, as we had nothing. No machete or even a knife, no food, no matches, no flashlight, nothing. Life was bleak. In my book, *Growing Up Yanomamö*, I wrote about this trip, the mosquitoes, the jaguar, and even possibly an angel feeding me that night, but the point I wish to make now is about something that happened the next morning.

The sun came up. It sounds simple, but you know, the sun is an absolute. In our jungle, located 3 degrees° north of the equator like we are, the sun rises in the east. You can take that to the bank. It always rises in the east. Using the sun as our compass, we walked out to the river. What we found out after finally getting home concerned the airplane that I was so positive I knew was coming from a particular place and direction, so we could use it to find the river. Well, I had total faith in my knowledge: I knew we were running right because I knew the schedule — but what I did *not* know was that the same rain that had gotten us lost had also delayed the airplane. So, when I heard the plane and thought it was coming from Parima heading back to TamaTama, I was really hearing the delayed plane which was actually on its way *to* Parima, not *from* Parima. I was 180 degrees wrong!

Oh, I had faith! I knew I was right, but you know what? It did not change the fact that we were running in the absolute *wrong* direction. We would never have gotten out of the jungle in the direction we were running. From that incident, I learned that what you believe is not worth anything if what you believe in is wrong. In life, we have to have absolutes. Just as the sun rising in the East gave us an absolute, God's Word is an absolute for our lives today. We can choose to run our own way, but it does not change the absolute of God's Word. There is a right and many wrongs. I think, way down deep, we all know it.

❖ ▣ ❖ ▣ ❖

Since that time of being physically lost in the jungle, I have had a greater sense of urgency when it comes to people whom I know are spiritually lost. They can be just as hard to convince — or even harder to convince — that they are lost as my friend Lucas was in the jungle there beside Tigre Mountain. Take, for example, old Justo. Dad and Mom met Justo back in or around 1954 and developed a real friendship with him. No one knew his age, as the Yanomamö don't keep track of their ages (it's hard to do when your counting system only goes to one, two and many), but Dad always figured that he and Justo were about the same age. Although he would always listen to Dad talk about *Yai Bada* and His Son Who had made a way to His land, Justo was more interested in the *jecula* he had and how to control and get more. So, while their friendship was real, Justo stayed in his "spiritual camp" and there was nothing Dad could do to convince him that he was lost.

I remember the last time I saw Justo alive. He was excited and animated as he motioned my boat over to stop at his village on the Ocamo River. "I've got Jesus!" the old witchdoctor beamed proudly. It's funny how memories can take you back years as if it were just a minute ago. In my mind's eye I can still see his gleaming eyes and broad smile as old Justo repeated himself: "Maikiwä, I got Jesus!" But I could also see the aftereffects of the drugs dripping from his nasal passages (never a pretty sight!).

Here is what brought the memories back. One evening, over coffee with Mom, Faith, Sharon, Keila, and myself, we were talking about near-death experiences we have heard discussed by different Yanomamö friends. From there, we started reminiscing about old friends who are no longer with us. These stories went on until Sharon mentioned old Justo.

As if it were yesterday, I remembered a meeting where the old witchdoctor Justo sat on the bench in our old mud-and-palm church beside me, while Yanomamö believers shared their faith in Christ. I could see he was under a lot of conviction. Also noticing his conviction, Gary moved over on the bench and sat down on the other side of the old guy. "*Shoabe* (Uncle), what do you think? Isn't it time you gave your heart to Jesus?" he whispered. "You have fought Him for a long time. I can see God's Spirit is calling you."

Old Justo nodded in agreement, but then slowly shook his head no.

"No, I can't." He shook his head harder as if his resolve had firmed up. "I can't! They are begging me not to," he mumbled. He turned his head and lowered his eyes. We sat there in silence until the meeting was over.

The next morning, we were disappointed to hear that Justo was leaving. Gary and I walked over to the port where he was getting ready to get in his boat and shove off. "We are disappointed you are leaving, *Shoabe*," Gary told him. "Why are you leaving early?"

"I could not stay any longer," the old guy told us. "My *jecula* were up all night long, crying and begging me not to throw them away..." His voice trailed off. Nothing we could say could convince him not to go. We sadly watched the canoe move out of sight.

A number of years later, I was over in the Ocamo area and Justo met me at the port, all smiles. "I've got Jesus! I've got Jesus now!" He beamed proudly. I was so happy for him and wanted to know details.

"Tell me what happened. I am so happy for you," I told him. "Tell me everything!"

"I was in the jungle and was thinking about all you all had told me about Jesus. Suddenly, I saw a bright light. So bright it hurt my eyes, but as I looked, a tall figure was standing there. 'I am Jesus. I have come to you,' He told me. I am so happy now."

I am not sure why, but something about the story bothered me. Maybe it was the fact that it was obvious he was just off a drug trip: the effects were still dripping from his nose. Witchdoctors have a way about them, and I could still sense something. I was not sure what, but I was uncomfortable with what I had heard. I continued to press him.

"*Shoabe*, what happened to your *jecula*?" I asked him.

"Oh," he beamed, "they are so happy too. They are just all squeezed into my heart together and Jesus has a place of prominence with them. They really like Him." I stared at Justo, and slowly shook my head.

"No, Uncle, Jesus would never share your chest with your *jecula*. They would never be able to stand the righteousness of God's Son that close. Jesus would never share a home with *jecula* that were kicked out of heaven." We continued talking for a while, but I never could convince him that he was only being deceived by a spirit masquerading as an angel of light.

How sad we were when, only a few short months later, we heard that Justo had died. How many opportunities he had turned down! Mom mentioned that, as one of the first Yanomamö they had met, Dad had spent hours patiently explaining the Gospel to him and yet, though intrigued with the power he knew *Yai Bada* had, Justo was never willing to give up the power he had in the spirit world in the here-and-now to yield his life to Jesus. He was willing to accept the counterfeit and died still deceived by the master deceiver. So sad that eternity is so long!

We have found, in working with the Yanomamö, that the norm is guys like Justo. We have lost the fight for their souls so many times that it is hard not to get discouraged, but then the times we win makes up for all the times we lost. Case in point is my good friend Carlos. Carlos is from the village of Seducudawä. He paddled down to bring his wife to the medical dispensary, as she had been stung on the foot by a large stingray and was in a lot of pain. Carlos had, at one time, been one of our most promising believers in Seducudawä, and was a big witness for the Lord there. His grandfather, uncle, and younger brother were all powerful witchdoctors, but we had believed the power of Christ had allowed Carlos to break the cycle.

A number of years ago, though, he had an affair and later on divorced his wife and married the other woman, and since that time has not wanted much to do with us. Then, about four years ago, he almost died of malaria, but slowly recovered. After his recovery, he attended one of our seminars and publicly made things right with the Lord and the church here—but for some reason, as soon as he returned to Seducudawä he fell off the deep end again. The next thing we knew, everyone was saying he had become a witchdoctor. It is hard not to take these defeats personally and frankly, setbacks like this are always hard to take, so we were feeling very defeated as far as both Carlos and the work in Seducudawä was concerned.

That's why I was surprised when he came in the other day and sat down to talk with me. For the past three-plus years our relationship has been strained and cold; to be honest, he mostly has avoided us.

I invited him in and after some small talk I asked him how he was really doing. "Not good," he admitted. "I am not happy anymore."

"Yes, I heard you had now become a *shaboli* [witchdoctor]," I told him.

He shook his head no. "I tried," he admitted quietly, "but I just never could make it. After chanting all day and way into the night during my initiation, I was slumped over in a drug-induced stupor when I saw the *jecula* coming. I was surprised when they stopped a short distance away from me. I watched in fascination as they walked around me in a circle, looking at me intently. They kept pointing and talking among themselves. I finally began to pick up what they were talking about. 'The Light is still there. We can't get any closer,' I heard one of them tell the others.

"The next day I chanted and chanted the chants the *jecula* had taught me to make the Light go out. Again, that night, the *jecula* came close, but they kept telling me I had to get rid of the Light before they could come in. I told the *shabolis* who were instructing me what the demons were saying and how they always stopped before coming into me. With their help, I made my heart as dark as I could, I took dope almost nonstop, I chanted all night long, but every time the spirits approached me, they would stop before they were too close, I would hear them talk about the small little Light in my heart, that it was still shining and would neither go out nor go away. I did all I could do, but the spirits finally even just quit coming. So, to answer your question, I am not a witch-doctor but I did try."

"Who do you think the Light was?" I asked him.

"I know it is God's Spirit. In spite of all I have done, He has never left me, so the *jecula* would not come. My heart is so heavy, but I just don't know what I can do."

"God's Word says if we confess our sins, He is faithful to forgive us our sins," I told him.

"Pray for me," he said. "I need to take my wife home, but I will come back and talk some more soon."

I posted this story about my good friend Carlos on Facebook back in 2009. Since I posted it, I have wondered at the truth of what he told me. There was no evidence of the Holy Spirit working in his life at all, and I was worried that he might only be deceiving himself. Then, during Easter 2018, in the middle of our Easter-week services, Carlos came down for the services. I was honestly surprised to see him get out of the boat I had sent up to get Danni, another good friend up there (whom we had sent out to Puerto Ayacucho sick and the doctors sent him home to die, but I am getting off subject).

The meetings are only supposed to go until noon, but in reality they have not let out until around 2:30 p.m. every day since we started. Today was no different. The entire congregation moves on down to our outdoor cookhouse and when all the meat has been eaten, the church provides yucuta, a drink made out of either casava bread or mañoco (both of which are made out of the yucca root). After most people leave, the church leadership sits around and I bring out our big coffeepot and we enjoy a cup of coffee before heading home to rest before the evening movie. We have three movies translated into Yanomamö: *God's Story: From Creation to Eternity*, the Jesus movie, and the Passion of the Christ.

Getting back to Carlos, as I said, I was surprised to see him down for Easter services and even more surprised to see him still sitting around relaxing with all of us. Since I spoke to him back in 2009, it was as if he was nervous about all he had told me. He had continued doing witchcraft and taking drugs and sure seemed sincere about everything he was doing, so I was left to wonder about that Light that he had told me his demons could see, and his claim that he had never really had the demons because they could not approach close enough due to that Light.

This time, he stood up and cleared his throat. "I wanted to tell you all that I have once again given my life to Jesu Christo," he began. "Many of you don't know it, but for weeks I lay near death. My son Lanzo had come up weeks ago and when he saw me so sick, he wept and told me to make sure my life was in order, as he felt I was going to die. I too felt the same. I was too weak to even make it out of my hammock to relieve myself. I could no longer stand up but could only crawl on the ground when there was no one around to help me. Then, a few days later, my wife left to go to the garden, leaving me alone in our house.

"I don't know if it was a dream based on my son telling me to return to the Lord so I would be ready to meet Him or what it was, but it was as if I heard a voice telling me to get ready. My days were running out. I thought back over my life. I remembered the joy I used to have as a child of God. I remembered my good friend Danni, we used to love sharing about God together. He is now dying but still follows the Lord. He is happy to enjoy the time he has left with his family and his God, while I am never happy any more.

"I was so sad to think of my wasted life. So many years I tried to live my own way; 'what a sad wasted life,' I told myself as tears ran down my face. Finally, I thought back about God and about the fact that God says if we repent He will forgive. I lay there in my hammock to weak to get out and started crying out to God. 'God,' I said, 'I want you to forgive me. I am sorry for my wasted life. I know my time is running out. I am sorry I have not served You. Now, if you give me more time here, if You heal me, I will serve You, but even if You don't lengthen my days here, that is fine. I want my last days here to be Yours.'

"Such a peace came into my heart. I could feel it warming my entire body. I fell asleep waiting for my wife to return, and when she dropped her big basket of firewood near our hearth, it woke me up. I realized I was hungry. I had not wanted to eat anything for days, but now I was suddenly hungry. After my wife gave me a bowl of *yucuta*, I slowly stood up and walked outside. Finishing, I walked back inside with my wife staring at me. Every day I am stronger. God healed me. Now, I truly want to live my life for Him. I want to publicly tell everyone that God healed me and I am once again right with Him. How thankful I am that God did not give up on me."

All I could say was WOW! We serve an awesome God!

Epilogue

The work and story continue. As I finish this manuscript, Venezuela is once again trying to throw off the yoke of a brutal dictatorship. We are bracing for a possible civil war, yet we are seeing God continuing to encourage and sustain us. Since the marches started, we moved our prayer time from 7:00 a.m. to 5:00 a.m. and we meet over there and beg God to have mercy and cause a godly man to become the leader of this once-great country. I smiled to myself as Jaime started his prayer this morning.

"Father God, it is me again. I woke up good again this morning and I say thank you for that. You know the problems we are going to face today, but thank you that in spite of the problems You are in control and You love me. This is enough for me! Thank you.

As I thought about his words, I realized that knowing God is in control and He loves me is also enough for me.

Other books by Michael Dawson

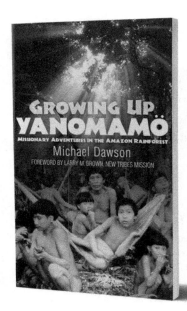

Available at GraceAcresPress.com
or wherever books are sold.

Growing Your Faith One Page at a Time

Grace Acres Press
GraceAcresPress.com
303-681-9995